Ride the Wind

~ Letters to and from Africa ~

by

Sophie Neville

~ SOPHIE NEVILLE ~

RIDE THE WINGS OF MORNING © Sophie Neville 2001

Illustrations © Sophie Neville

All rights reserved

The moral right of the author/artist has been asserted.

http://sophieneville.net

True Life: Travel~Animals~Autobiography

Also by Sophie Neville

FUNNILY ENOUGH

MAKORONGO'S WAR

ASHTON HOUSE PUBLISHING

Walhampton, Lymington, SO41 5RB, Hants, UK

~ The Author ~

Once a television director, Sophie Neville is now a writer, producer and established wildlife artist. Known for once playing Titty in the feature film 'Swallows and Amazons' she has never stopped leading an adventurous and inspiring life.

Ride the Wings of Morning **by Sophie Neville:**

"Real life jumps off the page with such warmth and energy I couldn't put it down." Fiona Lindsay.

"A delightful book and attractive concept." Virginia McKenna.

"Enormously amusing." Nick Archer.

"The content runs deeper than descriptions of far distant places. Today's readers need that. You weren't just travelling around Africa for the sake of writing a book, you were living there."

"It seems an obvious format - to write a travel book from letters that made their way back to England - but I haven't seen it done before. While it makes for light reading you get drawn into the warmth of the relationship between the three sisters and are carried along by the immediacy of their news, certainly by the romance. It's contrived but that's acceptable because it works."
"Oh, but they are real letters."
"You mean it's all true?"
"Yes."
"Good grief."

~ CONTENTS ~

News in Brief ~ I am off to South Africa
Chapter One ~ I never came to say goodbye
Chapter Two ~ Guess what I'm doing?
Chapter Three ~ All is well
Chapter Four ~ We have quite a few weddings
Chapter Five ~ What a simply dreadful time
Chapter Six ~ I found out that horses can eat meat
Chapter Seven ~ Here we are
Chapter Eight ~ We are appalled
Chapter Nine ~ Poor Dad, what did you do to him?
Chapter Ten ~ The worst thing about living in a rondavel
Chapter Eleven ~ I spent the day trying to finish a picture
Chapter Twelve ~ I know what it means
Chapter Thirteen ~ Great pangs of guilt
Chapter Fourteen ~ Stuffing my face
Chapter Fifteen ~ It was wonderful having you here
Chapter Sixteen ~ All the way to Norfolk
Chapter Seventeen ~ I'm in hospital again
Epilogue ~ Sometimes when you fall in love

~ SOPHIE NEVILLE ~

for
Sarah-Jane
who pioneered horseback safaris in
Southern Africa

and
all those who looked after me on my travels

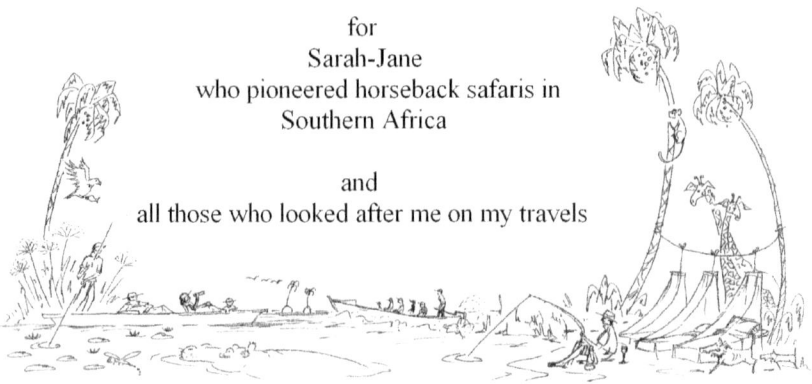

10th February 1992

~ *News in brief* ~

'Fifteen people were killed in the fighting overnight across South Africa. Sikhumbuzo Ngwenya, an ANC leader in the black township of Imbali, was shot dead on Saturday night as he left a restaurant. Six people were stabbed or burned to death in fighting, which continued into yesterday in the Johannesburg township of Soweto.'

The Guardian

I am off to South Africa. For my health.

I was grumbling about having to wait a few hours to change planes. It's strange though; it'll take a day to get from London to Johannesburg - but if you drove it could take five months. Birds fly to Africa all the time; well, once a year. I wonder if they know how long they're going for, or when they're expected back?

CHAPTER ONE

C/o Equus Horse Trails
PO Box, Marken
Northern Transvaal
South Africa
7th March 1992

Dear Perry,

    I never came to say goodbye. I'm sorry, I would have loved to have seen your new house; you'll have to tell me all about it. I hope everyone is well. I thought I would die on the aeroplane but the endless fatigue that was oppressing me seems to have evaporated in the sunshine. My doctor said the arid climate would help me get better and I think it has. I go to bed at night feeling tired instead of ill. It's such a relief. I look a bit pallid and have a spot right in the middle of my chin but Rebecca says that spots are good; a sign of youth and virility. She, of course, is beautifully tanned with a radiant complexion.

It may amuse you to know that I spent this morning removing ticks from sixteen horses before dredging green slime from a water reservoir supplying the house. Since the slime was particularly evasive I didn't do a thorough job. I did manage to move the washing line although it required the help of ten men. I know this sounds ridiculous but the whirly-gig sort of thing had been planted in a great block of concrete. Whilst doing this I had to supervise an idiotic plumber and do various office jobs for Sarah-Jane before spending forty minutes trying to light her gas fridge. (Failed; just got covered in soot). Before sunset I planted a row of lettuce seedlings, another of spring onions and collected enough thorns to bullterrier-proof the vegetable garden, which was most satisfying. The workload is quite something but somehow I find the strength, and the patience.

I'm living with Sarah-Jane, Rebecca and a tall blonde South African ranger in the middle of a newly established game ranch, three and a half hours' drive north of Johannesburg. It's quite a big property, about 42,000 acres with an enormous diversity of game. As I write I can see a small herd of waterbuck grazing in the evening light on the plain in front of the house.

The Waterberg is an amazing area, an old red sandstone plateau about 3,000 feet above sea level. On Sunday we were invited to a reserve on the edge of the escarpment where there's a frieze of ancient San Bushmen paintings. I lay on the rocks watching black eagles circling around the flat-topped mountains and felt glad to be here. And very privileged.

One of the game scouts found a python last week. It had obviously just eaten a small antelope and was lying in the grass looking bulgy, not moving at all. Rebecca, who is fearless, went quite close. A few days later we were riding along with a client, an old boy who had a bad stutter. He started to say, 'B-b-b-b,' but couldn't get the words out.

'Birds? er… branch?' I saw his horse pick up its feet and step over what I thought must be a log.

'B-b-bloody great snake.'

And it was too; another massive python. Andrew, who is the ranger, went over to see if he could pick it up. I dismounted too, as I thought it would make a good photograph. Well, don't ever try to catch a python. Andrew is 6'3". The snake reared up and lunged at his face, teeth bared. I was scrambling back onto my pony, but I think the snake thought twice about attacking us with so many horses about. It slid off under a thorn bush.

Andrew stood in the grass calmly saying, 'If a python does bite it won't let go; you have to cut the head off.'

Can you imagine? Getting out your Swiss Army penknife and trying to cut the head off a fifteen-foot snake with its teeth stuck into Andrew's nose? And although not poisonous, the fangs are so filthy you can get terribly infected.

We've only four clients coming this weekend. It's just as well. Although Sarah-Jane brought her horses up here about four weeks ago, accommodation for the tourists is not exactly in a state of readiness. She has been using the main lodge on the reserve but we need to move into our new bush camp about two kilometres from the house. There's still a great deal to do. I must get up and go and do it. You won't believe this, but I have to write menus. I, of all the people on this Earth, am to be the cook. Rebecca is teaching me as fast as she can before she leaves to work on hot-air balloon safaris.

My love to Robert,

Sophie

C/O EQUUS HORSE TRAILS
PO BOX, MARKEN
NORTHERN TRANSVAAL
SOUTH AFRICA

20th March 1992

Dear Tamzin,

You would love the riding here. There are miles of sandy tracks taking you through unspoilt bush with no fences; no gates to open. Well, there's a huge electrified game fence along the perimeter of the reserve to keep the elephants from wandering off, but we live in the middle so you can ride in any direction for hours without seeing a soul. Wherever you go there are birds; yellow-billed hornbills hopping about in the trees, brightly coloured weaver birds quarrelling incessantly over their funny-shaped nests and crowned plovers who shriek abuse at us if we cross the grasslands where they breed. We get followed by drongos all the time, rather smart black birds with forked tails, looking for insects disturbed by the horses' hooves. You see some of the same species we have in England, like barn owls, and the skies are full of swallows. The Warden is having to do something about their telephone lines today. They're rather low and the giraffe keep walking into them.

Sarah-Jane has quite an assortment of horses; one of every variety including a beautiful black Friesian who looks as if he should be carrying a knight, off to the crusades. Most of them are

South African breeds I'd never heard of, such as *Nooitgedacht* and *Boerperd*, bred for working with cattle. Some of them know how to triple, a strange gait between a trot and a canter, which made me laugh quite uncontrollably at first but it's very comfortable, especially since I sometimes find myself spending six hours a day in the saddle. Sarah-Jane's business partner, Wendy, has a little skewbald foal that comes into the house. And there are three bullterriers - Tigger and two naughty ones belonging to the Warden who lives next door.

I love being outside all the time. I wake up in the morning, pull on a pair of shorts and step into the bright sunlight. The acacias are in bloom and fill the air with their scent. Everything here smells different; I feel physically relieved to be away from the dankness of England, the traffic and the rush. We live in an old, white-washed farmhouse made up of an office, a rather stark kitchen with a humming strip-light and three thatched rondavels where we sleep. There's a biggish central area, once a sitting room, where Sarah-Jane has us organizing camping equipment and mending piles of tack. The horses have a 200-acre field with a couple of holding paddocks, and are herded into a yard every morning when we tie them up around a large Sourplum tree. Tiny blue waxbills hop about pecking at the horse food while a one-eared pony called Guido scoots around hoovering up the fallen fruit.

There are two grooms. One is a bolshie boy called France who is good at finding the horses but doesn't seem at all keen on working with them. I asked him if he was interested in learning about stable management.

'No.' He said scornfully, 'I want to be a panel-beater.'

I didn't know what a panel-beater was. The other chap is called Somewhere, but we can never find him. The tack shed is quite far from the big tree, so I spend most of my time lugging heavy saddles across the yard, wishing Somewhere could do it.

Andrew says, 'It'll make you fit and strong,' and then, 'Please let me take that,' and carries them for me as if they weighed nothing at all.

I can't get over how polite the South African men are; they don't just open the car door for you, they wind down the window too. It's very flattering. Mum would love it. But we are well and truly behind the *boerewors* curtain here. *Boerewors* are big fat farmer's sausages but the phrase has something to do with the white supremacy. Though not wanting to endorse this, Sarah-Jane feels she must offer work to the local Sotho people, and needs their help. We are separate. Their accommodation is the other side of the tack-shed but their hours are shorter than ours. They do seven hours a day and get paid, we work all the time for nothing.

Andrew is taking a diploma in Nature Conservation and is on attachment to Equus Trails for his practical year. He hasn't begun to think about the projects he needs to complete, he just rides all the time. Rebecca has adopted a baby rat and was suggesting he should study its development, but he said:

'Seeing it has a scaly tail, it would be classified as an exotic species and since it will inevitably become a threat to the environment, it should be despatched forthwith. Rather a short project.'

She was most offended. But Andrew is very concerned about this sort of thing.

'What's that?'

'It's an alien.'

'It looks rather beautiful to me.'

'It must be eradicated.'

'Why?'

'It's an invader species, encroaching on the indigenous ecosystem.' Was this a film we were watching; dialogue from *Gate Masters of the Universe*? No, we were looking at a tree. Apparently a South American one introduced by colonialists.

Andrew grimaces at the sight of a stray prickly pear or any other plant that wouldn't naturally occur here. He said that black wattle, originally introduced for tanning leather, is choking watercourses and getting totally out of hand in the Cape where it displaces the native fynbos. Australian gum trees are grown here extensively, for their timber which is good and straight, but drink so much they actively lower the water table.

The rat is called Isit. Isit because whenever you make a statement South Africans say, 'Is it?'

For example: 'I used to work in London.'

Reply: 'Is it?'

'I have a sister called Perry.'

'Is it?'

This flummoxed me until Sarah-Jane explained that the phrase is short for 'Is that so?' and is a symptom of politeness. If you say 'Hello' to someone, it's essential to ask how they are. If you forget they sometimes say, 'Well, and yourself?' as if you had anyway.

'Oh, yes.' Sarah-Jane said, 'The phrase will be used by complete strangers making business calls or even by people finding they've dialled the wrong number.'

What is currently worrying me is the health of our vegetables; a selection of alarming looking gourds and pumpkins which Sarah-Jane expects me to do wonderful things with.

'What is it?' I found myself asking as I peered at something that looked like a green flying saucer.

'Don't you know what a patti-pan is?' Gemsquash and butternut, sweet potatoes and great sacks of maize meal confront me before every meal; cooking here is a humbling experience. Somewhere and France (Somewhere in France?) have been most encouraging about what I manage to produce. All Sarah-Jane could say was, 'It had better be a steep learning curve.'

Thank you for taking me to the airport and for the lovely lunch before I left. You must think of coming out here; you'd love it.

Oh, Tamzin, I had to tell you. Rebecca and I found a street in Johannesburg called *Swartkoppie*. It means blackhead. Imagine having to tell everyone you lived in Blackhead Street.

Lots of love,

Sophie

CHAPTER TWO

**BBC Television
Elstree Studios
Borehamwood
Hertfordshire**
27th February 1992

Dear Sophie,

Guess what I'm doing? Another couple of weeks' filming, playing an expectant mother in frumpy clothes and greasy hair. Not glamorous. The BBC must have me down as a permanently pregnant actress. Only this time my bump is real and the 'wrap' is around 2.00am.

I'm sitting outside Make-up with a polystyrene cup of tea, waiting to be used. I must be mad to give up my comfortable suburban existence, but Robert is on leave from soldiering, so I might as well earn some pennies whilst I have a resident babysitter for Atalanta.

We are now well installed in Surrey. I was quite shell-shocked at first. The outside of our quarter is perfectly hideous, but inside is a great improvement on the last. It feels more like living in an ice-cream container than a tub of margarine. And it has a DISHWASHER, yes I'm becoming quite ordinary. Just to make you feel a million miles away I'll tell you about my local supermarket. Sophie, it is horrific – it has sixty, yes, 60 checkout tills. It takes half a packet of biscuits to get Atalanta around without whingeing.

The real walks here are great though, straight from the back door into the ferny woods. Only problem is that Teddy and his pushchair usually have to come too, so my relaxing stroll is spent heaving him over tree stumps and dykes. The Army keep spraying vanilla smoke everywhere, which is a bit weird. It turns your nostrils black.

Mum and Dad dropped in; Mum had just finished a two-hour photo session in London, dressed as a policewoman in a size 12 mini-skirt and high, black, patent leather shoes.

One of the other policewomen said, 'There's a man over there peeing himself.' (laughing)

It was Dad. He got glared at, which he said made him laugh even more. Mum said, indignantly, that she was doing it for an important German advertising company and was staggeringly well paid. She wasn't clear about what product they were promoting. By the time she reached us she was not in a good mood, demanding a hot-water bottle and a pair of Robert's socks.

'Daddy,' she said, tartly, 'has done nothing all week except strip the old paint off his boat. I hope he's not expecting me to go onboard.'

She hates getting cold feet.

Tamzin and Johnty came to supper. They were very naughty about the people coming to see their cottage. Tamzin took a brief look round and declared that my house looks like a squash court; it's quite true. Perhaps I should mark out the floor with red lines.

I need to get Atalanta a tricycle for her birthday – she wants a pink one, isn't that typical? Tamzin said her friend Raddy has a little girl who wanted a pink one too. Raddy found an old bike on the dump and just painted it herself. The child caught her at it but seemed quite satisfied, despite the fact that it definitely looked a bit ropey.

Your car has been a real help. We even managed to get £7 a month off the insurance for keeping it out of London - Damnit, you could have claimed for all that time you were staying with Mum and Dad in Gloucestershire.

I'm visualising your very different existence now. I bet you won't want to come back, but you will have to, to meet your new nephew/niece. I'm due in June, (if you can say that).

Lots of love,

Perry

Equus Horse Safaris
PO Box, Marken
Northern Transvaal
South Africa

Dear Perry,

I finally worked out how to light a gas fridge. You say to a man, '*Maak 'n vuur onder die yskas,*' and do you know; it works. I'm not sure why. A direct translation would be, 'Make a fire under the ice box.' When I needed something done at the BBC, I used to say, 'Would you mind…' or 'When you have time…' or 'Would you be very sweet and…' It doesn't work here. You have to say, 'You **must** make this **beautifully** clean; **now**.' Otherwise nothing gets achieved at all.

We have a great big Afrikaans builder called Johann, who just sits in his beaten up *bakkie* (or pick-up truck) swigging brandy, while he watches his labourers *slowly* clear the ground. We have clients arriving at the weekend and need the loos, or a 'communal ablution block', as he insists on calling the facility, finished and **working**. This, he fails to comprehend.

I said, 'Johann, would you **like** to collect the cement **sometime** this afternoon?'

He looked at me, laughed and said 'No.'

He was so frustrating that I ended up hitting him on the chest with my pen. Standing in the middle of the bush surrounded by lavatory bowls. Word has gone around that I clobbered him, which everyone seems to think very funny. I expect it's because they all want to 'bop him one' too, as Mary-Dieu would say. Anyway, you can just imagine me striding round saying, 'Do this, do that,' sounding more like an archetypal film director than I ever was when I was one.

There's still terrible, green algae coming out of the taps. We don't have a dishwasher, or a washing machine, but Sarah-Jane has found a redoubtable maid called Nelly. I asked her to teach me to speak Northern Sotho but she insisted we should concentrate on Afrikaans, saying I will suffer at the Co-op otherwise.

Afrikaans seems a very odd language. A hose is a *'tuin slang'*, which means 'garden snake'. You don't put water into a kettle, you fling it in ~ very descriptive. And then you have a *'koppie koffie'* as there are no Cs. While a *kop* is a cup, a *kop* is also a head, and I'm sure I asked Johann if he was a coffee head, instead of asking if he wanted a cup of coffee. Whatever I said, Andrew, who is bilingual, walked out of the room making grunty noises. I think he was laughing. Johann must just think I'm mad. I have to say he proceeded to add six teaspoons of sugar to his coffee.

Learning Northern Sotho is worse. The word for a child is the same as for a man, only with a different intonation. In my great effort to make conversation I asked Nelly's friend how many children she had, only it came out as 'how many men do you have?' It might have meant 'how many men have you had?'

Either way, she didn't take it well. I looked on, speechless with horror, as she put eight spoons of sugar into her baby's bottle.

At this stage, while Nelly was busy with the laundry in an outside wash-sink Johann breezed past referring to her as a 'Black-a-matic'.

I was so outraged I could neither speak nor hit out before he swung into his *bakkie* and disappeared in a cloud of dust. Sarah-Jane assured me that he was just doing it to get a rise. Although I fell for it hook, line and sinker, Nelly was completely unperturbed.

The clients seem devoid of obtuse attitudes and all seem to speak English fluently, thank Goodness. I can readily identify with them. Taut executives arrive all hot and prickly, but once you get them onto a horse and into the bush they begin to relax and laugh a bit, discarding all their tension and tight clothes.

'This is the first time,' one man told me as we were watering the horses, 'that I've been to a place where you don't hear manmade sounds.'

It's true. You look out over miles of untouched bushveld without seeing a single light. Sarah-Jane and I sit round the fire watching our visitors become real people again. You would so admire my hostess skills; I get them to lie on their backs and look at the stars through binoculars, pointing out constellations of the southern hemisphere like Orion and the Southern Cross. My knowledge of astronomy is not particularly wonderful but I feel that by chatting about Taurus and Betelgeuse I'm justifying my existence as a safari guide, while Nelly crashes around with the washing up. Does this qualify as 'Imperialist guilt'?

How do you cope with putting on endless Army dinner parties? I suppose electrical gadgets do help. I have to cook on an open fire here. Rebecca even makes pudding on the fire. When it was my turn everyone got handed a baked banana with chocolate in the middle. Thankfully they couldn't see very well by paraffin lamp.

The bush is beautiful. You ride across wide, open plains with warthog running around; past hartebeest standing on anthills, and then drop down into gorges where great red blocks of sandstone rise from secret pools of water. There's always a lot of barking as you approach because baboons like roosting on the cliffs at night. They have sentries who sit high up in the gnarled fig trees that grow straight out of the rocks, rocks worn smooth by the feet of their ancestors over thousands of years. We, who invade their territory so haughtily, take drinks and sit watching them as the sun goes down.

Funny isn't it? I thought losing my job in London was such a disaster but if I hadn't fallen ill and been forced to give up my career I wouldn't be here, drinking all this in. I'm learning so much. Andrew has been teaching me about the indigenous trees. I can now tell you about *Diplorhynchus condylocarpon*, the wild rubber. It has pods, which are full of what looks exactly like Copydex and can pretty well stick your fingers together. This is not something you want to do when you're sitting on a difficult horse. Actually none of the horses are difficult except for Sarah-Jane's own pony Jigsaw, who is a black and white demon.

'He's just sensitive and highly-strung,' she's telling me.

He is not too bad with girls, but hates men, especially men wearing hats, probably because he was once badly treated. I suppose human personalities get damaged in the same way. But the other problem with Jigsaw is that he wasn't castrated until he was about seven and still behaves like a stallion. He even managed to father a foal after he was cut. She is called Puzzle, and is a funny little grey and white thing.

Jigsaw is fine once you manage to get on top of him; responsive with a good sense of direction. This is a great relief when you're leading the ride, as he thinks nothing of plunging into unknown territory. We are exploring the whole time so you need a horse that will cross marshy ground or take you up rocky zebra paths into the hills without getting lost. He snorts when we come across wildebeest. They snort back or sneeze at you. We had giraffe at the camp today, which was exciting. They must think we are most peculiar. I suppose we are.

Sarah-Jane's partner Wendy, who looks after the marketing and accounts, drove up from the office in Johannesburg for the weekend with her boyfriend Donald. Donald is tall with bright red hair and freckles. He adores animals and thought Rebecca's baby rat was sweet. I don't.

'It can't stay,' Sarah-Jane said, 'You'll have to take it ballooning with you.'

Donald is good at fixing things. Rebecca said, 'Donald, there's something wrong with the electricity in this kitchen.' There was too. He found two dead rats in the fuse box. They had been electrocuted.

'ROUSES!' said Sarah-Jane at the top of her voice. Her bullterrier, Tigger, who normally spends the whole day asleep on the sofa, sped into the kitchen and started looking about frantically. Donald moved the fridge. There was a streak and another rodent, the size of a cat I might say, was exterminated.

'They have to go,' said Donald, the animal lover, 'Or you will attract snakes.'

'Not snakes,' (me).

'Right,' said Donald. 'The feed shed.'

And went striding over to the place where the horse food is kept. A primeval instinct to hunt rose within me as I started moving tools and Donald heaved sacks around, urging Tigger on. It was all dust and mayhem. After a completely hectic fifteen minutes we managed to find one small mouse. It was dispatched very quickly.

I don't know why everyone is so besotted by Rebecca's pet. She stayed behind to nurture it while we packed sleeping bags and food onto the horses and rode off to camp down by the Palala River with the clients. We had to; Johann was still finishing the loos.

It is such varied, stunning country. The vegetation changes dramatically as you ride towards the river and the view changes at every turn. We started coming across hippo tracks when we were still high in the hills. Donald told me that they'll easily wander two kilometres from the river at night in search of grazing, but I was amazed that they had tackled such steep, stony tracks. They're deemed dangerous, being responsible for more deaths than any other animal in Africa.

'Apart from the mosquito,' Sarah-Jane put in.

As there was no sign of hippo in the river we tied up the horses on a picket line and climbed along a ledge under a high cliff face to find more Bushmen paintings; little stick-like people and exquisite pictures of animals.

There were enough tents for the guests, but Donald, Sarah-Jane, Wendy and I slept out by the horses. This sounds romantic, but it wasn't. It was smelly. The horses exude so much methane you can't breathe. They don't sleep much, they only need about three hours and spend the rest of the time chomping away or bickering. You'd think you could lie on your saddle blanket, but you can't. After riding all day they're drenched with sweat.

We slept on a groundsheet but the moon was so bright that I kept waking, thinking someone had left the light on. The next moment it was like trying to sleep in a disco. Sheets of lightning were flashing around us and rain started to come down. Donald wrapped the groundsheet round himself, but us girls barged in on the clients without any warning or any shame; Sarah-Jane and her revolver with one man, Wendy with another and me with two rather terrified girls. Luckily they all made it back.

Must go and make twelve beds and a vat of beef stroganoff.
Lots of love,
Sophie

CHAPTER THREE

Bellevue,

Quellington Green,

Hampshire.

England.

Dear Soph,

Here are medical insurance papers you asked for. I hope you don't need to make a claim.

All is well except that Bellevue has been on the market for two weeks and we've only had one couple round.

They called everything 'quaint' or 'feature' and loved the crass name. (So much for Raddy telling me to change it to get a better sale). They were worried about the noise from the sawmill at the end of the garden. I said it was infrequent and didn't bother me. (This is a lie). They're coming back for a second gawp tomorrow, when no doubt the circular saw will be going all the time.

We went to see Perry and Robert's new house. It's odd; open-plan with the most enormous sitting room. You could stand fifty people in it. Or park up two tanks. Atalanta zooms around in her Noddy car. Oh, how I long for such space.

I spoke to Mum last night. With more violence being reported from South Africa, she is anxious about you and needs a letter. She had an interview for a job as a dinner-lady yesterday, so is excited but isn't happy about Granny, who after another bout of 'flu is threatening to go into a nursing home again.

Raddy is rather upset. She made friends with a man she thought would like to rent Mum's cottage, only to discover he is a sitting-tenant with a strange past. Last week he was walking down the track that runs above her farm and started chatting to her while she was feeding the chickens. This wouldn't normally be alarming, but he was wearing surgical rubber gloves.

Her husband is away for a week so she has set up booby traps in case the creepy man comes back.

I shall keep you in touch with house developments.
Lots of love,
Tamzin, Johnty, Maude, Bod and Thelma xxx

PS: Johnty only noticed the organic under-blanket, the sheepskin you gave me, last week when I stripped the bed. I've been sleeping on it for over a month. He wanted to know what 'all that revolting white hair' was.

EQUUS HORSE SAFARIS
PO BOX, MARKEN
NORTHERN TRANSVAAL
SOUTH AFRICA

Dear Tamzin,

I'm rather wishing that I brought out the dead sheep Johnty is complaining about, so that I have something to lie on in the bush. I did have a blow-up Thermarest mat but lent it to Sarah-Jane who rolled it out onto paperbark thorns. It will never inflate again. The suede chaps that you persuaded me to buy in Farnham are a great success. I just zip them on over my shorts and ride, without having to squeeze into jodhpurs. As I don't think I've owned a pair since I was fifteen, this is just as well. The chaps stop me getting scratched by acacia bushes and are useful for cooking in. I'm meant to be the chef, which entails trying to do complicated things like roast a whole chicken on the campfire. I struggled with this, getting hot legs, but have found the answer:

You say, brightly, 'We're having fillet tonight.'

It's not expensive here, and, it's a man's job, as Perry would say, to cook the meat.

A South African *braai* is completely different to one of our barbeques. A huge emphasis is made on collecting dry wood, preferably stuff baked so hard by the sun even the termites have rejected it. A fire is lit but nothing happens for a while except that numerous cans of beer are opened. Then the man in charge takes a *graaf*, which is a spade, and drags out the coals, lifting them onto a higher level area where he cooks, while everyone else can still sit round the fire. I just have to make a few salads. And lay the table, search frantically for the horseradish sauce, take round snacks, do something about potatoes, and make a pudding. The same sort of thing applies to starting diesel pumps. Our water has to be pumped two kilometres, which entails starting a massive engine. I just stand looking at it. I thought I was a practical person, but this thing's bigger than me and only starts if you can turn the flywheel. You need to weigh more than 80kgs to do this. I only weigh 47kgs.

We had the strangest guests this weekend. A gruff looking man arrived with his little daughter who was keen on riding. I put her on Guido as he trots all the time. Well, it turned out that the man, despite being small and quite weedy looking, was a Colonel in the Special Forces, the *Koevoets*, which, I gather, means 'crowbars' and is the South African equivalent of the SAS. He told Andrew, who was recently an army conscript, all about his time fighting on the Angolan border. He was there seventeen years. One job was to spring ambushes. To make a lasting impression on the enemy his men would chop off their ears. He said he had quite a collection. And there was his little daughter, trotting along happily on her one-eared pony.

I took out an evening ride with two sweet old ladies, 'here on a jaunt' and a rather good-looking Swiss chap who had never been to Africa before.

I packed drinks in our saddlebags, and thought we would sit watching the sunset before riding back in the moonlight, which is an amazing experience. You can see quite clearly; the moon is so bright it casts shadows.

Only I miscalculated things. The sun went down and then it was dark. Pitch black. There was no moon at all. I had to lead them back, through the rocks, along a streambed, winding through towering reeds and thick vegetation, across a dam wall and over open country for a good hour in **starlight.** It's not like going through the woods in England either. The clients said all they could see was the white top to the tail of the piebald horse I was riding, so they followed that and were amazingly cheerful, considering it was rather dangerous. I learnt how well horses can see in the dark and how forgiving people can be. Sarah-Jane was good about it and the old ladies assured me that the reason they had come was for adventure. As we reached home a huge moon rose over the flat-topped trees. We could see quite clearly when we got off the horses.

We're so busy that my attempts to learn an African language have gone right out of the window. As Sarah-Jane has never attempted to speak anything but rather precarious Spanish, she's 'Looking for local staff who can speak English.'

Somewhere, whose real name turns out to be Samuel, rather alarmed her by asking for 'flesh' at 6 o'clock in the morning. He meant meat.

Nelly, who works in the kitchen, said:

'This English makes me tired. Why can't everyone speak Northern Sotho?'

'Well, Nelly, Northern Sotho isn't an international language.'

Although English does appear to be becoming the language of this world, I'm assured that when we get to heaven it'll be Afrikaans. Better try to extend my vocabulary.

Nelly is horrified that I don't have a boyfriend, 'The blood,' she said, ominously. 'It will go to your head.'

Andrew explained that African girls are told you will die if you don't get enough sex but it's more likely they'll die if they do. AIDS is hovering over the people here. A nurse from the government clinic, who drives around the farms providing contraceptives, told me that anyone with a sexually transmitted disease (and these are rife) is probably HIV+. She said that South Africa has been largely protected by the trade embargo. Because AIDS is mainly spread from place to place by lorry drivers who use prostitutes, the fact that trucks couldn't cross the border curtailed the spread. Until now.

There has been a National referendum. Being English Sarah-Jane couldn't vote but she made Andrew go.

'Why doesn't he take Nelly?'

'Sophie,' she said looking at me as if I was mentally disturbed, 'Nelly doesn't have a vote; that's the whole point.'

Apparently the Prime Minister, FW de Klerk, has asked all those who are enfranchised, ie: the white people, if they support him in pursuing a new constitution, ie: whether forthcoming elections should be multi-racial.[1] And this is 1992. I suppose it marks the end of apartheid but all round Marken there were posters saying NO. Andrew thought this quite funny. But while most of the rest of South Africa voted YES, the people round here did, indeed, vote NO.

You will be so impressed; I've learnt how to cure acne. We have a shrub with huge pods called the *Sumac bean*, which does the job. I always wanted to make a television programme on acne. Seriously; some people get so depressed about having bad skin that they resort to suicide. My proposal was entitled; *'Spots'* with that song *Spotty Muldoon* played over an opening sequence composed of famous acne-fied people. I didn't know any offhand, but thought I could ask the film library to look for shots of spotty world leaders.

Here's a porcupine quill I found for you. Don't touch the tip, it's poisonous.

Lots of love,

Sophie

Bellevue,

Quellington-on-Sawmill,

Hampshire

15th April 1992

Dear Sophie,

Thank you for your letter. I was *fascinated* by the ear collection. What kind of ears? Does he still have them?

We went home the other day to celebrate Mum and Dad's wedding anniversary; 35 years. I gave Mary-Dieu your address but she says she never writes and isn't going to start now. She was there with Daisy, who is two now and chatting away quite confidently.

I was listening to one of the neighbours telling me how much money her husband earns, thinking, 'I don't believe I'm hearing this,' when Mum announced to one and all that she can, henceforth, be seen as a large, smiley dinner-lady in a pink nylon overall, pushing around fifty trolleys of dirty dishes.

'Oh, no, Mum. Where?'

'Through the streets of Birmingh-gam,' she said, putting on a funny accent and taking another drink. 'It's for a Fairy Liquid advertize-ment; I'm going to be gracing the bill boards.'

How can she do this to us? It happens time and again. The embarrassment.

I told Dad about the ears. He said that during the Second World War the Ghurkhas collected German ears. They were paid half-a-crown for each one. He read your letter and said that Spotty

Muldoon died in the end but met lots of acned angels in heaven and was very happy.

I actually entered at The County Show last week. I put Bod in for the 'Handy Hunter Class', which means the judge has to ride your horse. She wouldn't ride mine. No sense of adventure.

It wasn't too disgraceful except that my number came loose and was flapping around. There was a shout from the crowd.

'Don't worry,' called a voice, as a rather dishevelled woman ran towards me. 'Your Mummy's here.'

And Mum ran into the arena with her arms outstretched, about to make the necessary adjustments. I didn't even know she was at the show.

We came second to last.

I had Atalanta to stay for a week. She was great and only cried once when she fell out of the wheelbarrow. Her favourite thing is to sneak up to you looking totally expressionless and then raise her eyebrows up and down.

Raddy and her husband have been skiing, leaving me with *all* their animals – my penance as Raddy kindly lets me stable my enormous horse on her farm. Before they left, Raddy made the most of April Fool's Day, I can tell you. My April Fool was a dead rat hanging out of Bod's feed bin.

However we had a shock far worse than that. Every time I went to make up Bod's food I could smell something really foul. Raddy and I went to investigate. We moved a huge pile of wood to no avail. Just as we were about to give up, Raddy said that she was going to look in the old pram… Ha ha ha. She went white with shock. I went over to investigate. Inside was Henry, the ginger cat. He'd been decomposing for over three months. The smell was dreadful. We wheeled the pram backwards up into the wood. Raddy removed him with a spade, buried him and cried a lot. I said to Raddy that I would take the pram in the back of the Land Rover to the dump and burn it. She was livid and said she was going to sell it at the Quellington Car Boot Sale.

Not much acting work about. Richard Eyre, the director I once worked for in a BBC *Play for the Day*, asked me to be in *Tumbledown*, a drama series about the Falklands war.

When I turned up at Brize Norton, he took one look at me and said: 'You're not pregnant.'

They must have muddled me up with Perry, as I'd just been told to come dressed in my own clothes, as a soldier's wife. I had to play the part with a quilted jacket stuffed up my front, which was a bit difficult. You try running across an airfield, bringing on the tears with a padded arm determined to fall down between your legs.

We've still had no luck with the house. Raddy will have to think of a better sales ploy than changing the name. We have to move for Bod's sake. I need to find a place with a bit of land for him. And Maud. She started chasing cows yesterday, the naughty little dog, and got a wallop, but then I dropped a tin of cat food on her head and was instantly immersed in guilt. You must treasure bullterriers; they're such angel creatures.

Write soon,

lots of love,

Tamzin and Johnty xxx

**Equus Horse Safaris
PO Box
Marken
Northern Transvaal
South Africa**

Dear Tamzin,

When I asked Andrew about the collection he said they were Cuban ears. Would you warrant it? Cubans were employed as mercenaries by the Angolans.

Sarah-Jane's boyfriend, Billy, was in the South African Defence Force Mounted Division and used to patrol the Namibian border on horses. They would ride through the desert with Bushmen trackers; the idea being that the enemy could be approached silently. But what about land mines? Military service is compulsory for all South African men, well, all the white ones. There is no obligation if you are black.

We have a new guide called Andy, so now we have Andrew and Andy, both of whom are blonde and rather good looking. Andy has come from a smart game lodge in the Eastern Transvaal called Londolozi and is going to teach us all he knows. I can now identify an agama, a gymnogene and wild gladioli. The only thing he can't do is ride.

'But Andy, I thought all Army recruits have to learn how to vault onto a cantering horse and trot endlessly without stirrups,' Sarah-Jane said in dismay.

'Yes, M'am, but I served in the Air Force.'

We put him on an old grey mare called Smokey Joe, but she trod in an aardvark hole and he fell off onto his head. All the guests were looking.

We have an unpleasant group staying; nine men led by a pompous and autocratic nitwit wearing an eagle feather in his hat. He arrived early, 'to inspect the horses' and, without asking us, plonked an Austrian Army saddle on Jigsaw, Sarah-Jane's frantic horse, who stood there snorting and twitching in revolt. It was far too big for him. The man had special, handmade canvas saddlebags for his video camera, which he slapped on behind the saddle. They had emblems on the sides; little shields which he'd drawn on, in felt-tip pen.

'I intend to take video footage while we are riding along.'

'That saddle slipped and Jigsaw bucked like a two-stroke,' Andrew said later. 'I found the video camera swinging from a branch.'

I wish Perry was here to organize the kitchen. I did manage to make marmalade from our own oranges. They are so bitter it tasted quite good but every single thing in the kitchen was sticky for the next week. It's difficult cooking impressive food when you have a low budget, especially when the nearest supermarket is 100 kilometres away. Marken, where we post our letters, consists of a mortuary, a doctor's surgery and a farmers' co-op; the *Ko-operaserie* of the Northern Transvaal, where you can buy farm implements and diesel. There's a sort of café shop, but it just stocks plastic bottles of Handy Andy. Marken must be the last outpost of apartheid; you find two different counters at the post office, and separate examination rooms at the surgery. I haven't asked what happens at the morgue.

In each of the last three groups of riders at least one person has been a professional chef, and they can tell how hopeless I am. When I made macaroni cheese; everyone was late and it turned to concrete. I tried to roast potatoes in the traditional way, using an iron pot on the fire. They turned to mush. I should have pretended it was some new dish. Then I attempted to cook *gemsquash*, vegetables that look like dark green tennis balls, by putting them around the fire. I knew you had to bake them but didn't realise they ought to be pierced first. They exploded in all directions.

I have to use tinned tomatoes. Oh, the shame. As I was walking down to the dining-tent with their breakfast, some English clients were talking about what good tinned food you can get and what amazing things they managed to find to take on their boat.

'But it has to be said,' the husband declared resolutely. 'Tinned tomatoes are absolutely h o r r i b l e.'

At this point in time I placed before him a great, steaming bowl of the long red Italian type, pathetically sprinkled with dried herbs.

We go to a neighbouring farm, about fifteen kilometres away, for eggs. The farmer's wife is a sweet lady called Meisie. *Meisie* means girl in Afrikaans. She always has bright make-up and

wears delicate lacy dresses with her hair set immaculately in a doll-like way, but she is about seventy-five. She has an old-fashioned farm shop, which sells everything under the sun. A white bullterrier ominously guards her fruit trees. Meisie loves receiving customers and flutters from shelf to high shelf collecting all the things you need, writing a long itemised receipt in neat, loopy writing. All the food is terribly expensive and all the funny things she has had for years are ridiculously cheap. You can buy a reel of thread for about 2p, but as Sarah-Jane pointed out, it is so decrepit it would perish if you tried to use it.
Lots of love,
from Sophie

CHAPTER FOUR

Goodwood Close,
Camberley,
Surrey
23rd April 1992

Dear Sib –

I'm busy babysitting someone else's child who is asleep, and as Sumo wrestling is the best thing on telly I thought I'd write to you - high time anyway.

We have quite a few weddings coming up; Atalanta can't wait to be a bridesmaid. Actually it's me who can't wait, as she has no idea what to expect. Godfather Jiminee and his bride-to-be came for lunch today and took her vital statistics. Her dress is going to be so pretty. We took them for a picnic by the lake in the college grounds and Robs sold our car just after they left. So now we have none but your Chrysler Sunbeam ☼. It's still running well and is used every day, but those brakes can be quite alarming.

Granny rang and said her lodger was an evil, wicked woman because (despite her other perfect lodger qualities) she'd propped the letterbox open with a twig and caused a draft. Mum had thought up a scheme whereby Mary-Dieu could take Daisy to Bedford and live with Granny but the idea did not prove exactly popular with any of them. Mary-Dieu is not exactly destitute and there's nothing Granny likes less than babies, even her own great grandchildren.

Mum is still worried about the violence in South Africa but we seem to be more at risk in Surrey. The Army have declared that we are no longer allowed to walk on Barossa Common – the endless woodland at the back of our quarters. Some sort of psychopath pounced on a woman there. He had his hands around her throat but as her Alsatian leapt out of the bushes and bit him on the elbow she managed to escape from his clutches. Despite soldiers being sent in to assist the Police, the attacker cannot be found and is thought to be living rough. We've all had photo-fits shoved under our doors. He looks the epitome of an escaped convict – matted hair, rotten teeth, a scar on his cheek and cold sores round his mouth. The men refer to him as Barossa Bob.

Tamzin says Johnty has been pro-active about intruders but it rather backfired. He woke up late for work on Friday, something that has **never** happened before, flew downstairs to let the dog out and found a large tabby Tomcat bearing down on Thelma. I do not know why, she is the most unattractive cat. Johnty made the huge mistake of trying to pick up the Tomcat. It ran up his chest, puncturing him with its claws, onto his shoulders, turned digging its claws further in and dropped down his back before running off. Poor Johnty. He staggered back upstairs to ask Tamzin to treat the lacerations. She was furious that he should wake her up so early, only to discover he was quite badly hurt. His pyjamas were in shreds. Blood was pouring everywhere but he made the error of telling her what had happened. Tamzin couldn't stop laughing, which made him even more upset.

'I'm meant to be at work.'

'Stay still. You can't go dripping with blood.' She was trying to put sticking-plasters over the wounds but couldn't do the scratches as they were so long.

When he eventually reached the office a call came through for him.

'Meeaow.' It was Tamzin.

She couldn't resist ringing back a bit later announcing herself as Eartha Kitt.

When do you think you'll come back? London is dismal and nothing ever changes here – I wouldn't rush, except to see the wolf cub of course.

My tummy threatens to pop early again. I'm still quite compact, but feeling full. Full to the brim.
Tons of love from us all,
Perry xxxxxx

Equus Horse Safaris

Dear Perry,

Sarah-Jane and I are in despair. Andrew, who managed to teach me about the plants and animals here in five weeks, is leaving us to work as a ranger on the main game reserve. He gets to wear epaulettes on his shoulders.

Andy is also leaving. A local farmer tried to strangle him.

Sarah-Jane's mother, who was staying, took us all out to dinner at the neighbouring lodge where the farmer became very drunk. This was OK when he was asleep but he woke to find Andy was (kindly) driving him home, in his car. He was so cross about this he grabbed Andy around the neck while they were going along. A bit like Barossa Bob.

Andy was stone cold sober, not amused and only escaped by flinging himself out of the vehicle, which then started hurtling back down the road towards the Palala River. Andrew was lying, half asleep, in the back. He managed to dive over the seats and put the hand brake on just before they reached the river.

Apart from all this, Sarah-Jane has booked herself on a six-week holiday to Bolivia. Nelly and I can't run this place by ourselves; we have eleven people coming to stay this weekend. Andrew says that he'll be around to start the pump. Ha ha; he'll be busy cutting hiking trails and doing rangerish things with his Zulu scouts. I'm stocking up the freezer with stuff like lamb curry that I can heat up when we get in from riding but things are never easy. I had to deal with a truck that arrived with a load of frozen chickens this afternoon at the same time as one that turned up with three hundred bales of lucerne – feed for the horses.

Is the wolf cub you refer to your baby? Will you have to call him Wolf if he's a girl?

There's a baby white rhinoceros here. He is about the same size and shape as a bullterrier; the sweetest thing. The bush is starting to turn golden now; it's autumn and beginning to get quite cold at night. I'm rather short of clothes. I do have Mum's 1971 safari jacket but need something a little warmer. We have to wear khaki, 'and look smart,' as Sarah-Jane says when we tumble out of bed at five o'clock in the morning.

It's OK for her; she looks like a fashion plate in beige shorts. I look more like a Hitler Youth.

There's time to write now as I'm at the camp waiting for guests to arrive. It's easier to get through everything here than at the house where there are endless things to do. We just have a big old safari tent with raised sides, lending its shade to a dining table and two sofas where people relax after they come in from riding. We light the whole camp with paraffin lamps at night and always have a fire, which we sit round on canvas chairs. Since there's no phone or electricity it is very peaceful – nothing hums or rings, only there's a bird that has a call exactly like an alarm clock.

There's a little swimming pool here and five dark green Hemingway-style tents, each with it's own verandah. They're quite large ones, furnished with proper beds for the guests. I think even Aunt Reinhild would find it comfortable; Mum would love it; you must persuade her to come out. And come out too, whenever you can.

Wendy has just rung from the office in Johannesburg saying, 'Don't worry,' (about the chronic staff shortage) 'I've found you a really good looking man of thirty-four. He knows all about the bush and speaks masses of languages.'

Well, I can't wait.

Lots of love,

Sophie

Equus Horse Safaris

Dear Tamzin,

I'm immobilized. Jigsaw slipped in deep sand and fell over, trapping me beneath him. My knee is squished. A nurse, who happened to be staying, told me that all I can do is wait for it to un-squish. On top of this Nelly has left. She turned out to be an unmarried mother of five.

'Five?'

'I knew she had children but didn't realise how young they were,' Sarah-Jane said, locking the safe. 'It seems her mother is fed up with looking after them, although this seems to be the lot of grandmothers in Africa.'

'Nelly said working here was too dangerous,' Andrew said, looking in.

'Is it?'

'I did find her peering out of the kitchen at the camp looking rather anxious,' Sarah-Jane muttered. 'The buffalo had been around and gave her a fright. They went away when she started banging pots and pans but not before chasing her into the loo. Rather a sweet Zulu girl called Lindizwe, who said she is not frightened of wild animals, is coming to replace her.'

'All the way from Zululand?'

'No, she's the girlfriend of one of the game scouts. Since you will be the guide, Sophie, we are going to have a proper cook.'

'Yes, Sarah-Jane.' Relief flooded through me.

DANIELLE VENTER

Originally a voice down the phone declared she would come up from the Cape for a month, as long as she didn't have to slaughter a warthog. I was expecting a funny old lady, but a girl with long hair, dyed BRIGHT purple has arrived. Danielle. She can make a horse perform like a dancer, cooks the most complicated meals quite effortlessly and arranges flowers. Well, sticks and stuff but it looks impressive. She wanted to put fruit bowls in the guest tents but they attracted ants.

Another staggeringly attractive girl, called Nicki, with long dark, crinkly hair, a nose stud and very short shorts has arrived to manage the horses. She says 'isit' a lot. Isit and 'Howzit?', 'Now' for soon, 'Now-now' for 'straight away' and 'So-long' for 'in a while'. 'Ach-shame' means 'what a pity', 'dorph' means 'particularly stupid' and everyone is 'man', regardless of gender, but otherwise she does speak English.

What I was excited about was the tall, dark, good-looking man Wendy had promised. Well, Tamzin, this complete weirdo called Vincent has pitched up. His languages include Afrikaans and Zulu but he can't actually engage in conversation. He just hides behind his dense, fuzzy beard, and eyes you up. He knows the bush, but he's been living in a remote, mountainous area of Natal, all alone for seven years, and can't actually impart any of his knowledge to other people.

Danielle was instantly wary of him, saying, 'If you saw him in the street you'd lock you car doors from the inside.'

'*Ach. Ja, man,*' Nicki said, laughing. 'I checked him walking along the pavement outside Wendy's house.' She'd been sitting in the car with her father, waiting to go for her interview. 'I thought, "No ways." Even Dad told me to lock my door quickly.'

The clients think he is peculiar too. I sent him off for the day with one girl who arrived back saying she was slightly concerned that he'd rape her. Wendy said this was utter nonsense but I had

Lindizwe, the Zulu maid, standing in the office in tears saying that he'd been trying to get into her room at night, demanding favours, asking for sex. I told him that she was indisputably out of bounds, but men from his background resent being told what to do by women.

He is demanding when it comes to meals and won't even clear his own plate from the table, let alone take orders from me. I've been insisting that Tigger sleeps on my bed. She snores, but since I'm alone in the rondavel in the garden I want her to bark and wake me if he tries the door at night.

the Liquidizer......

Danielle has rigged up an alarm system at my window consisting of a series of tins balanced on top of a defunct liquidizer. My own liquidizer.

'It's experienced baptism by full immersion,' she explained. 'I don't think the South African electrification programme has reached Zululand yet.'

She'd just extracted the whole thing, plug and all, from the sink.

One thing that was quite exciting is that I found a snare. It was a noose of wire that had been laid in a game track, which I came across as I was taking out an evening ride.

Vincent said a poacher had laid it down and that he wanted to look for more. We left him tracking footprints while I radioed through to the Warden, pleased that we were making a tangible contribution to conservation. I can't bear the idea of an animal being left suffering in a trap, desperately trying to gnaw off its own foot.

Vincent is certainly good at tracking. He found eight more wire nooses and the poacher; he was the little old gardener who works for the ranch mechanic. Vincent and the Warden, who is quite young, started interrogating him. As the staff on the ranch are on salaries and receive food with their pay it's not as if the animals are being trapped to feed hungry children.

I suppose they find it exciting. I know rare animals like pangolin - scaly anteaters, the African equivalent of an armadillo - are sought after by witch-doctors who will pay up to R40 (£9) for each scale. The gardener wasn't forthcoming.

'I threatened to pull his teeth out.' Vincent muttered, 'with pliers.'

I think they bashed him about because the owner of the reserve was furious, came over and threatened to chuck us off his property; horses, guests, the lot.

The next morning I was out at 6.30am wondering where our game-drive vehicle was. All I could see was Andrew coming towards me in a huge Ford pick-up.

'You've got problems, Sophie Neville.'

'Have I?'

'Yep; I know what's happened to your Toyota. Vincent used it to spend the night whoring, only he chose the wrong girls to visit and all my scouts are up in arms. Start blockading the farmhouse,' he said as he drove away. 'And bring in Michael Caine; you've the third Zulu war on your hands.'

I rang Wendy.

'I'm sorry, but you're going to have to find another guide; this one is a complete liability.'

She was not pleased that I was questioning her judgement, but when I looked out of the window a Zulu scout was swinging his knobkerrie and shouting at Vincent.

I sent him off to take a group of six stoic women walking down a ravine, but that night he let the water tank overflow onto the electricity junction box for the farm. When I spoke to him about the danger, he flew into a rage.

Tamzin, I prayed. Wendy is not prepared to sack him, Sarah-Jane is in South America and I was in a state. Although I felt sorry for Vincent in a way, I knew I had to get him out of here. Only couldn't think how.

In the morning Danielle walked into the office, swung her purple plait over her shoulder and declared, 'Vincent has blood emanating from his anus.'

He had a ruptured colon of all things. I sent him straight off to hospital in Pretoria, and somehow don't think he'll be coming back.

Love from a girl with a bullterrier now determined not to get off her bed,

Sophie

CHAPTER FIVE

Bellevue,

Quellington Green

3rd June 1992

Dearest One,

What a simply dreadful time you had with Vincent… what a horror. Perry has someone lurking in the bushes too, so just wait; it'll be me next. I do feel sad, however, that it took such a grim situation before you could discover the JOYS of sleeping with a sweet bullterrier. They're so sensitive.

We are having big problems selling our cottage and may have to lower the price. Finding a house is another ball game; all we can afford is a hovel. V. depressing. Raddy and I were riding past a lovely old redbrick farmhouse surrounded by apple trees and I nearly wept with longing. It's quite dilapidated but I would love to have a place like that, with space to breathe. We are going to Scotland this weekend for a wedding, and then Johnty is taking me on holiday to Greece so I'm trying not to complain.

Mum and Dad had a film crew at home recording *The House of Eliot*, which was great as they were paid quite well and the production team put covers over all the downstairs radiators. Dad thinks it amusing that his house is being featured as 'a love nest' in the storyline. He had a small part as an auctioneer and seems to be enjoying his new career as a jobbing actor. I'm beginning to loathe the very thought of it.

I had an awful journey yesterday to an audition in Bristol, which I didn't even get. It was the first rain for weeks. It rained and rained; I couldn't see the road in front of me.

Last Friday I had to play a glamour puss in a video for the AA, which was embarrassing as it was made outside Tesco's (my local). The stupid director hadn't asked permission to film and we were nearly kicked out.

Then, Oh Sophie, then I was in an advertisement for *Mr Kipling's Cakes*, shot in Birmingham. I went off gaily thinking how we could live off the repeat fees for years, but somehow I think not. I found myself being a 'young mother', with a twelve-year old child. The notion. I couldn't believe it. Do you see me as matronly? I don't look vaguely maternal, and would have had to produce the child when I was sixteen or something.

They gave me a yellow shirt-waister dress, in which I had to whirl round, smile and eat a lemon slice. Not just a nibble either. All of it. I must have had to eat nineteen. I can't tell you how much my 'son' ate. I couldn't look at the child. After each cut, we had to spit the contents of our mouths into a bin-liner, only he didn't – except after the final cut, when he was sick.

Mum said that she had to drink so many cups of coffee for a commercial once that she became quite delicate in the bladder region, and had to wear nappies coming back on the train.

Well, I had driven to *Mr. Kipling's* shoot. Perry had lent me your car – it was a Sunbeam in the rain. By the end of the day my tummy had blown up to such an extent that I could only waddle and could hardly get behind the steering wheel. I drove straight into a roaring flood; water two-foot deep rushing along the main road. It must have been the result of all the rain. I had no option but to turn into the Holiday Inn and stay the night there, all by myself, feeling bloated, while surrounded by leery businessmen. Not funny. Mum thought it was, for some reason.

Must go –

Love,

Tamzin

EQUUS HORSE SAFARIS

Dear Perry,

Your time must be near upon you. Push hard. Has Mummy sent you anything to bite on? I should have sent you a stick of *biltong*.

My Afrikaans is coming along. Andrew assures me that it is the most descriptive, lyrical language but I'm not fit for heaven yet. Under Nicki's influence I've learnt to swear. I can say, 'Fling it on the compost heap' only I do get confused with the grammar and end up blabbering incoherently. 'Throw the horses on the compost muck.' The Africans are too polite to laugh but Andrew isn't. I've been reading the writing on biscuit packets and notice boards in an attempt to learn normal words. I can tell you that a *winkel* is a shop and a *wortel* is a carrot. You say vinkel and vortle. A *boing-kie* is a bean, only it is spelt *boontjie*. We've just driven 100km to a place called *Vaalwater* to buy horse food, passing a sign to a place called *Vier en Twintig Riviere*. Nicki said they couldn't be normal places:

'Vaalwater means 'grey water'- dirty water.' You must pronounce the V: F and the W: V with long A's, as in Farl-vater. 'The other sign says twenty-four rivers; you couldn't call a village Twenty-four Rivers. Think of living there.'

But there was a sign on the way into the town saying, '*Dit is die Volkstaat*'. Nicki could only explain this as being a declaration that we were entering a Rightwing stronghold. I looked all over the place for Eugene Terre'Blanche[ii] but only met the rather gorgeous grain trader. He is called Janneman. I'd love to have a boyfriend called Janneman.

Nicki, who is frankly so attractive she leaves men gasping for breath, already has a huge number of admirers, including a rather sweet young farmer who arrived with another load of lucerne, fodder for the horses. He hardly speaks English at all. When we had him in for tea he spent the whole time trying to think of a cool way of asking her out.

In the end he plucked up his courage, drew a deep breath and said, 'You must come up and see my lucerne sometime.'

Naughty Nicki couldn't help herself and burst out laughing.

She had a long love letter from another Afrikaans chap.

'How's this? You're going to have to see it to believe it, man,' she said speaking to me.

He'd written most poetically, comparing her to a rose:

'Only you are more than a rose,' he wrote. 'I think of you as a hole rosebush.'

'Ah, shame man,' Nicki said 'I must write back so-long.'

It's extraordinary: when you go to a party out here the men and women separate. Men talk about their time in the army at the bar or standing round the *braai*, women sit on comfy chairs and talk about sex. Only Nicki can manage to combine the two.

I've gone and done a rash thing. I bought a horse. He is small, red and stands with his neck arched and feet together like a

Chinese statue. He bucks like crazy. Nicki and I had been told that there were two Thoroughbreds for sale on a neighbouring game ranch, only he isn't a Thoroughbred at all, must be an Arab/Saddlebred cross, but we both decided he was rather fun to ride and bought him for £100. He seems to be quite versatile, but I'm not sure what Sarah-Jane is going to say. His name is Sam the Great.

An odd thing happened today, which rather unnerved me. I was in the office, going through the bookings, when I heard a knock at the outside door. For some reason I decided to peer sideways though the window to see who was there before answering it. A long, brilliant green snake was sliding up the white door. If I had opened this, it would have fallen down on me. Andrew came to catch it declaring it to be a *boomslang*, the most poisonous snake we have. Apparently the fangs are at the back of their mouths, so it's hard for them to actually get a good bite out of you, but I was so glad it didn't try.

Now he says we must be careful of puff-adders which tend to hang around old houses.

'Their venom is cytotoxic, often causing necrosis. You're likely to lose any limb bitten to gangrene.'

Let me tell you I have the dog searching my bedroom every night. Donald and Wendy arrived on Friday evening to find me rushing round in my nightdress, wearing dark glasses and gumboots, looking for a cobra with a broom.

'It helps if you have a hairy chest and wear a gold medallion round your neck,' Donald assured me. 'If they do decide to spit they aim at the speck of light in your eye, but will go for whatever is more shiny.'

So, there you are.

I saw the baby rhino again this morning. He was with his mother in a dry lake near the camp, chasing a bird. White rhino have poor eyesight and send their young in front of them; the cow was beginning to get quite confused.

If we go quietly we can find up to about fourteen different mammal species when we go out riding now. We almost always see warthog, who graze by dropping to their knees, small solitary antelope with huge ears called steenbok and herds of impala that scatter as Go-away birds squawk from the trees, giving away our presence.

Because climatically we are in an intercontinental convergence zone, there's a wider variety of plants and animals here than you might find in East Africa where Uncle Tony taught me to identify game. Here the kudu are huge with magnificent, spiral horns so heavy you wonder how they can run, but apparently they can jump a twelve-foot fence from a standstill. We have oryx on this ranch and forest antelope called Nyala. There's a big herd of eland that I'm longing to find, and I still haven't seen the elephant. There are ten; a small herd of young ones translocated from the Kruger National Park when their herd was culled a year or so ago. I come across their footprints and follow them endlessly but they seem to be shy, living on the most inaccessible and rocky escarpment.

I learnt how to cook bread on the fire last night; you mix an ordinary packet of flour with a can of beer and put it in an iron pot, spading coals onto the lid. We made some with sea-salt and roughly crushed garlic on top, which was delicious. Danielle says she'd show me how to make an oven in a termite mound so we can bake our own pizzas.

My new pony is doing well. He loves jumping and Nicki is hard at work, building a cross-country course. Andrew seems to be terribly keen on building it too for some reason.

Lots of love

Sophie

**Oak Tree Road,
Cape Town
South Africa**

20th June 1992

Dear Tamzin,

I'm in Cape Town, looking up at the mountain and taking a break so my poor squashed knee has a chance to recover. It was getting awfully awkward hopping everywhere. Sarah-Jane returned from South America with a big smile and a huge, fuchsia pink Bolivian jersey, which I'm wearing since winter has arrived and it's quite chilly.

I'm staying with an old friend who S-J, Rebecca and I once drove down through Africa with called Judith. She took me to Stellenbosch yesterday, for lunch with Danielle who has returned to running a Cape Dutch homestead where they take about ten guests in enormous splendour and luxury, with towering flower arrangements and great bowls of fruit in all the bedrooms. There's a staircase up the side of the white thatched building, which was originally built for goats kept in the attic. I suppose there were lion in the area then, but imagine living beneath a herd of goats. Mind you, the Masai keep livestock under the bed.

When we went around the wine estates I found one vineyard had a funny little Rapunzel-like tower with a conical, thatched roof. Instead of a girl with a long, golden plait there were goats living there too. They get to the top by walking up slats of 2"x 2" wood and then sit in the doorway sunning themselves. The cheese is terribly good but I've no idea why the goats live in a tower.

Despite my cronky knee, Danielle took me riding through the dunes and down to the sea. I was hurling along on an old racehorse when it suddenly put its head down and stopped. It had seen a mole. A mole.

Danielle roared with laughter as I struggled back off the horse's neck into the saddle, but we had been going so fast that mole could have killed me; much more dangerous than anything on the game reserve.

We saw children running across the dual carriageway as we drove into the city. Judith said you have to be careful because many Xhosa families have only just arrived from rural areas and their children don't have any experience of traffic.

She took me into Kayelitsha, a vast shantytown made up of corrugated iron shacks piled on the sand dunes beyond the airport, where she takes sewing classes and a Sunday School. I found myself in a room with two hundred and fifty children, all looking up at me expectantly. I had no idea what to do. None of them speak any English. I don't exactly have any Xhosa.

Judith came out with the only international word she could think of at the time, which was 'Hallelujah?' and they all burst into song. They sang on and on in beautiful harmony for about twenty minutes, when someone came along and told them a story. I couldn't have managed two hundred and fifty British children for five minutes but these children were so responsive, so happy to be there and so well-behaved that two hours flew past. We came back glowing.

It was more worrying when we returned to Kayelitsha to take a sewing class. None of the ladies turned up and I could see men walking around with guns. A white girl was shot recently for driving into the township and drunken violence with shooting is an almost nightly occurrence. Most are retribution killings. Rape and abuse are almost part of normal life. The children see it all.

We left, driving past pitifully thin dogs covered in sores. The worse thing I saw there was a horse, harnessed to a cart loaded with scrap metal. It was so thin and worn out I couldn't bear to look.[iii]

It's difficult to imagine Africa as being wintry, but I've never felt so cold as I do now. I've actually started knitting myself a jumper in desperation. Can't think how Harry the Hottentot managed to survive without one. After a week of sparkling clear days, when we climbed Table Mountain and walked through the harbour where the fishing boats come in, a thick mist descended and everything's dank and wet. None of the houses are heated and it seems impossible to get warm. I felt for the people in their tin shacks. We drive north soon, through the Karoo and back to Johannesburg, but I'm told it's colder there on the Highveld. I never imagined it to be like this, but it is freezing.

Lots of love from your frantically knitting sister Sophie

URGENT -

The wolf cub has arrived - 40 minutes ago - 20th June 1992. I'm writing from my labour bed. 8lb 2oz. Clever boy - to be called Hastings. Sprinkling of brown hair. Looks like Robert with a strong nose and not like Atalanta at all. Mum is looking after her; they should visit later. In fact Mum was so late arriving I couldn't sit down in the car and only just reached the hospital in time. What a panic; I nearly had him kneeling in the back as there was a traffic jam in Aldershot. I thought, 'I'm going to give birth to this baby with all the other drivers being able to see.' It got so bad I screamed, 'Drive over the top of the roundabout, Robert.' but he couldn't as it was covered in trees. Will write properly soon.

Tons of love Perry and Robs xxx

I hear that the stork has been! Congratulations — thinking of you all - lots of love Sophie

✉✉✉WELLDONEGIRLKEEPMEABREASTOFDEVELOPMENTSLOVEAUNTSOPHIE✉✉✉

Equus Horse Safaris

Dear Tamzin,

Please give the newborn babe my greetings. I'm horrified to hear that he was nearly born in the back of my Chrysler Sunbeam. I thought Perry was so organized. I have to tell you that at the time in question his aunt was being whisked off to Swaziland by an old Etonian. I arrived in Johannesburg to find James Money-Kyrle was up at Equus looking for me with Rebecca, who has bought herself a yellow jeep with a bullet hole in it. A real bullet hole.

James returned, declaring that riding horses was most uncomfortable and that he was taking me to the seaside. While Rebecca went off to sort out a problem with a hot air balloon that had landed in Hartebeespoort Dam, we hired a car and sped off towards the mountains.

'Wake up James, we're at the Swaziland border.'

'Oh, just wave my passport at them,' he said without opening his eyes.

'James, you're not in the EEC anymore; this is an African border.' It was too; a hot, colourful, sweaty one with armed guards and an array of ladies in bright dresses with baskets piled on their heads and babies tied to their backs. As we drove on, winding our way up into the hills, children danced by the roadside in grass skirts, trying to get us to stop and buy carvings. We spent two nights at a lodge near a place called Pigg's Peak where I made James swim under icy waterfalls, and then on, driving through the spectacular little country. Did you know that Jamie, our cousin not this James, was at boarding school with the King of Swaziland? When he was seventeen the King fell in love with a Dorset girl who worked at the greengrocer's in town. Jamie said a VHS tape showing a selection of nubile and topless Swazi maidens arrived, and the whole sixth form helped him to choose a wife from his own kingdom. I've always wondered how the girl at the greengrocer's felt. I don't suppose she would have been happy as Queen of Swaziland. There must be a tremendous number of other wives by now. The King's father had 600[liv].

We were intending to put up tents and camp but ended up driving along in the dark and had to stay at a motel in a town called Big Bend. It was called the Big Bend Motel. The beds were bedecked in brown nylon with Scottie dogs looking up at you from the surface of the wastepaper bins. Nothing seemed to work and since the wiring looked a little precarious I was rather wary about touching anything to do with electricity. There were a lot of towels on a rail around the green tiled bathroom, folded so they read BEND, BEND, BEND.

'James, you must see this.'

He didn't think it funny at all.

The dining-room tables were lit with red light bulbs encased in hanging shades that looked like great big mop caps and we were presented with a meal of fried spam. Travelling salesmen stared at us, swigging beer out of cans.

We finally made it to a dazzling place by the sea called Kosi Bay where the Warden, who is a friend of Sarah-Jane's, took us whizzing in his motorboat through a series of coastal lakes filled with spectacular bird life. We watched Samango monkeys in the Tarzan-like forest and snorkelled in the river mouth amongst swirling schools of fish. I had an even more amazing time swimming with sardines that were trapped in a tidal pool at Sodwana Bay. The shoal would twist and turn around me, glinting in the sunlight until I felt as if I was a fish myself. James was a little sunburnt by the time I put him on the plane, but he was happy we had survived each other's company and he said we must do it all again sometime.

Back to work as a guide now, with a large group of teenage girls to entertain and a horse manager who is in love. It's very gooey and rather revolting to watch, but I'm quite jealous as I long to be loved and in love. I have Sam. I suppose he takes me out, but only riding. I hope you have fun at the dinner in London. You're so lucky to be married; even if you get rather used to the love bit; you do at least have someone to take you dancing.
With all my love, for what it's worth,
Sophie

Bellevue still,

Quellington Green,

Dear Sophie –

It wasn't your car Hastings nearly arrived in but Robert's Jag; far more of a consternation. He didn't want his leather seats spoilt. Guess what…having decided that life as a baby-bearing machine would be pretty gruesome I discovered I'm having a child. Quite a shock, but we are very excited. We found out in Scotland (so it will have to be called Jock) and I'm due on Valentine's ♥ Day. No dancing for me.

Now I really am pregnant do you think I'll get any telly work? I suppose I could emulate a greedy Smurf. My bosoms, stomach and bottom have ballooned and I feel sick most of the time. Can you imagine me a mother? I don't know what we are going to do. Johnty went off the other day, came back about half an hour later and I said, 'Where's Maudie?' He'd left her tied up outside the village shop. What is he going to do with a child?

Raddy rather stole my thunder by declaring that she is going to have a baby too; her third. It's brilliant though; they can grow up together. She says that sadly the pram that we found the dead cat in was given to a friend who took it to Hong Kong, or I could have had it.

We had a great weekend in Scotland. When the bride and groom went away on their four-wheel drive quad-bike, it shot up into the sky, out of control and smashed into a great aunt's Volvo. Everyone roared with laughter except the great aunt. And the bride's mother.

You're wrong about being married. Johnty hates going out, let alone to parties. He couldn't make the last formal dinner in London and had to ask his friend Nigel to take me.

On being introduced by Dad to the ghastly vicar who married Johnty and I, Nigel said: 'Hello, I'm Tamzin's Lover.'

Dad nearly fainted. The meal was dire and went on and on. Poooor Perry (who was heavy with the wolf cub) was sitting one down from a woman who fainted. As sick poured out of her mouth Nigel remarked, 'I didn't like the pudding much either.'

Johnty did manage to get away from the harvest long enough to take me on a week's trip to Corfu. We stayed with some friends in a villa that belonged to the chap who discovered the Hitler Diaries. It was in a village opposite Albania where I think you filmed *My Family and Other Animals*. You would have loved it, but the steps down to the beach housed a family of snakes, which didn't make me happy, so I walked round most of the time with an olive branch, singing loudly. We hired one of those sloppy boats, which was the most terrifying thing I have ever been on in my life; I don't know how you managed to cram a film crew onto one. Johnty fell off it.

We did have a lovely day water-skiing, although I had to miss out on account of Jock and I found myself worrying about where we are going to live. I phoned Perry to get the news…. The wolf cub had been born under a full moon. But she didn't know about my house. Then, as I was walking down the steps to the beach, singing away, a little boy ran up and thrust a note in my hand. It was from

Raddy. Written in pencil. It said, 'The old man who owned the farm we rode past has died. His relations need to sell-up. I've put in an offer for you at the full asking price.' The FULL ASKING PRICE...

Johnty just said, 'Impossible, especially since we have no buyers for our cottage. And how on Earth has Raddy been able to send you a note?'

But there it was, in her distinctive handwriting. I flew into a terrible angst and ended up walking all over the island as an outlet for my emotions.

We arrived home to discover we did have an offer on Bellevue ~ from the people who had come to see it five minutes before we rushed off to catch our plane. The lovely 18th century farmhouse had just come on the market, with thirty-five acres and an old-fashioned barnyard. It's wonderful – no modernisations, no heating, no inside loo, just splendid. Unfortunately other people think so too and we are going to have sealed bids on Friday, 12.00. I'm in real turmoil now, pacing the bedroom all night. My next letter will tell all. Raddy, who is jumping up and down with excitement too, said she'd rung everyone, frantically trying to get hold of me in Greece before the farmhouse went on the market. In the end she found an old school friend of hers was renting a villa in the same village as us and rang her with the message. The friend sent her son over with the note. She does have similar handwriting to Raddy.

We've seen the wolf cub. He has black fur and dark brown eyes. Perry is looking great and her tummy is totally flat again.
Lots of love, Tamzin.

Equus Horse Safaris

Dear Perry,

I'm so glad you didn't give birth in my car. We have a new chef called Josie, who once cooked for Roald Dahl and has a lot to say about unexpected deliveries. Another lorry load of frozen food came today. She thought they were bringing penguins, but they turned out to be more chickens, which we had no idea what to do with. Penguin was just the name of the company.

Anyway, it is wonderful news about the boy. I'd better start looking for a pony for him straight away. Why is he called Hastings? Was he conceived there?

On Sunday afternoons, just as we are about to flop, a rather dismal child of twelve comes over for a riding lesson. He calls me Tunnie, which means Auntie, but I can't bear it. I don't feel old enough and as Sarah-Jane says, it's like being called a tuna fish. Nicki says you spell it *Tannie* but they say Tunnie. Repeatedly. Anyway, he spends the weekend with his daddy and comes here to ride before being collected by his mother and her new husband.

Today the enormous father, Dupe du Plessis, arrived, clad in a light blue crimplene safari suit with long knee socks to match. He sat down on a small white chair in our garden and started drinking from a bottle of vodka he produced from his otherwise empty briefcase.

It was terrible. He stayed all afternoon and started crying when his son was driven away. Great big tears were splashing into his drink. I hardly know him and had no idea what to talk about, so started watering the vegetable garden, which is coming on well.

'Spinach!' Dupe said in disgust. 'Why are you growing spinach?'

'It's for our guests.' I announced brightly.

'*Kaffir* food,' he said, sneeringly. 'You're nothing but a *kaffir* lover. And do you know something?' He went on as I stood there trying to jam the hose back onto the stand-pipe, 'There's nothing I hate more than a *kaffir* lover. You *Rooineks* are all the same. I'm telling you; I am going to murder you and no one will find the pieces.'

At this point Josie came along and asked if he would like to stay for supper.

'Don't offer him spinach.'

We didn't. We ate, appropriately, *Potjiekos*, a *Vooretrekker* stew that Josie heated up from the night before.

'Nicki, you must help,' I said under my breath. 'He's roaring drunk.'

She normally doesn't eat in the evenings but speaks Afrikaans and I thought would be able to placate him.

'Oh, he's just desperately lonely. Imagine having to go back to an empty house tonight.'

And she proceeded to pour him another drink. Once he got going I thought he'd never stop.

'This country was bought with blood.' he cried, thumping the table till we clutched our plates. 'And the river will flow with blood again; YOUR blood,' he said pointing at me for some reason.[v]

I heard a crash and looked out of the window.

'Buffalo.' Josie cried. 'There are buffalo in the vegetable garden.'

'My spinach! They'll trample the spinach.'

'*Ach*, no problem,' said Dupe, lurching to his feet and out of the door. 'They're just *wildebeeste*,' he said disappearing into the dark.

'They're not,' said Josie.

We all looked at each other appalled. Buffalo are terribly dangerous and will gore you to death without any hesitation. We peered into the gloom. There was silence and then a lot of crashing. A buffalo charged out from beneath the orange trees, leaping the cattle grid at the end of the drive.

'A knife.' Dupe was shouting. 'Get a knife. Get a knife.'

'Oh, flip, they've *donnered* him,' Nicki said opening the door.

She went cautiously outside, followed by Josie. I rushed into the kitchen where I obediently found a carving knife then walked, tentatively, past the bougainvillea looking under the orange grove. Dupe was lying on his back at the end of the garden with one leg raised awkwardly, while Josie and Nicki dropped to their knees beside him.

'Where is that knife?'

I ran down to find the girls were completely helpless, rocking on their heels, in gales of laughter. Dupe was lying on his back, trapped with one leg in the air, sticking up at an odd angle. His long, powder blue knee-sock was twisted round the garden tap, at the top of the stand-pipe. He needed me to cut him free.

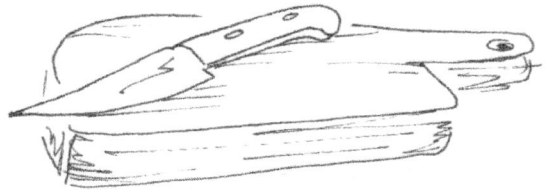

My new horse, Sam, is amazing; intelligent, amusing, tough and brave, with perfect manners. Now I just have to find a man like him.

No qualifiers here. All we have arriving are four colts; big black Friesians. Sarah-Jane has told me that I am to break one of them in, if you please. I'm completely terrified as Nicki has been wandering about with chains to use as leading reins.

With love from a very tired spinach eater,

Sophie

EQUUS HORSE SAFARIS

Dear Tamzin,

I have to tell you that snakes can't hear; they have no ears. They're sensitive to vibrations so when you are in Corfu, stamp like crazy. No one on *My Family and Other Animals* complained about the sloppy boats there, but they went out with so many people crammed on-board I expect the weight made them more stable. I can remember the film crew getting on with great polystyrene reflector boards, the 16mm camera and all the sound equipment; about seventeen men with Hannah Gordon and a sausage dog. I looked down at them from the jetty and couldn't resist putting on Mum's voice and asking, 'Now, have you all done wee-wee?' They all looked at me, looked at each other, knew they would be at sea for a good two hours and piled out of the boat again. The director sat there shaking his head but couldn't complain because he needed to do wee-wee too.

I hope the bairn is being good inside your tummy. I've just spent a gruelling day with Walter, our vet, castrating the four beautiful Friesian colts that arrived yesterday. What terrible things we do to animals. Their destiny is to provide heavy men who can't ride with a safe and steady passage past unpredictable wild beasts. I caught the castrations in a bowl and offered them to the grooms for supper, but they were instantly rejected. I'm sure Mum would have relished them.

While Nicki has introduced the cheery rhythms of Radio Jacaranda 'your soothing companion' 🎵 to the yard, the grooms are still proving rather a problem. I keep giving them lists of which horses to saddle up and quite different ones are brought in. It didn't occur to me that they might not be able to read.

Now Somewhere has disappeared somewhere else, and France (I now learn that you spell his name Frans) has been so belligerent and unreliable Sarah-Jane had to sack him.

'I do hope you find a job as a panel-beater,' she said, crisply sending him on his way, before explaining to me that he had been taking small boys into the Lucerne shed.

An old man, Nicki instantly called Madula, has come to look after the horses instead with an even older chap called Wisdom, who is, by all appearances, a Bushman - only his traditional dress seems to be a boilersuit. Neither of them speak a word of English but they ride beautifully. *Madula* means 'revered one'. He was (visibly) dismayed by the sight of my vegetable garden and to my great relief has rather taken it over. I got Lindizwe, who now has a hairdo consisting of thirty little plaits sticking out of her head at different angles, to ask him if he'd ever grown tomatoes before. He looked at me. Wisdom started laughing. Apparently he has grown thousands. Literally acres and acres of them, farmed commercially on the Palala floodplains. I felt rather stupid. Nicki chucked a book called *Painless Afrikaans* in my lap. Fascinating reading. It says, 'Consonants are sounded exactly as in English with a few exceptions ~ B,D,G, and J,K,L,R,V,W, and GH,KS,KW,SJ,TJ,N.' That is virtually all consonants. The vowels are odd too. They spell Zulu: *Zoeloe*. As in *hoepoe*. The bird.

Something we don't have is a dung problem; enormous beetles fly in and take it away.

'Oo, what are these called?' one particularly smart French lady asked.

'Dung beetles.'

They love horse manure. They chop the dung up, make it into balls and, by pushing with their hind legs, roll balls of dung precariously across the hot sand before taking them underground to use as a good medium in which to lay their eggs. Males push while the female can often be seen balancing on top. Mum would be fascinated. I don't think she'd find the vultures so appealing. They were pretty well wiped out from this area when DDT was sprayed everywhere to eradicate malaria in the 1950s, but a giraffe died recently and two vultures were on the carcass within hours. They must be cruising high in the sky, beyond our visual limits.

'How did the giraffe die?' I asked Walter, who had come to do a post mortem.

We once had a terrible storm with great cracks of lightning when two were struck and died, but this one wasn't burnt.

'Poverty.'

I didn't understand, but he explained that even though this reserve seems vast to us it has been dry and the giraffe haven't been able to get the nutrients they need from the trees. In the past they would have migrated further afield. This one was pregnant, reaching full term. He reckons she died through lack of access to the right species of acacia.

Tigger was expressing a great interest in the head that was lying in the back of Walter's *bakkie*, on the way to be analysed further in the Government laboratory. They'll test it for infectious disease in an effort to detect and prevent potential epidemics spreading through wildlife populations.

More rhino are being re-introduced. I've been taking the clients to see a beautiful, young female called Tracy who is in the holding boma; a pen made of solid, upright posts, where she can acclimatise and adjust before being released into a bigger paddock and then into the main reserve. You can get quite close, so I've been going along with my sketchbook. She wears an earring and has beautiful eyelashes. Atalanta would have been quite overwhelmed.

I was ill and couldn't speak for four days last week. It's no wonder the vegetable garden is ailing. I slept all day, which was amazing since the mattresses here are literally on wooden boards. To begin with I thought, 'No, I can't bear it, the M.E. is coming back again,' as the same grinding fatigue hit me, but it must have been 'flu and after a couple of days I was sitting up in bed, drawing. After a while Andrew came round and said I must come and see Tracy's boyfriend, Rodney.

As it was overcast and windy, Andrew was wearing an Italian Army jacket over his shorts, only this looked odd because you couldn't see much of the shorts, just long bare legs, with red-laced hiking boots on the end. I plodded through the bush after these legs, clutching my sketchbook until we came to a high fence made of tight meshed, galvanized wire. Rodney, an enormous, dark rhinoceros stood the other side eyeing us. I started drawing him. Rhino have the most elegantly formed ears like arum lilies.

It's just my animal magnetism Sophie

'He's vicious, this one.' Andrew started telling me. 'He had us all up trees yesterday. I was in that floppy one,' he said, pointing to a bent sapling. None of the trees around us were at all substantial. I was looking at the spoor on the ground. Huge prints from a rhino outside the boma were heading towards the fence. I followed them round the corner of the enclosure.

'Andrew!' He hadn't seen that there was a massive hole in the galvanized mesh. One of the resident males in the reserve must have charged it, trying to attack the new bull. There was nothing between Rodney and either of us but two flimsy strands of wire.

Andrew is naughty; he does it on purpose. I now gather that despite the fact that most bomas look like fortresses, white rhino can be kept behind cattle fencing. I think he's getting bored. He has to take clients staying at the main lodge on endless game drives.

'Why is that tree marked with a cross?' One of the tourists asked him.

'Oh, we're studying their migratory movement.' And they BELIEVE him. None of us have any idea why there's a cross on that tree, least of all Andrew. But he can't help it. People ask the most stupid questions:

'Is Nelson Mandela still in exile?'

'Do giraffe hunt in packs?'

'What kind of meat do horses like to eat?'

'What do you call a herd of zebra?'

'A herd of zebra.' I assured them.

'They're also known as a dazzle,' Sarah-Jane told me later. 'A dazzle of zebra. You normally find one male with a harem of four females.' Umm: Andrew with Nicki, Josie, Sarah-Jane and me.

Someone asked me, 'Do warthog charge?'

'Yes they do.' I had a terrible fright. It was a cold morning and I was looking after a couple from Yorkshire who could hardly ride. There was a big warthog hole in our path, so I stopped and started to explain why you should never walk in front of the entrance. Well, as I was talking, describing how the warthogs enter by reversing down the hole, an enormous male rushed out, turned and came hurtling towards me. Sam stood his ground, so the pig turned and went for the others. I was shouting at the clients to get away, as warthogs can rip through a horse's stomach with their tusks, but by this time the female and three piglets had run off with their tails in the air and the male joined them.

Those clients were rather odd. The man had his hair plaited like an African girl; only it doesn't look so good when it's flat and mousy. 'How do they keep it clean?' Wendy wanted to know.

'Like tack,' said Nicki. 'They wash it and oil it.' Think of that as you're cleaning your bridle.

Love,

Sophie

Camberley
Surrey

10th July 1992

Dear Sib -

You have been a long time on my mind, but I've waited and waited to send you a photo of your nephew and at last they're back from the developers. He is such a sweet little boy - just like a mole. He snorts and grunts and squeaks. He and Tadpole can do a fine duet - *'The Baby and the Bullterrier'*. He is called Hastings, not after the place, Thank you, but after Hastings, our Great-grandfather.

At two weeks he helped supervise his older sister being a bridesmaid. The evidence is stuck in the next film due for the developers, but what a weekend…

We arrived, *en famille*, in Leicestershire at 10.00pm, having been stuck in M25 traffic all evening. We woke to a miserably rainy day, then off to the bridesmaids' lunch at a relaxed household. I sat spooning shepherd's pie into my mouth whilst sewing rosettes on ballet shoes. Atalanta looked enchanting and was telling everyone about 'white shoes' and 'flowers in hair'. She came right down the aisle behind the bride and at the reception she PERFORMED; she laughed and clapped and pulled flowers from the bride's bouquet, running around delightedly. Quite nerve wracking. And I had to keep disappearing to whack a boob out. At the end of the day we threw Atalanta into bed and drove on to Hertfordshire for another wedding – dancing into the night with Hastings in the hippy sling on Robert's tummy.

On the Sunday we went to Granny's. She gave us a bin liner, a suitcase and three cardboard boxes of 'useful things'. Well, Robert and I laughed and laughed. You see, we were just so exhausted we were almost hysterical when we unpacked moth-eaten jumpers, old anoraks, and a vile, putty coloured doll for Atalanta. (It's made in Mongolia and is, very definitely, a boy).

But Granny has given me a set of silver hairbrushes. Tamzin got a gorgeous china bowl and a sherry decanter. She must have put something aside for you but I didn't ask. It is so sad that she is packing up all these loved and familiar things and giving them away but she seems to be enjoying it all.

This weekend we are going to a regimental thing; church, lunch, polo and stuff. Princess Alexandra will be there so I'll have to squoosh my bosom into something smart for my curtsey. The summer ball Robert organized was brilliant with excellent jugglers and stilt walkers, a jazz band, a raunchy singer and a good dinner. I couldn't miss it and went, four days after having Hastings, leaving him upstairs with the cloakroom ladies. I even managed to wear Tamzin's slinky, lace-up-the-back dress, which the poor ladies had to keep undoing so I could feed the baby.

We go to Wales in August for two weeks. I can't wait to get out of suburbia for a bit. Barossa Bob has prevented our going on walks for ages and ages. He still hasn't even been arrested. I said to Liza, 'Oh, come on. Let's just go. We'll be together and have the dogs.' So, there we were, pushchairs and all, keeping nicely to the paths when Tadpole rushed ahead and jumped up, tail wagging, to greet a scruffy man dressed in green with a **gun** slung over his shoulder.

I said to Liza, 'Don't look. Just turn round and walk as though nothing has happened.'

'What, what?' She said, twisting round. Luckily he had run away from us, into the trees. We met a crocodile of soldiers being yhomped through the woods and said,

'Barossa Bob's right there.'

They got very excited and rushed off to seek him out. The Police ought to use Tadpole as a tracker dog.

Hastings's christening is on 27th September but presumably you will still be away. Do you plan to come back this year at all? I can't imagine Shepherds Bush really tempts you. Sorry for being so bad at keeping in touch.

All love from us all,

P + R + A + H + Tadpole.

Equus Horse Safaris

Dear PRAHT,

I've been having such a lovely time. I'm breaking in one of the young Friesians. We've called him Xian. His little brother is called Limpopo. Tamzin would be so impressed. The first time I rode him a whirlwind came straight towards us. I feared he would shoot off at full gallop but he just closed his eyes and waited until it spiralled past us, tearing leaves and insects up into the sky.

Nicki is on leave but we've been joined by a nineteen-year old boy called Wayne, who thinks living in the Northern Transvaal is the funniest thing. 'Are there any girls in Marken?'

'Yes,' I said, thinking of the one working at the post office.

'Do they bark?'

Wayne alarms me. He wears nothing but a pair of rugger shorts even when it's quite chilly.

'I get dirty working in the bush and it's quicker to wash my body than my clothes, as-well.'

'Good idea,' Sarah-Jane said approvingly, 'But please wear a shirt with a collar in front of the guests; you might shock one of them. And please don't say *aswell*.' Her boyfriend says *aswell* the whole time and it annoys her. It's another South Africanism.

Wayne was brought up on a dairy farm in the Eastern Cape where they study things like plumbing at school. And call men 'oaks'.

'Oaks?'

'The oak who taught us plumbing.'

'Please don't call the customers oaks.'

Wayne says that he has five horses, one of whom is called Moment, 'Because one moment you're on and one moment you're off.' When he was in the Army he had to teach a group of Bushmen to ride but he said it was impossible to get them to wear boots, or accept the concept of sleeping in a bed, let alone climb on a horse. They ended up loving it, insisted on charging about everywhere and taught him about tracking game. Now he's teaching me. I wanted to introduce him to Wisdom who actually rides rather well and can track from a cantering horse but he seems to have completely disappeared. In fact Wayne is replacing him.

A friend of Andrew's called Fred arrived from Cape Town last week. I had interviewed him there and thought he would make a good addition to our team as he is amusing and can cook. He was a farrier in the Army, but Wendy pointed out that as he's 6'5" tall he would always need to ride one of the few big horses and won't employ him. She is size-ist. I'm embarrassed as he has come all this way of his own accord, but he is staying with Andrew next-door where the Warden used to live and seems to be happy helping him on the reserve. Wayne is far more interested in what they're doing than mending things for me and I can see he wants to join the bachelor herd. The social dynamics of our group have changed radically in Nicki's short absence.

I found out that, whilst the house we live in once belonged to Meisie, Andrew's cottage was her old shop. Sarah-Jane said she came round and was furious that we hadn't watered the guava tree. I had been but apparently not nearly enough. It hasn't rained since I first got here. Whilst the sky is clear and blue the ground is rock hard and cracking. I was wondering if Meisie had voted 'No'.

'Very probably,' said Fred who had come in to use the phone. 'She's of that generation. It's the corruption factor that worries these old farmers. They don't want to see all they've strived for go down the drain. There's plenty of evidence that it will: you only have to look north of the Limpopo.'

'Well, excuse me,' Sarah-Jane said, 'but that is our company phone you are using. And our pen.'

Perry, I've been, quite seriously, chased by a rhinoceros. It was our own fault. Wendy wanted us to go out riding, without clients but with cameras, as she needs publicity photographs. To get decent pictures of people game viewing on horseback you need time to get the riders close to the animals. Well, the wildlife tends to run away when you do and it's difficult to line up a good shot, but off we went. We were lucky and soon found a young male rhino on the Serengeti-like plain beyond the camp. I had a zoom lens and was trying to get a shot of the rhinoceros in the foreground with Wayne, Josie and Fred looking at him. I did; I took quite a few shots, but had to get so close to the bull myself that we ended up surrounding him.

It's dangerous taking photos because you think, 'If I could get just a bit further to the right…' and end up taking risks you never would normally, provoking the animal. Rhinos are surprisingly agile and can accelerate much faster than a horse. This one spun round and came at me with his head down. I'd no options. My little red horse shot off, leaping over anthills and past thorn bushes, thundering over the hard ground with me clinging on like a monkey. The others thought this funny, although it wasn't. We rode on trying to look for giraffe but the horses were too excitable after that and Josie ended up coming off near the dry lake, breaking her lovely new camera. She scrambled back on in case the rhino was still following us, but I think he'd run far enough.

Mum is coming out in September. I hope she'll be able to cope. I think I'll take her to sit safely in a hide. Andrew took us to one he has built near a waterhole yesterday evening and we sat, very still, while literally hundreds of different animals came down to drink. It was quite different being so near the rhino when they're unaware of your presence. A bit stiff-making though.

A Law Enforcement Officer from the local Nature Conservation Headquarters came and gave us a lesson in shooting today. Not animals, people. *Tsotsies*, as they call the lawless, bent on murder.

'You must learn,' Andrew told me looking serious for five seconds, 'Dupe du Plessis was held up by four thieves armed with AK47s last week.'

I now know how to use a semi-automatic assault rifle and pump-action shotgun. Our teacher was so incoherent Wayne had to show me how the things work, but I got the message that I'm meant to be sleeping with a firearm under my pillow.[vi] I don't think I shall; I'd probably let it off by mistake. And you can get banged up for eight years if someone steals it.

'Live by the sword, die by the sword', as Dupe would say.

Wendy has just arrived with the photos we took. After all the risk-taking mine were hopeless, all crocked and into the sun. The really brilliant one came out of Josie's broken camera. The light is gorgeous. It is a shot of a rhinoceros with me on a tense horse, trying to take a photograph of it. I'm sitting very badly.

Lots of love, Sophie

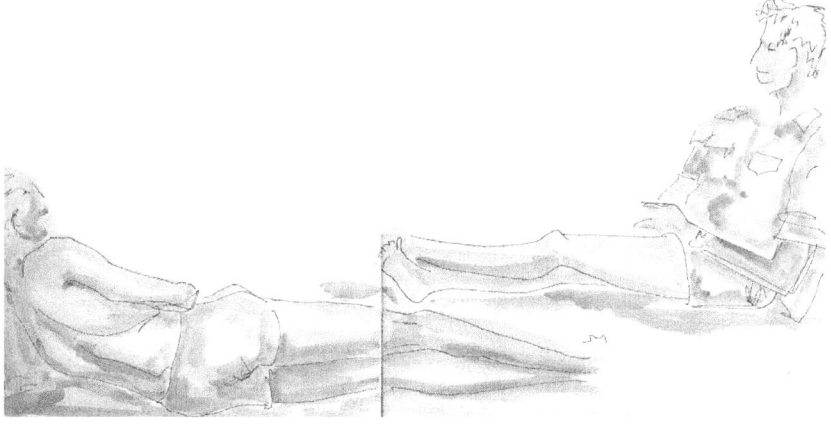

CHAPTER SIX

Equus Horse Safaris

Dear Tamzin,

I found out that not only can horses eat meat, but have also been known to survive when fed nothing but dried fish. It's dry here. Most of the trees have lost their leaves and, from a distance, stand out as blue against the yellowed grass. The nights are still cold but as there isn't a cloud in the sky the days are bright; blindingly bright and oppressively hot. My vegetable garden looks pitiful. So much for my spinach. I've planted my second generation of beans but it probably won't rain until October. The ranch has only had 150mm all year, which is serious as they normally expect 650mm; the same as London. The watertable must have dropped as there are days when our borehole runs dry. We have to share the bathwater, making it last for three people and then baling it out onto the guava tree. Josie was deeply shocked by this command and hates it, as she is usually the third person in the tub. But we are comparatively fortunate; Zimbabwe has been hit so hard by drought that hippo and elephant are starving to death, even in National Parks like Gonarezhou.

We've had few clients and I spend my days at Wendy's old sewing machine, mending tents and patching clothes. 'If you don't stitch up Wayne's rugger shorts he probably won't wear anything at all,' Sarah-Jane said, flinging me her holey jeans. As there's also a financial drought in this business we have to make or mend everything, economising, saving and mixing tins of old paint donated by Donald in an effort to enhance the appearance of Johann's loos.

Andrew is, at last, stuck into his academic projects. I suggested he looks at grazers and how much protein they must gain from accidentally consuming spiders and other insects living in the grass. But no, he is doing one on tourism. He goes round asking visitors what animals they most want to see. Ha. They all want to see cheetah and lion, which haven't been re-introduced in this area yet as they would annihilate everything else, including the riders. I wrote on my questionnaire: 'Want to see guide overcoming threatening situations.' It's true. The women spend most of their time gazing at Andrew's legs anyway.

What we have been getting is one or two good sightings of leopard. I reckon they have an easy life living off baboons that colonise the cliffs, but until a few years ago they were prone to getting shot at or trapped by farmers and are wary of people. This was cattle country - originally a million acres or so of land leased from the Government by the Oxo family, and later surveyed and divided into extensive farms. The aim now is to bring fences down between the private game reserves and form one massive conservancy.

Nicki arrived back from leave like a whirlwind, amazing both Fred and Wayne with her audacious vocabulary. As Wayne said, she can turn the air blue with her language.

'I'm not sure I go for her nose-ring,' Fred said. I think he comes from quite a conservative, rural background. 'My brother had his ear pierced once. When he came home my father looked up and without hesitating said, "Fred! Get the pliers."'

Sarah-Jane has found two young Sotho men to help with the horses. One is called Lazarus and the other Macaroni. Lazarus is very enthusiastic and insists on wearing gumboots and a bobble hat despite the heat.

'Macaroni doesn't exactly appear to be a high achiever,' Sarah-Jane sighed. 'He just stands around smiling. But it's always nice to have someone who laughs at your jokes.'

Andrew said their names are not that unusual. 'I knew a Malawian cook who called his four sons, 'Benson, Hedges, Special and Light.'

'It's trendy to have a name like Storm in England.' Sarah-Jane said from the depths of her desk. 'And Rebecca wants to call her children Saffron, Thyme and Coriander or something.'

'Tarragon.'

'Well, there you go. It's perceived as quite normal to be called Flip or Bossy if you're Afrikaans.'

Wisdom did come back, after about three weeks away. 'Where did you go?' Sarah-Jane asked him.

'I had to take my mother to hospital,' he replied in Afrikaans.

'Your mother.' She said in amazement. 'Do you still have a mother?' If he does she must be ancient.

He stayed a while, but seems to have gone walkabout again.

Sarah-Jane gets all the luck. She has seen aardvarks three times from the horses. They're nocturnal and while you see evidence of their diggings we never see them. Last night she was riding along with two guests and they found themselves being followed by one who snuffled along behind them for forty minutes. They're quite large animals, like pigs with big ears and a long, broad tail. She said it smelt like a sweaty old man. Aardvarks spend their whole time looking for termites, and eat thousands upon thousands of them every night, digging up more earth in their search than anyone would be able to with a spade. Fred said he rather wishes he could employ one. He has to lay a water pipe right across the reserve.

I'm rather worried about Fred. He and Andrew were filling applicators with a chemical called Deadline, which keeps the game clear of ticks. The idea is that animals are attracted to a tub containing salt, and as they reach inside, their necks brush on an upright pole with dip trickling down it. The chemical, which is highly concentrated, is mixed with oil of citronella so it spreads over the animal's body. It has just spread all over Fred. He was standing, filling the container at the top of the pole, without realising the tap was open and it poured out over his shorts. It burnt him terribly and I found him sitting in our office with an ice pack in his lap.

'Go and wash it off!'

'Oh, don't worry, I scraped most of it back into the container with a piece of cardboard.'

'Cardboard?'

I made him go and take a shower. It will make him infertile.

Andrew keeps making jokes about Fred needing to meet his Deadline, but I wouldn't dip the horses without wearing rubber gloves. Perry would approve. I'm not sure if she would be so thrilled about my clothes. It's still so cold at night that I made green tracksuits for everyone to wear. 'Is that a fashion statement you're making?' Andrew enquired. Well, no. Nicki and Sarah-Jane have such good figures they manage to look rather sexy in theirs but I look more like a broadbean. I'd better find some decent trousers. My friend Nick Archer, who is a diplomat and wears smart, well-cut clothes, is coming out to stay. He'll definitely notice what I wear. Must get a striking hat. I'm very excited that he has booked in, except that his visit seems to be coinciding with Mum's arrival.

Hoping the Hampshire housewives are happy,

Love,

Sophie

'Fred meeting his Deadline'

Hampshire

12/8/92

Dear Sophie -

Disaster has struck ~ the house sale has fallen through on Bellevue. Great gnashing of teeth. The man who was buying says that his girlfriend, (who we all thought was his wife) has run back to her husband + that he is having a nervous breakdown and wants to commit suicide – he was *so* pathetic that I couldn't even yell at him. I told him to talk to Johnty, who was really kind and understanding. We were a few days away from exchanging contracts. It's all so stressful and depressing. We were *so* lucky with Hardacre Farm and *won* the sealed bid by a whisker. The other people who were bidding just wanted it for storage use: a tyre company, a second-hand car dealer and a market gardener (plastic tube greenhouses growing exotic gourds for Leicester and Bradford) so we are in rapture.

We just don't know what to do. Bellevue is back on the market and we will continue to live here until the farm is liveable in. If we can't sell we are in BIG trouble, so pray like billio.

Perry, Robert and their cubs are holidaying in Pembrokeshire, so can't update you on their doings. Granny is eating well in her old people's home and writes with glee to tell me about the 'Old Biddies dying'. She says, 'For Goodness sake tell Sophie to cut her hair; she looks so much better with it short. And tell her to buy a nice A-line skirt.' I think she is worried that you will never get married. Mum is very well and excited about her safari. We haven't seen her for ages as she has been doing otter things with Princess Michael of Kent. ie: things with Princess Michael and her otters. I dread to think what they get up to.

Oh, Sophie, this will thrill and delight you: I went to the doctor for the usual tummy prod around and asked her if she could possibly give me her opinion on the Rice Krispie that insists on growing behind my ear. She took one look, started to laugh and called it a horny something-or-other which, joy of joys is a virus related to a wart, so I have to go to Dr. Eldred's Wart Clinic to have it zapped with a hydrogen gun – the indignity. Johnty thinks it is unmentionable.

Haven't exchanged yet on the farm… dreadful smell of cow muck and Milton fluid lingering there.

Lots of love,

Tamzin xxx

17th August, 1992
Camberley

Darlin' Sib,

The Gumby family and their dog have just returned from Wales. By tow van. Not for your Sunbeam but Robert's new Jag. Near disaster either side of the holiday. We had arranged to go with friends since February. I packed the car to the gunnels on Friday night, all set for a speedy getaway on Saturday morning:

Robert: "Can you ring Angus and ask him what drink he's bringing?"

Me: "Angus, hello. I've just unearthed half the boot to get out my address book for your number."

Angus: "What do you mean, 'Half the boot'? Why?"

Me: "All set for tomorrow morning."

Angus: "No. You mean NEXT week…" We didn't.

Amazingly they were able to come, though Angus did have to go up to spend two days in London while we were there. We stayed in a cottage on a working farm (big delights at milking time) about five miles from Parrog. Atalanta caught three crabs in the rock pools there and we had a few sunny days on Newport Sands.

When we were on the beach, Robert thought he'd give me some peace and took Hastings off in the hippy hammock to fetch lunch. I was worried my baby would come back sunburnt, but no. Two-and-a-half hours later he arrived back BLUE. Robert was wet up to his chest because he'd missed the tide and had to wade across the estuary. He'd given the Cornish pasties priority; they had been held above his head and were as dry as a bone while Hastings, six weeks old, was forced to swim the Atlantic.

The holiday was quite hard work. I had to feed H. at night by torch-light, but Atalanta loved every minute and burst into tears when we returned, crying, 'Holiday home.'

My old flat-mates came to supper last night, for Lucinda's hen night, which was great fun. Six girls; poor Robs. Actually, he loved talking about Wonderbras. I told them all that you had left your belly-dancing outfit to him in your Will.

Actually, I need to borrow it as I'm going to James Money-Kyrle's *Round the World in Eighty Days* party. Where is it?

Your car, with a push and a shove, a dodgy garage and £500 passed its MOT. We didn't mean to spend quite so much, but it's good for another year. People are very nice to me about it, but it is a bit embarrassing being in a Sunbeam. It still starts effectively. In fact it's good at starting the Jag too. I don't know when you want it back?
Tons of love
PRAHT

Equus Horse Safaris

Dear Tamzin,

Nick Archer arrived… with his girlfriend Fiona who writes for *Country Life.* They both have glamorous riding clothes. 'Don't my chaps look vaguely sexy?' I asked Sarah-Jane in despair.

'Well,' she tells me now, 'The problem is that your shorts bag out at the back and it looks as if you're wearing nappies.'

I had to send Wayne, 'Waynus' Andrew calls him, to collect Mum from the airport. She was delighted as he was so good about taking her bags and they passed donkey carts trotting along the road on their way through the hills. 'Enchanting.' She is determined to ride the big Friesian I've just broken in but he is big; colossal, and the only way we can get her on top is for Waynus to shove. He is phlegmatic about this.

'And so he should be,' said Sarah-Jane but even she was brought to a standstill by the prospect of finding a way for her to dismount.

'You need a loading ramp,' Mum insisted. The nearest one was at the rhino boma.

Mum loves her tent but I'm not so sure that Nick enjoys the hardships of camping. I thought we ought to do something adventurous and packed up the saddlebags, so we could spend a night sleeping by the river. We rode right down to the south of our area and along the Palala as it cuts through wild untouched country. At one point we came across a family of hippo, sunning themselves on the opposite bank. Nick didn't manage to get a good view of them before they plunged into the water, so we got off the horses to watch them from the rocks above the pool. Mum decided she might never get on again so I left her to look after our ponies while I was fiddling around with binoculars. She looked, but she didn't HOLD onto them. As I came back Fiona's horse, Zambezi, ran away with Sam. I managed to grab my naughty horse by the tail, but Zambezi was off. I knew he would run all the way home. It was disastrous as he had Fiona's sleeping bag and tent tied to his saddle with her wash-bag in his saddlebags. Wayne was great. He tore off his shirt and ran after him for about two kilometres, racing up a steep, stony hill in the heat. We trudged after them, walking the horses over the boulders, me praying that by some miracle Wayne would catch the pony, but it didn't look possible. Fiona was furious with me for not making sure Zambezi had been properly tied up. It was OK for her; she was riding my horse.

I stomped on, trying to work out how far we were from home; miles. By now I could see Waynus doubled up, panting at the top of the hill. Zambezi would gallop all the way home and ruin his feet.

Mum was great, she said, 'Don't worry darling; Sarah-Jane will be standing at the top of the hill holding him with a big grin on her face.' Strangely enough she was.

Sarah-Jane had realised that we'd forgotten to pack the *braai* grid needed for grilling meat and decided to take extra horse food down to the river for us in the truck. She'd just reached a fork in the road and was looking for our tracks when she heard Zambezi coming and managed to catch him.

By the time we reached our camping spot Nick was muttering about his favourite mode of transport being a London taxi, but Mum, although she'd been quite scratched when the Friesian went under a hook-thorn tree, gamely put up her tent and jumped in the Palala.

'Excuse me Sophie,' Nick asked, 'But what are the arrangements for drinking water?'

'Oh, we just drink from the river.'

'But your mother is swimming in it.'

We had a big fire that night, but Golly it was freezing in the morning. I was a bit worried about everyone.

'Mum, were you cold in the night?'

'Yes, Darling,' she said. 'But I found a pair of knickers and put them on my head.'

Nick was all right, he was sleeping with Fiona, but he said she took all the blankets. His main worry was the accumulation of dust on everything.

'I don't think I've been this dirty in my entire life.'

He was still looking immaculate. Wayne was staggered.

Fiona, being on holiday, didn't want to think about writing an article but when I took her to visit our nearest neighbour, a great big, red-haired farmer called Hendrik, she nearly started taking notes. Oom Hennie, as he likes to be called, was busy making *boerewors* and *biltong*, which she'd asked if she could try. But it was the house that was fascinating. I think he just converted an old cattle shed. We went into a dark, cavernous sitting room, crammed with possessions. Enormous game trophies hung from every wall, looking over wagon wheel furniture. There were glass cabinets filled with china ornaments, which on closer inspection consisted of a collection of mugs with rude jokes printed on the sides. Fiona sat marvelling at it all, sipping sweet Roibos tea she'd been given.

'Oh no! What's **that**?' Oom Hennie and his family burst out laughing. She was looking at a stuffed jackal that had been placed under the coffee table, so that it looked up at you when you set your cup down.

Ornate and brightly coloured flower arrangements sat in alcoves at intervals around the room. One was pink, one was yellow and one was blue.

'Ooer, you're liking the *blometjies*?' Oom Hennie commented, looking at his children endearingly. 'I gave them to my wife, one every time she had a baby.'

His freckle-faced girls started to giggle. Little Hennie, his tall, gangly son, sat stroking a tame mongoose and stared at Fiona, open-mouthed. The flowers turned out to be made entirely of feathers.

Mrs Hennie is so thin you wouldn't have thought it possible for her to produce a family. She only has one arm, but is a chicken farmer and manages to lift great trays of eggs by flinging them into the air and catching them with her right hand.

I could feel Fiona wanting to say 'Cor, can you do that again?'

I returned, full of *biltong*, to find Mum had done a runner. She'd gone off with Josie, our cook, to rescue donkeys. She has realised that the way they're treated by the Sotho people is not so enchanting and that they can get badly rubbed by makeshift harnesses. These usually consist of coarse webbing tied together with bits of old wire that cut into the donkeys, especially when children put them on inside out. I had to stop a cart recently. It was so badly weighted that too much pressure was falling on the donkeys' necks, which were raw and bleeding. What made me cross was that having improved the cart, I saw the same donkeys pulling it the next day, suffering because instead of accepting my advice the driver had put the weight even further forward. The animals' blatant injuries were being totally ignored. I once saw a bridle with a bit made out of a piece of twisted wire. It's quite illogical; the donkeys will behave badly in their pain and die young. Mum is on another rescue mission right now. She rattled off, equipped with a pair of pliers, string, pieces of old carpet and a bag of Sarah-Jane's snaffle bits, declaring to the local population that her name is *Mama Donkey*. She doesn't care what anyone thinks; she just muscles in doing whatever needs to be done. It has added enormous fulfilment to her holiday. Josie said that people are rather baffled. Mama Donkey could have one of two meanings; Mother Donkey ~ in Sesotho or *Mama Danke,* Lady Thank you ~ in Afrikaans.

We riders had rather a thrilling time today. We were cantering along a track, all riding black horses when a herd of wildebeest came running out of the bush and started galloping alongside us. They must have thought we were running from danger and came to join us. You would have enjoyed it.

Lots of love,

Daughter of all donkeys.

Equus Horse Safaris

Dear Perry,

I'm sending Mum home with this rather odd christening present for your boy. I'm afraid Marken doesn't have that much to offer. It was this or set of spanners. Fiona says that all boys love gutting fish. I had to take her to see the doctor as she had a sore throat, but stupidly forgot to warn her about him. 'Was he drunk?'

'Well, he did ask me if I would like to try something called *Mampoer*. I presumed it was for my throat.' It's the local brew, made illegally by distilling Marula fruit and must be 50% alcohol. It would probably kill any infection lurking in Fiona's throat stone dead.

I think Mum enjoyed herself, what with the donkeys and everything. She enjoyed the food.

Mum: 'Could I have some more?'

Nick: 'Could we stop you?'

Mum: 'I'm a growing girl.'

We were all having lunch one day when Lazarus ran up, politely put his hands behind his back.

'Madam,' he said looking worried. 'There's a large animal urinating in the bush.' He was completely serious.

Mum was intrigued, actually left the table and crept stealthily through the undergrowth. She came across an enormous green thing on legs. Someone had left the pump on. It was the camp water tank, overflowing.

We spent some time wandering along the river looking for otters together but found nothing more than a few crab shells on a rock. Mum told everyone about her conservation work saying she has volunteered to hand-rear another short-clawed Asian otter. A deep conversation with Andrew ensued, as he sees 'extension work' or raising public awareness, which is essentially what Mum does in the UK, the key to the survival of African wildlife.

'If you don't educate ordinary people on the value and importance of ecology, wild animals could be lost within a generation.' There's already nothing left in countries like Ghana; it has all been eaten up.

Sitting in the hide Andrew built for the local children proved a dead loss though; we were there ages, getting stiff and bored. Nothing came along at all. I also made everyone wait around endlessly outside what I was sure was a freshly-dug aardvark hole.

We did have an encounter with a zebra stallion. Mum was riding a little Basuto pony, a mare that must have been in season, because the zebra went nutty and trotted in front of us, braying endlessly for miles. Mum began to get quite worried, but Nick said he'd be right behind her should a problem arise.

'When are you going to return to work in television?' Mum wanted to know.

'Oh, not just yet.'

It's so lovely here. She could see how much we have, what a wonderful way of life it is. I don't earn any money but have so much more than I ever had in London and so appreciate feeling well. Although I know she is ambitious for me, she can understand that living in the country is so much more enriching than battling away at Television Centre. I want to see the year out, at least. It's so exciting watching the seasons change. Spring is just coming, with green leaves and blossom appearing on the trees, despite the fact that we haven't had a single drop of rain. Swallows and bee-eaters are arriving from Europe.

I heard a nightjar singing last night; a fiery-necked nightjar. And we've been dancing. Andrew and Fred have rigged up a sound system and we Rock and Roll like you wouldn't believe, outside under the stars. I walked out into the paddock last night, wandering amongst the horses. I'm so fond of them all. They've become like my children. I couldn't bear to leave yet.

Mum's worried because there's no sign of a husband on the horizon.

'But I'm hardly surprised;' she declared, 'These young men are very contradictory.'

'Well, Mum, I'm meeting more people here than in London.'

Presumably, if you go and do something you enjoy you'll meet someone who is like-minded. Anyway, it's not entirely my decision. I reckon if God wants me to get married he'll be able to arrange for me to meet my husband wherever I am. I've told him that he must make the choice; as if I do I'll only make a dreadful mistake. Nicki has been trying to convince me that Dupe du Plessis, who owns a prosperous bottle store half way along the main road to Potgietersrus, is longing for a girl like me, but somehow I don't think we are terribly well suited. This is a pun.

'I bet you,' Sarah-Jane said ruefully, 'that he wears his knee-socks in bed.'

If Mum says anything about me being featured in *Country Life*, please don't encourage her. It is NOT going to happen.
Love
from
Sophie

Camberley

Darling Sib,

   Thank you so much for the lovely fish smoker. It's delightful and I'm sure Hastings will be able to use it on his forth-coming holidays in Wales.

   We read that aardvarks somersault backwards when alarmed. Is this true?

   Oh dear, I haven't been good about writing have I? Every evening I just seem too busy or tired, which is ridiculous as I have an au pair. Actually I have to pick Tanja up from her English lesson in fifteen minutes. The hungry Hungarian left at the end of September and we now have the thin Finn. (Very nice and very good).

   Atalanta goes up the aisle again next week, following Godmother Lucinda. Oh the excitement. Her dress has a silk top, red sash and a long, wide, skirt made totally of tulle, that frothy netting stuff which is usually used for petticoats. Sweet. When Lu Llewellyn last came over we decided her bridesmaids - not that she is getting married yet - should wear tutus and hold glitter stars on sticks.

   Well, the boy is now officially named. We had a lovely HAPPY day. (Everyone was happy except Johnty who has done something to his leg). It was sunny and the service was special except that the Padre started calling him a her until we all giggled. Hastings was sloshed with water and didn't cry. Liza said later that it means he still has the devil in him. What a dreadful thing.

Then we had lunch in the mess with a GIANT salmon Mum and Dad brought along, and I had no clearing up to do.

Lots of love,

Perry

Dear Sib -

Can I borrow your belly dancer's costume and if I can WHERE is it? Please answer ASAP.

We went to see Mum and Dad and put Atalanta on Len with the old donkey saddle - he is great. Nothing changes there except, perhaps, that it gets more chaotic.

Dad's study is worse. Piles of papers and books slide down on top of you when you walk inside.

He was trying to sort out his new computer, 'It's even more exasperating than your mother.'

The bed on top of the chest of drawers was piled high with clothes, and 'Don't look up there.'

It's where he keeps his Christmas presents. I don't think your boyfriends would be able to sleep in it anymore. Mum maintains that she is a neat person.

'You lying toad.'

'Alright, I'm a lying toad, but I'm a well organized one.'

Tamzin came over yesterday, dreading her first move.
I'm on my ninth.
Lots of love
P, R, A, H & T

We've been making pancakes!

Equus Horse Safaris

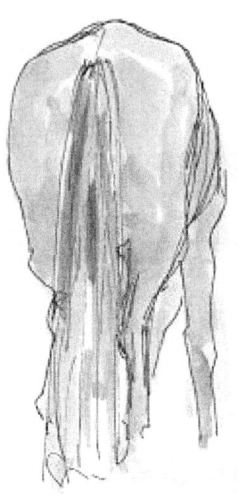

Dear Perry,

We heard that there was going to be a dance in Marken and I did so wish I had the belly dancing costume here, but it's in the bottom of my wardrobe, to the right. You'll find it with a jewel for the tummy button. There's a long, white sash Robert could wear as a turban. I told Nicki that as a teenager I was made to go to Pony Club discos wearing a bridesmaid dress and ballet shoes. She couldn't believe that until I was fifteen, Mum dressed the three of us alike, in matching coats and bunny fur hats, but Sarah-Jane's face crumpled in sympathy.

In the end I went off to the *Sokkie Jol*, as Fred called the dance in the Farmer's Hall, in my khaki shorts and jodhpur boots.

Waynus and I took two of the clients. We just got off the horses and went. The hall, which is marked out for sports, was brightly lit with overhead florescent lights. Everyone was dancing the Two-step to accordion music; there was Meisie and her husband, Mr Labuschagne the ostrich farmer with the girl who can bark, and our inebriated doctor. I was grabbed by Johann, the man who constructed our lavatories, tucked under his *beer bop* (as Nicki calls his tummy) and whisked around the floor. All the grannies were sitting around the perimeter, tapping their feet and watching avidly, while children slept under their chairs in bedrolls. Dupe du Plessis was there in his powder blue suit, with a lady friend who apparently answered an advertisement for a wife that he'd put in a magazine. I didn't dance with him, I'm afraid. I waltzed around with Wayne until our English client said, 'I'm not sure if I can stand these accordions much longer,' and went up to the self-styled DJ. 'I don't want to compromise your culture or anything, but have you got any *Right said Fred*?'

Perry, he was there before me. *Sierra smile, legs that go on for miles and miles.* I was picked-up, incredible though it may seem. And by a really sweet farmer. He is called Hano Gerkin. 'Would you mind if I phoned you?' he asked. Truly. (Why don't we have men that ask such questions in England any more?) And he came to visit me, the next day, bringing a present of two boxes of tomatoes. He'd grown them.

'Just what we need,' Sarah-Jane said coming briskly round the corner. She picked them up and took them off to the pantry. I was going to keep them in my bedroom, to look at, like a bunch of red roses. I made Hano a cup of tea (Why didn't I offer him beer?) and asked him about Marken.

'Everyone at Church was talking about you.'

'No, what did they say?'

'Oh, they said,' he told me, blushing, now having to admit to the truth, 'That your legs are like walking-sticks.' Anyway, he came riding and I'm going over to his farm next week. I can't wait. It's the place where our groom, Madula, used to work. Hano is wonderful looking, with dark eyes and long, brown legs. He wears football socks and walking boots with green laces. Josie is going to cut my hair and make it look pretty.

Lots of love,

Sophie

"LEKKER BY DIE SEE, NÊ"

Camberley

Surrey

October 1992

Dear Sophie,

It was Lucinda's wedding last week. Atalanta was so looking forward to it. She knew what it would be like this time and had been talking to herself about weddings and pretty girls for days. I had been lying in the bath listening to her chat away to herself at night. She really was beautifully behaved and looked enchanting, gazing up at the flowers in the church; whirling round to make her skirts fly out and blowing kisses to the bride. I was with her for the cutting of the cake but then I had to go off and feed Hastings.

When I returned there was a horrid smell in the tent. I was thinking, 'How foul, I wonder who has made that stink,' when I realised it was the smell of burning and overheard a group of anxious people saying:

'One of the bridesmaid's dresses caught fire.'

'She must have got too close to the marquee heater.' And then,

'It was the little one with the red hair.'

Sophie, I froze. I couldn't move. Tulle is the most flammable material. I stood there clutching Hastings, the blood running like ice through my veins, looking and looking. It was just a sea of hats. And then I saw Robert coming towards me with Atalanta in his arms. She was in her vest and white tights. Someone had clapped out the flames of her burning dress with their bare hands.

    I thought she would never want to go to another wedding again, but No, she wants to get married to Liza's little boy. They see each other nearly every day. Tanja and their nanny are good friends. The neighbours think we are VERY rich having nannies, which is so funny as all our husbands earn the same. Anyway, we get GOSSIPED about... Poor Robert has an exam all day tomorrow - he has made himself sandwiches to eat at his desk. Doesn't it make you weep? Prince Andrew is in his group. He drives the same car as ours, but in navy blue, so R gets the guards standing up stiffly as he approaches and then they slouch, their salutes withering, when they see it's only him.

    What else has been happening? Well, I'm going to the dentist tomorrow. There are lots of spiders coming into the house now it's getting colder. Atalanta is going riding with Tamzin on Friday. Guess what? Her un-separable, best toy is bloomin' Mongolia, the hideous 'boy dolly' Granny gave her. She calls it Golia. I suppose ugly things must be loved.

Lots of love from us all

PRAHT

    - Atalanta was sweet. When I was looking at the horrifically melted tulle she looked up at me and said, 'Mummy, dress broken.'

CHAPTER SEVEN

Quertington Farm,
Hampshire

1ˢᵗ October 1992

Dearest Sib –

Here we are, living in Raddy's barn, happy and relieved to have sold Bellevue. Thank you so much for the splendid guineafowl shirt – I'm wearing it at the moment. It accommodates my growing shape rather well. You won't believe this, but last week as I was driving along, a guineafowl ran straight in front of my car and off into the bush, not unlike Africa.

I collected Mum from the airport when she returned from visiting you. She was feeling 'a bit sweaty Betty' so came back here for a bath before heading straight off to the Newbury Show to be *re-united* (as they'd say in tabloids) with her baby otters. The energy.

Johnty was pleased though. I can *reveal*, as the self-same journalists would say, that he won a cup at the show for the best trade stand and his photo was in the papers. The poor chap; when he jumped off the boat in Greece (back in June) he hurt his knee and it's still swollen and sore. He is having to have a camera inserted – the thought. So what with Johnty limping and me waddling, we make an attractive couple. We staggered off, in this fashion, to Sandhurst church for the wolf cub's christening. Dad was standing outside with a large fish. Johnty's face.

'It's for lunch.' Mum said, swooping past in what can only be described as a marquee, making me, despite being five months pregnant, feel slim. (Did you know that the average dress size for a woman in this country is a size 16? Mum said she found it a comforting fact).

Happy Happy Birthday: you will have to have your proper present when you come back as I can't find anything light enough or flat enough that is nice. Do have a lovely, lovely day; I'll be thinking of you.

I'll write when I have news on Hardacre Farm. It's proving almost as difficult to buy as Bellevue was to sell. The lawyers who are in charge of selling it are totally hopeless. They keep ending letters saying, *Please find attached document* and failing to attach anything. Typical.

I don't know what I would do without Raddy's kindness. Imagine; she is having us, all our furniture and all our animals to stay. She even stays relaxed when Mum arrives with swollen feet and eats eight slices of toast.

Love,

Tamzin xxxx

PS: I've had the scan of my baby. It looks like a salami to me but I'm assured he has 2 arms 3 legs and a big nose, so I hope the poor little creature is a boy.

EQUUS HORSE SAFARIS

Dear Tamzin,

Being well covered is considered a sign of wealth and beauty in Africa. The greatest complement you can give a woman is to tell her that she is looking fat. Perhaps not. It would be even better to say her baby was fat.

I'm thirty-two now, which seems rather elderly. Thank you so much for the scarf. It was just what I needed for my date. I went for a *braai* at Hano's house and met his parents. Josie came with me. We were both bowled over. You have never seen such a beautiful farm. The Gerkins are Dutch and have geese and goats and everything. They live right under the Waterberg escarpment where a great rock chimney rises hundreds of feet above the plain. We drove around looking for leopard. I was rather alarmed by a stuffed one that they had in the sitting room. There was a baboon in the hall, sitting on a plinth with his mouth wide open in a terrifying bark. Hano's father had shot it when it was raiding their tomato crop.

They do have a problem with snakes there. Mrs Gerkin told me she once killed a black mamba with a fishing rod right outside her bedroom. A bite from a mamba will kill you in ten minutes. It was whacked to death. She is quite a lady. Some baddies tried to hijack her car when she was taking Hano to school in Potgietersrus once, but she said she drove up onto the verge and accelerated hard, managing to run one of them over. We ate the most delicious food: *toebrootjies*, onion and tomato sandwiches tied up with string and toasted on the *braai* with delicious bushbuck steaks.

We gave a leaving party on Thursday for my Zimbabwean friends, Jane and Ged who were running the lodge. Hano came but Josie didn't seem to be about much and I was so busy cooking I couldn't spend much time with him. What was apparent by the end of evening was that Josie was spending a lot of time with Fred; and I'd never noticed. Wayne thinks I'm completely blind.

I'm actually preoccupied. An old friend of Sarah-Jane's wants to start horse safaris on the Nyika Plateau in Malawi. I thought this would be wonderful and wrote, offering to set it up for him. He has replied, asking me to come and see the concession area, so I'm off, planning a trip that will take me up through Zimbabwe and on through Malawi to Tanzania. I should be able to reach Kenya by Christmas, and take the train to Mombasa to stay with Uncle Tony and Aunt Reinhild on the coast over New Year. Girls have to wear skirts in Malawi and men aren't allowed to have long hair. It's against the law.

Hano came over while I was packing. I don't think he has ever been out of South Africa. Until recently citizens were prevented from entering other African countries and there isn't much money for travel. Farming is a great tie. I tried to encourage him to think about visiting Zimbabwe, and as he drove away in the dust I thought, sadly, that I'm not ready to live under a mountain like Mrs Walton. Not yet. Perhaps Waynus is right and I'm completely mad. What I will be able to do is to come back home in February, so I can be with you when your baby arrives.

Lots of love,

Sophie

Guess what I did? I ran ten kilometres. In a race. A victory for me as it proves I'm well and truly over the ME: 'they shall run and not grow weary; and they shall walk and not faint.' I went into training with Andrew and Wayne and ended up coming third, which wasn't bad as the road was rough and we ran against a hot wind coming straight from Botswana. You will have to tell Perry. Andrew said his running shorts chafed him so badly he had to take them off. Just like in the Bible. Look up *Hebrews 12 verses 1 & 2*. It doesn't say anything about looking for the shorts afterwards.

Camberley
Surrey
Another dark, wet November day

Darling Sib,

The Indian man at the post office said it was very sad that I was only buying one aerogramme.

'One is a lemon'. He must feel that I only have one friend to write to.

We've just come back from a ghastly cocktail party where I'd been given champagne with crème de menthe in it, but otherwise everyone is fine. Atalanta goes to ballet in a pink leotard and plays a green recorder. The latter is agonising, but I keeping nodding and try to look encouraging.

Even Robert was impressed by your race. I'm flabbergasted. It's hard to believe that I once won *Vitrix Ludorum* for running. While I take no exercise at all but should, Tamzin has had to be given a lecture on exactly what would happen if she didn't REST. Raddy has enough energy to run the lights of Regent Street and interrupts Tamzin every time she tries to lie down, so she is coming over on Monday - to sleep.

We've had a busy weekend with Robs playing rugger in a league thing. They won so he's a happy frog but what a horrible game rugby is. Thugby. He was quite beaten up. He looks like he has a bran flake stuck to the side of his nose and I've been at him with my handbag. I'm cross with him though. After standing, queuing in the post office, he now tells me I don't need an aerogramme after all and can send you quite ordinary letters.

Lu had us for supper on Friday. Now she told us a funny story: she was at a wedding in Norfolk and went to say 'Hello' to the bride who was chatting to the vicar. She was then left talking to the vicar and he said, 'Goodness, you look just like my Goddaughter, Sophie Neville.' If she'd been sitting on a chair she would have fallen over backwards.

I ended up going to the *Round the World in Eighty Days* party in a dress covered in crisp packets. Robert's inheritance could not be found even though Mum turned everything upside-down.

'Why are you children so messy?'

Right, I'm off now to draw/colour Robert's knickers. I'm doing him a set for his birthday with the regimental motto painted across the front. It's a skull and crossbones. Very smart. Everyone is going to want a pair; do you think I could make my fortune?

Six weeks to go until we follow the drum to Nottingham, which I can't bear the thought of, so I won't think.

Lots of love,

PRAHT

Nyanga Highlands

Dear Perry,

I'm in Zimbabwe, having spent two days travelling north on a double-trailer-ed lorry laden with a cargo of Vaseline. Apparently there's a tremendous demand for Brylcream in the Congo. Waynus and I went up into the mountains on the Swaziland border before coming here, to stay with Billy, Sarah-Jane's old boyfriend who works for the National Parks Board as a game ranger. He patrols his territory on horses and had asked us up to help trim their feet. That didn't take long (Wayne did it while I picked off ticks) and we found ourselves riding endlessly over the grassy mountain slopes where black wildebeest run, looking down into gullies choked with jungly vegetation full of chattering monkeys.

Billy is furious that Sarah-Jane gave him the boot but he hardly ever saw her, insisted on calling her his *skellem* (or bit-on-the-side) and spent one evening too many getting plastered with Andrew when he was last at Equus. It's fun riding with him; he complains in English, shouts at his scouts in Swazi, swears at his horse in Afrikaans and provides the Latin names of plants for me, all in one breath. He told us that people still bring drugs through his reserve, but his real problem has been with poaching, not of animals but plants; ancient cycads that grow on the high slopes. They made forty-eight arrests this year and recently prosecuted a

Greek for stealing R4 million – nearly £900,000s worth. I sat in his garden guarding five. They were very dull.

BILLY'S GARDEN

Russian firearms used to be smuggled from Mozambique through Swaziland and over these mountains but Billy thinks that this is coming to an end now that it looks as if the ANC will come into power without an armed struggle. He said that until recently the situation in Mozambique was so desperate it was possible to buy a Kalashnikov for a loaf of bread. A lot of automatic rifles have ended up in civilian hands. 'It's replaced the knobkerrie as a traditional weapon,' Billy told me sardonically. He never goes anywhere without a 9mm revolver, which he can draw and spin like a cowboy only he wears it on his left hip and brings it across his body. 'It's easier with real guns than with toys; they're heavy.' Security seems much more of an issue in the Eastern Transvaal than where we live. I never even take the car keys out of the ignition on the ranch. We'd lose them.

It is special to be taken round by someone like Billy; so interesting. I've written to Alastair Fothergill, putting forward an idea for a wildlife series based on the concept of spending time in the African bush with someone who works with the animals. You'd be with a different expert, in a different environment every week, using a different mode of transport. I know it's something Alastair would love to do himself. Having been banned from the BBC car park for years, he is now Head of the Natural History Department and has a named space. This caused instant mayhem; his girlfriend left her briefcase standing by the back wheel of his new executive car, which resulted in a full-scale bomb scare. They didn't just make an announcement, they detonated it. He said that she'd had a nightdress inside and tiny bits of her clothing are still scattered everywhere, hanging from unreachable places.

When they're not looking up the names of strange plants, Wayne and Billy both draw and gave me lots of time to paint. I'm now staying with an artist in the Nyanga Highlands. She is married to a British Army officer out here with BMATT, providing military training for the Zimbabwean Forces. You would love the posting. My friends spend their spare time fishing in the Pungwe River, picnicking on gigantic granite boulders while their children splash in the shallows. There are parties here all the time, and unlike in South Africa, where men talk to men and women with women, they actually interact normally. I am assured this isn't always so in the local community but Zimbabweans tend to be outgoing and rather fun. I went riding with a farmer's wife called Pixie. She had one little girl called Burgundy and another called Summer Rain. They rode their ponies bareback, jumping them over gates and fences without hesitation. I'm heading for Victoria Falls by train next week and after going down the Zambezi plan to fly up to Lilongwe so I can drive up through Malawi to the Nyika Plateau.

I didn't realise how bushed I had become at Equus. I hadn't taken a day off in four months ~ hadn't used my own money, watched television, worn anything accept khaki clothes, had hardly driven on a tarmac road or been to a town since I was in the Cape. It's strange adjusting back to life on the open road and making decisions alone. Being able to wear turquoise. Having time for myself.

Very, Very Happy Christmas, I'll be thinking of you all singing away. But why did you wear a dress covered in crisp packets?
Lots of love, Sophie

Fishing on the Pungwe River

Dear Tamzin,

Three hundred and eighty people died when a bridge collapsed under the train going to Mombasa. I might have been on it but I wasn't, I took the last plane out from Lake Malawi before the rains washed the airfield away and returned to South Africa for Christmas. I was all set to go north but was praying about my plans and knew, as if I'd been told, that I had to come back.

I've had my hair cut short at last. This was a mistake; I look so like a boy that a man at a petrol station in Malawi said, 'How are you my young brother?' The Nyika Plateau was like Scotland in Africa; rolling grasslands cut by wooded valleys, with wild flowers growing everywhere. Klipspringer and blue monkeys leapt from the rocks as we drove up into the open country where big herds of eland and roan antelope were grazing. Spotted hyena and porcupine were wandering around in the middle of the day and there were zebra everywhere. You feel as if you're on top of the world. I would love to ride there, but it's isolated ~ three hours on dirt roads from the nearest town. I felt that it would take almost ten years before you could start to make money out of a horse safari business based up there and didn't think it was for me. I spent a few days painting by Lake Malawi but am glad to be back at Equus. The Kenyan elections were not a bundle of fun and Aunt Reinhild said they were stuck inside the Muthaiga Club for days on end.

On Christmas Eve we had the naughtiest client ever. Not a tourist at all, but a local farmer called Charles Baber who arrived in a Mercedes. A golden brown Mercedes. How I would love a car here. *'Oh Lord, won't you buy me a Mercedes Benz?'*

Charles brought his tall blonde daughter, his even taller son and a short pretty dark girl from overseas. Sarah-Jane, who is 5'9", looked up and then looked down. I could see her thinking. Thinking about which horses they could ride. We didn't have one big enough for Charles but he swung himself up onto a Friesian, said, 'I rode around this area when I worked on the 1953 census,' and he was off. By himself. I had to rush after him.

'Do you know where we can go to church tomorrow?' I asked the Babers later as we were eating watermelon for breakfast.

'You can come to our church.'

'Will the service be in English?'

'Yes. We don't have a minister so it's Do-it-yourself, and it's me tomorrow,' Charles said, laughing. 'Juliet's playing the organ.'

His daughter smiled, telling us that her mother used to play and her granny, and her great-granny before her when Charles's grandfather would take the service.

'My aunts asked Sir Herbert Baker[vii] to design the building in 1914. When he sent them the bill they were quite horrified and told him to ask the Lord about it.'

'It's just a little thatched church in the bush.' Juliet told us. 'We won't all fit in but you must come.'

It turned out to be at the place called Twenty-four Rivers. There weren't any rivers there at all.

We had to go wearing straw hats. Well, Sarah-Jane and I had to. An extraordinary boy called Alan Dryden had just arrived, looking for work; only there's no job as Sarah-Jane is now employing Fred. Alan claimed to be a war photographer, saying he was waiting for South Africa to explode. It hasn't yet. Instead he fell, instantly, for Sarah-Jane. We had no guests; so at five o'clock on Christmas Eve we stopped work and sat down to have a drink in the garden. He was so focused on her that he wouldn't speak to me and didn't notice when I went into the house and came back wearing a white towelling dressing gown, a Father Christmas hat and a cottonwool beard.

Josie came outside, took one look, squawked and rushed back inside, only to emerge five minutes later dressed as a reindeer in Fred's hiking boots and army jacket with impala horns and a red nose. Alan noticed this. By the time Hano arrived Sarah-Jane had dressed up as the Christmas Fairy and Fred was busy handing out presents.

Alan then decided it would be fun to rub flour and water into my head and Sarah-Jane's hair. Vigorously. It doesn't come out. We tried washing it, which was disastrous. The hot water made it set hard, in nasty bogey-like globs. I looked bad but it was terrible in Sarah-Jane's long brown hair. And the Babers were expecting us for breakfast after church. I lay with my head in Josie's lap all the way over to their farm, while she tried to crack off the gunk with her fingernails. They were very polite about our appearance but Alan asked Charles for a job, somehow inviting himself to stay with them on Christmas Day. I was so embarrassed. He is going to 'sort out' their horses.

I had a fight with a praying mantis today. It nipped me quite hard. Fred says they're carnivorous and eat their husbands. I wish they would eat more of the other insects. There's a cicada making a noise like a drill and hundreds of owl moths fluttering everywhere. We have so many in the mess tent it is as if the whole ceiling is moving. The house has been invaded by little black beetles. They smell vile. Oily, chemically. Nicki calls them Stink Bugs. Someone left the light on and I came into the kitchen this morning to find the whole floor covered in their dead bodies.

And there was a rat in the loo. 'Fred!' I shouted. 'There's a rat in the loo.'

'What's it doing?'

'Swimming around.' He came and peered inside.

'Can't you kill it?'

'How am supposed to do that?' Tigger put her face into the lavatory bowl and snapped its head off, quick as a flash.

We have a bullterrier puppy. He is chestnut with four white feet. Sarah-Jane calls him PK after the little boy with white boxing gloves in *The Power of One.* He isn't her dog. Andrew brought him as a present for Nicki after they had a bit of a contretemps but PK thinks he belongs to Tigger. He is actually a rescue case and looks like being rather hard work.

I'm coming back for The Great Event, hoping to stay in England for three weeks or so.

Lots of love,

Sophie

Did Perry survive Christmas?

Notty, Nottingham

4th January 1993

Dear Sib,

They were *Phileas Fogg* crisps, so I thought the packets appropriate, but it was rather crinkly and odd to dance in.

We are looking forward awfully to seeing you in February. Your little nephew will probably be crawling by then. I found his first tooth on New Year's Eve.

Christmas in Gloucestershire was jolly. We missed you enormously. There were seventeen of us. Mum worked very hard. Mary-Dieu, it has to be said, was in a grump for most of the day but Daisy was sweet; probably better behaved than anyone.

Gregory the Dachshund was in church and Atalanta helped the vicar light candles, looking pretty in her bridesmaid dress (not the burnt one). Big disappointment that you and Tamzin weren't there, as yes, we sang about joy. Not only singing either; the children had to hold up big letters saying **J-O-Y**. I had a frightful giggling fit, almost rated as bad as last year but worse, as the man behind cleared his throat and I was glared at by the Church Warden.

Robert says God is a happy God and therefore encouraged me. Awful. I was snorting. No one understands how difficult it is to cope with carols when you have a name like mine.

Tamzin, enormously pregnant, has just moved in to Hardacre Farm. It's freezing there but Johnty is buying her a massive Aga. It's green. I'm green with envy. The whole place looks like a demolition site but she has just discovered Victorian fireplaces behind plasterboard in two of the bedrooms.

As Clerk of Works, Tamzin is in charge of the builders: a Mr Hindleson, who is about eighty and his son Eric who has terrible problems with an allergic reaction to underarm deodorant, or so he keeps telling her.

I found Tamzin talking to Eric very seriously about stench pipes while dressed up in her elf outfit. She was off to help with a nursery school play. Raddy wanted to suspend her from a tree to greet the audience as they arrived (I'm being perfectly serious). Tamzin actually thought this a good idea but they couldn't find a branch that would take the weight. I might say Raddy, herself, was scheduled to give birth the next day.

We are now established, behind security wire in another red box. At least it's safe here. There's no need for a burglar alarm; we have armed guards. The house does look out over fields one way. They're deep and crisp and even.

There's a big yellow skip at the top of the hill so the whole patch can dispose of their unwanted stuff. The soldiers' wives put their rejects ON; the officers' wives take them OFF. There's a big race up there after the weekend turnouts. I spied some brilliant pram wheels I thought I'd try to make into a go-cart for Hastings. I later found my neighbour re-upholstering a children's pram in her garden. She said, 'Guess what, I've just found this brilliant thing on the skip; the only trouble is that I'm going to have to get some wheels.' I had to come clean.

Robs is enjoying his new job but the civilian staff think it odd that he takes the dog into the office. He left her there by mistake on Sunday and Tadpole had to be brought home by the Brigadier's driver, the madam.

Lots of love from us all, Perry Joy

ROCK HYRAX AT OTTER POINT

Dear Perry,

Thank you for all the children's clothes. It was a bit of a thing lugging them over but they were so appreciated that one poor baby has been called Sophie, after me. Her mother is already back at work with the little thing strapped to her back.

It was lovely to see you all. I had a good time in England but wasn't any help to Tamzin at all; she was stuck in hospital.

When Mum and I went to visit her she looked fine but said, 'Hughie is in Intensive Care,' and burst into tears.

'Shall we go and see him?' A huge baby boy that looked like a rugger player to me was bawling its eyes out.

'Shut up, Hughie,' a nurse was saying.

He wasn't ill at all, but was in for observation having swallowed fluid in his enthusiasm to get out into life. Mum found being in a room full of incubators most distracting.

'He looks just like your father-in-law,' she said, pointing to the wrong baby.

The nurse patiently corrected the mistake but Mum didn't seem all that interested in her own grandson.

'Look at all these goldfish tanks they put babies into.'

She started peering into another incubator with a look of sheer fascination on her face.

'Oh, my Goodness,' she said, looking at two miniscule twins in horror. 'There are two in this one. Why are they so hairy? How revolting; don't tell me those have any chance of survival.'

We had to remove her.

We returned to Tamzin's room to find a (male) electrician fixing the bedside light and a (female) health worker in a tight, white, nylon trouser suit who'd come to give her a little talk.

'Now, have we been doing our pelvic floor exercises?' She asked in a singsong voice.

Tamzin just gritted her teeth and looked murderous.

'Ooo,' Mum said, jogging up and down. 'Pelvic floor exercises. What are those? Can I do them?'

'Everyone should be doing them,' chirped the nurse, showing me a gruesome looking diagram on her clipboard.

'Are you doing your pelvic floor exercises?' Mum asked the electrician.

Raddy created mayhem by leaving her six-week-old son wrapped in a car rug on the floor of the corridor outside the Intensive Care Unit, which she'd marched into without permission. One nurse thought Alexander was an abandoned baby case, and another that Raddy was a baby thief.

The Sister took one look at Raddy, skinny as anything in her drainpipe jeans, decided she must still be at school and said she wasn't prepared to release Alexander until the mother arrived. Raddy laughed and told her not to be so stupid but was hopeless when it came to proving the child was hers. Tamzin came along to find quite a fight going on and had to sort it out. Wish I'd been there.

Dad was upset because he put his smart new shoes on the roof of his car outside Tamzin's house and drove off losing one but not the other. He was wondering what he could do with one new shoe.

I heard of a woman who left her seven-week-old baby with her husband while she went shopping; her first break since the birth. His friends rang, persuading him to meet them at the golf club. He took the baby in her travelling seat outside, unlocked the car and went back to get the changing bag.

It was only once he was driving along that he realised that he'd left the baby, in her seat, on the roof of the car. By now he was on the motorway. He stopped and found the car seat, with baby, was still there. On the car roof. This is true.

I told this story to Mary-Dieu who said she wasn't a bit surprised.

'That's why women over the age of fifty can't have babies; they'd put them down and forget where they'd left them.'

You were right about Tamzin's builders; they've been off for a week.

'The problem is,' the doddery Mr Hindleson insisted on explaining to me, in his creaking voice, 'Is that our Eric will send off for these mail orders.'

The purchase was a seven-day deodorant. He thought he had to put it over his entire body, the idea being that he wouldn't have to bath for a week, but something went wrong.

'I took him to the apothecary,' Mr Hindleson went on, 'And the apothecary said they'd never seen anything like it and sent us to Casual-tee. Casualty said they'd never seen anything like it and gave Eric ointment which turns the skin to plastic.'

Poor Eric did look like a nuclear fallout victim: the boils on his face were coated in pink 'plastic skin' that was coming off in ribbons. Even the palms of his hands were in a state.

It was a bit of a thing adjusting to Hampshire culture. Having battled to learn Afrikaans I kept coming out with phrases while I was there.

The words for 'Thank you very much' are *Baaie Dankie*. You pronounce this: 'Buy-a-donkey.'

Well, you can imagine what I told them to do as I walked out of Quellington Green Post Office.

I must go and tack-up fourteen horses. This takes an hour and a half to get on, about two minutes to take off. Why?

Lots of love

Sophie

Equus Horse Safaris

Dear Tamzin,

It's quite disorientating to fly back into summer, especially after such dismal weather in England but it was wonderful to see your boy. I hope you're both doing well now you're back at home. Johnty said he only just managed to get the carpets down and the heating working in time for your return from hospital, did he tell you?

We have a new cook who is in love with Sarah-Jane. He is actually a chartered surveyor, but once met her on the bus to Lake Turkana and said he couldn't forget her.

Everyone falls in love with her the whole time, but he took a chance, came over and found her unattached. Why does this never happen to me?

'You weren't on the bus to Lake Turkana.'

Anyway, this chap Jez is making a frame to keep birds off my strawberries today. I have to be grateful for the crumbs that fall off the plate.

Fred and Josie flew to England soon after I arrived, and are living in Buckinghamshire where Josie is working on a cookery book called *Revolting Recipes*. It is. She is devising recipes so that children can cook all the things Roald Dahl described in his books, like snozzcumbers.

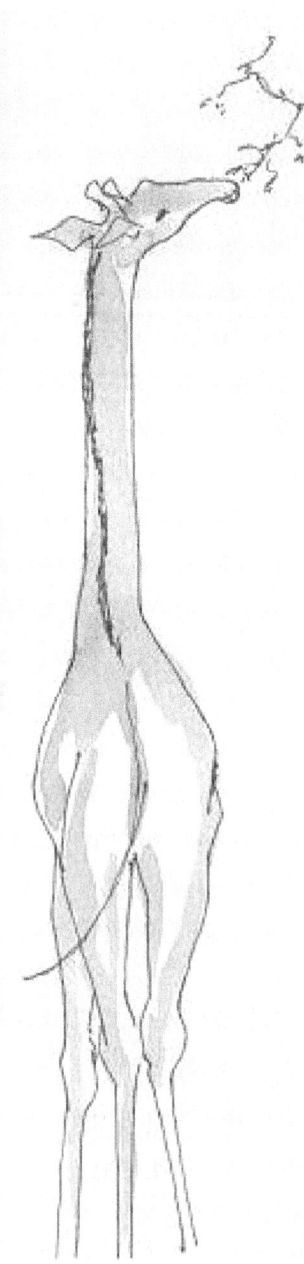

Fred devised the edible wallpaper. I suppose Mum might try making it. Instead of a Mercedes I bought Fred's rather rusty, blue Nissan *bakkie*. He calls it 'The Blue *Bliksem'*. *Bliksem* means lightning or getting a whack. I hope I don't. Nicki has left for Scotland of all places, and Andrew, newly graduated, has gone to work in Alaska. I've told them they can think of each other while they're both being bitten raw by midges. So, it's me and Jez and Sarah-Jane with Lindizwe, who seems to have taken to the bottle. A qualified veterinary nurse is coming up to help with the horses. She said that she has been working for the Blue Cross in Kyletsha, bless her soul.

Have to rush, but I'll write again soon, love Sophie

Hardacre Farm

16: III: 93

Dear Sophie –

Is it bliss to be back in Africa or are you missing Mummy's cuisine? Hughie is very well indeed and now weighs in at 9lbs 14oz.

Quite a bit has been happening since you left. Mum went and advertised the empty room in their cottage in rather a hurry. It read:

<u>Single woman</u> seeks another to share remote cottage: £35 per week. Lovely rural position.

Well, I mean to say – surprise, surprise – she has had a pervert ringing her up. Luckily he phoned when Dad was around.

Mum asked the caller 'What did you say?' He repeated it, and Mum said to Dad: 'I have a pervert on the phone!' And then blasted him with a wolf whistle.

Sadly this did not deter him (although he's not so keen on speaking to Dad), so she went to the Police Station. They had her write down what he'd said – can you imagine how embarrassing – and now British Telecom are tracking all their calls. I'm sure it's the man Raddy met, who was wearing surgical rubber gloves.

To top the pervert story on the head, we now have New Age Travellers a few fields away. I've just spent £37 on padlocks, but we still have one field without a gate. Meanwhile, we keep getting wrong phone numbers, strange men calling at the door etc, so I'm a bag of nerves. Dad came up to stay for two days in bodyguard mode, which was great, especially as he cleaned out the woodshed. It was full of old rats' nests.

Poor Thelma. Johnty decided she really ought to go back to the vet. Sophie, she has skin cancer again. Instead of having her put straight down, he insisted they operate once more, and she came home with a shaved head as well as no ears – a bald cat with no ears – she looks at best like a strange monkey. Then Johnty said, 'Thelma needs to be kept warm and quiet,' and that she must live in the kitchen by the Aga. But since old age has set in she has lost the will to think and has forgotten to use the litter trays. And I'm sure cats do dreadful things to babies. I cried and cried and eventually Johnty put her in the old dairy with a heat lamp. She is still ugly.

We have an electric fence up, so it won't be long before we have around 200 sheep for Maudie to play with. I don't suppose I'll be so excited about them when they start baa-ing outside our bedroom window, or munching away at the garden. I have to find a friend for Bod now, so hope to borrow an old chestnut pony.

The most extraordinary thing happened to Raddy's mother. She was walking in our field when a hare looked up and stared at her. She stood, quietly looking at this hare, and do you know, it came up to her and punched her hard on the shin. So hard it drew blood. She was shocked and rather badly scratched by his claws. Raddy had to bandage up her leg. Dad says he is not a bit surprised because animals get territorial at this time of year. He keeps finding that badgers have dragged stones off walls or up out of the stream onto the meadow grass. He reckons they return later to turn the stones over and eat the slugs and insects that have accumulated underneath. In a way you could say the badgers are farming, but Dad says it annoys him as the stones are quite big and he keeps hitting them with the mower. That would infuriate Johnty.

Things are going well with the builders; great excitement in the bedroom this week. As I was stripping the old wallpaper, shaky writing was revealed beneath, stating the pattern and date the wallpaper was hung in 1945.

'Look. Mr Hindleson,' I said, 'A piece of history.'

'Ooh, yes, Miss Tamzin,' he said prosaically. 'I put it up myself, when I was an apprentice.'

He'd never mentioned this before. Johnty wanted me to have a 'firm word' with him about the seriously bad drips in the new paintwork. Ever the diplomat, I approached the subject with tact.

'Mr Hindleson, isn't it irritating how we get all these drips? Is there anything you can do about it?'

'Oooh, no, Miss Tamzin, you need a few drips in a house like this. It adds character.'

Eric got in a bit of a state yesterday: 'Where's my bradawl? Has anyone seen my bradawl?'

'I'm terribly sorry, I haven't seen it anywhere.'

Actually, I had no idea what a bradawl was until I found naughty Maudie eating the handle of a carpentry tool in the garden.

Perry has left your Chrysler Sunbeam here, parked outside my house as a cold-caller deterrent. All my friends will think I have moved the New Age Travellers in with us.

Lots of love, T xxx

EQUUS HORSE SAFARIS

Dear Tamzin,

OK: if the sheep start to eat your roses this is what you do: you put lion poo around the garden. It might even deter the New Agers, you never know. Fred told me about it. He has been working in Buckinghamshire as a gardener. They have muntjac continuously eating whatever they try and grow.

Fred went off to the zoo and asked if he could have some lion dung. He put this around the flowerbeds and the deer haven't returned. They leap into the garden but think better of staying there. You would think lion poo might, logically, keep away antelope in Africa, but isn't it amazing that Chinese deer in middle England should be wary of it?

A huge stick insect in flight, like something out of *Alice through the Looking Glass*, has just landed beside me. I feel like the Red Queen, running as fast as I can just to stay in the same place.

A German technician, who had never been outside Berlin in his life until this week when he flew to Johannesburg, is demanding my every waking moment. He was rather threatening at first but I think it was because he was just concerned about yellow signs he'd seen along the roads of the Waterberg. They say '*Bonsmara is die race*'. He wanted to know if it was an apartheid thing.

I didn't think so. Bonsmara are the local breed of cattle.

'Don't deny it,' Jez has just pointed out. 'You revel in revelations.'

I do. Jörgen works on the underground system and normally lives in darkness, sleeping during the day, like a termite. He can't get over the space and freedom, is intrigued by the wildlife and as he rides quite well; we go out all day, for miles. I feel as if I'm showing him a new world.

We've given Jez a lady American client to look after. She is about sixty, knows everything about everything and is a world traveller, 'come to see big game'. While Jörgen and I go quietly and see all sorts of animals she yacks constantly, making so much noise that any living creature scarpers before they get anywhere near.

She wanted to go on one of the 'Luxury Safaris' Wendy has been marketing, so we sent Jez off towards the Bushmen paintings, while Sarah-Jane went ahead to set up a camp for them, frantically trying to get a long-drop dug before they arrived. Jez took ages.

'He rode in just before sundown with a 'Don't ask' expression on his face,' she reported.

'The woman talked all day long,' he told us later, 'On and on and saw nothing. Nothing at all. I managed to get to a good cliff for lunch so we would at least have a view of the river and possibly spot hippo but there didn't even seem to be any birds around. There we were,' he went on, 'munching away on sandwiches, me desperately looking for something when a baboon came along. "Look. Baboon." I hissed. As she turned round another baboon came up behind the first one and thrust himself upon her. They stood there, right on the edge of the cliff, bonking away. I didn't know what to do or where to look.'

Poor Jez.

'"OK," the lady said. "Now, could we see a rhino do that?"'

I've only actually seen a rhinoceros do it once. It was when I had a large group of schoolgirls who, to my surprise, seemed bored by the spectacular event. I was intrigued. The male was on top of the female when we rode past at the beginning of our ride and was still there, quite motionless forty-five minutes later. They hadn't moved at all. It must be quite hard work for the cow; the males can weigh over two tonnes.

Jez's strawberry netting weighs nothing at all, but, as Sarah-Jane says, looks as if it should go to see the doctor.

It was me who had to go to the Surgery. I woke with terrible stomach pains, which I suspected could only be amoebic dysentery.

Feeling quite nauseous, I drove into Marken only to find the doctor had painted his house in pink and purple stripes. Truly. All the other patients were sitting on a low wall under the carport, so I joined them, desperately hoping I wouldn't need the loo. I heard the phone ring.

Dr Grobler stuck his head out of the door and said brightly, 'Ach, Sophie, man. How are you?'

'Not at all well, actually.'

'It's Sarah-Jane on the phone. She says can you go to the Farmers' Co-op and buy a ball-cock?'

I didn't want to hear this. I could see a gasping Sotho woman lying on the examination couch, obviously in urgent need of attention but Dr Grobler took me by the elbow and steered me round the corner to a frilly waiting room, which I could only conclude was reserved for white people. I then realised he was deeply inebriated. Jez says it must be something to do with living in Marken.

Our poor animals have been in the wars. It always happens when Sarah-Jane goes to Johannesburg and the full weight of responsibility lies on me. Luckily the veterinary nurse had arrived. This time, Nicki's puppy, PK, found a cobra in the garden, about six foot from where we were sitting, and started barking at it. It spat in his eye. I had heard that you should wash the venom out with mother's milk, but couldn't find a mother. Walter, our vet, told us to use running water. PK seemed to respond well to an antihistamine injection, but I'm sure it was all very painful.

Then Nicholas, the naughtiest of all the horses but Sarah-Jane's darling, tried to walk over the cattle grid. Well, he fell in. It was late at night and when I rang the vet he said we'd probably have to shoot him. We could see why. He kept struggling to get out, but every time we tried to get near him to help he would panic, bashing himself terribly.

The only person who wasn't in a panic was Jörgen.

'You need a flat board, that is large,' he said prosaically.

It occurred to me that we could use the thick slabs of hardboard under our mattresses. While Jörgen and I pushed my bed-board under the horse Jez grabbed one of Nicholas' back hooves and pulled it out. Quite brave as his hands could easily have been squashed. After he extracted the third leg Nicholas was somehow able to struggle up onto the board.

He is still a bit bruised and shaky but it was a great triumph. He isn't even lame.

Jez has now filled the deep cattle grid with sand so anything falling in will only go down about three inches.

What with sorting out Nicholas, and nursing PK I didn't get to bed until about two, and then, after I had the jabberwocky flying around my room all night, Jörgen wanted to go on another marathon ride.

Love from a tired girl guide, Sophie

Hardacre Farm
31: III: 93

Dearest Sophie –

You're tired? Just try having a man cub. Hughie is well and will be six weeks tomorrow. I can't believe it. He eats, sleeps and wails all day long (not forgetting nappy filling; usually a large mustard explosion, which no nappy known to mankind can hold back. It covers him from neck to knee).

Thank you for the information on lion poo. I actually want to know about bird tables, although I don't think Thelma would be too much of a threat anymore. She is still no beauty. I took her for a check-up and the woman sitting next to me in the waiting room said, 'Oh, Good Gracious, what's that?'

I said, 'It's a cat.'

She said, 'You would never have guessed, would you?'

Mum did manage to find a female to rent her ugly Nissen hut of a cottage, but the hopeless woman backed over Atalanta's pink bike. She squished it flat, which caused a major to-do, I can tell you.

Raddy and I found out that the man in the surgical rubber gloves was a con artist of the first order.

The Police said that 'The gloves were 'a pointer', indicating that he didn't want to leave fingerprints anywhere.'

I told Mum, who got frightfully excited when a man knocked on her door, wearing not just rubber gloves but heavy duty ones. He turned out to be coming to pump out the cesspit.

Granny is in terrific form, driving me dotty phoning all the time. She says she is worried about you, and prays for you constantly.

Johnty has been lugging corrugated iron around, in an effort to dismantle numerous old pigpens.

He says he always wondered how Robert kept your car outside his house without dying of embarrassment… Thank you Sophie; we are thrilled to have it to stay. It is with the fertilizer, so with any luck may be backed into by a tractor. Hoping Lu Llewellyn will buy it, but she hasn't called back yet.

Having gone to great lengths to have all their phone calls monitored by British Telecom, Mum's pervert has not called back yet either.

Lots of love

T xxx

Hughie's hand. (Outline included) not a good likeness as he wriggles so much.

PS: Sophie – have just spoken to Lu who does not want to buy your car – Listen, what are we going to do with it? Perry wants to claim back the £25 left on the tax disc, but I don't want to take that off until it has been moved.

It can't stay here indefinitely, and I'm afraid I don't want to sell it through the paper. Please could you give this a great deal of thought and let me know.

PS: Hughie is now 6 weeks old and 11lbs 1½ oz.

Equus Horse Safaris

Dear Perry,

We've suddenly had a lot of people to stay, all of whom have been good riders. I've never covered such an enormous amount of ground but nothing seems to tire my horse. He is starting to find game for me. I didn't actually think of training him to do this but he knows that when we do come across wild animals, he'll be allowed to eat as letting the horses graze seems to calm the game.

We found a roan antelope today, with thick scimitar horns, which was special as they're rare and I know there are only a couple of males on the reserve. I also found myself riding past two rhino who were fast asleep. Their ears were moving independently like radar sweepers. I rather wanted to stop and draw them but was leading quite a large party, so couldn't.

Having not seen much of the elephant, I seem to keep on coming across them whenever I ride Jigsaw. I was out with two people from Cornwall, when I heard a great crashing in the trees and our horses stopped dead. Ten elephant came charging through the bush within yards of us, trumpeting with their trunks up. They saw us, looked disgusted, turned and ran off in the other direction, disregarding any bushes in their path. It was quite something.

Jez pulled out all the stops this weekend and cooked a breakfast under a marula tree in the bush. Poor Jez, he had it all looking so well organized, but he was approached by a group of ostriches determined on stealing the fried bacon. I found him chasing them off with a folding chair. The ostrich often scare the new horses but ours are immune to their vagaries, thank Goodness. It's because they live out in the wild. A great flock of francolin rose up right in front of Sam the other day and he totally ignored them although they gave me quite a fright.

After consuming Jez's sausages we sat, eating the ripe marula fruit, which look like greengages with thick skins and large stones.

'It was the fruit that was meant to make all the animals drunk in that legendary wildlife film called *Beautiful People*.' Jez started telling everyone. 'It didn't. A baboon couldn't get tiddly on fermenting fruit, let alone an elephant. They drugged them for the sequence.'

But the fruit did have a strange effect on us. We all ended up with rather badly behaved tummies and I only ate two.

Just when everything was going well and the bookings book was, for once, full, our horses started to get sick. There's a midge here, which spreads an horrific equine virus simply called horse-sickness. We inoculate against it, but the virus mutates so quickly that the injections only protect the animals from old strains. The first we knew of it was when one of the guests complained that the horse she was riding ~ a beautiful skewbald called Patches ~ was sluggish, so Wendy trotted everyone back to the yard. I could see the pony had great swellings over its eyes, which is an early symptom of the disease. Just before they set off again, I noticed another horse, Rocky, had swellings too. Patches died in the night. Walter said that trotting back home would have put too much stress on his depleted system. Wendy is devastated. He had such a lovely, gentle nature. He belonged to her cousin, so she feels dreadful and she can't stop crying, asking, 'Why, why, why?'

Rocky became feverish and his neck blew up terribly but looks as if he'll pull through. Xian, the lovely Friesian colt I broke in, is ill now and I think we will lose him. He is wheezing terribly and keeps getting up and lying down.

It's heartbreaking. I feel as though my child is dying. I was with him all morning but there's nothing more I can think of to do for him and Sarah-Jane said the best thing would be to let him rest. She is frantically taking temperatures to make sure that no other horse with any sign of a virus gets ridden, but it's hard as the camp is full with ten guests. I've been taking them out on game walks but don't think I can struggle on physically much longer.

Mrs Baber came to help and her son Anthony has been driving over with bales of hay for the enclosed horses. He tried bleeding the sick ones with cattle syringes to reduce the swellings.

We are all pulling together but everyone is tired and emotional, on edge. Keeping the awfulness from the guests, who are after all on holiday, is becoming a strain. They keep asking awkward questions we are not up to answering just now, like, 'What's under that tarpaulin?' when it's a dead horse.

I find it difficult to keep on being gracious when the clients fuss about little things and have you running about in the heat altering stirrup leathers when you need to be with sick animals.

I've been asked to stay near the Kruger Park for Easter, so I'm hanging on until then.

Lots of love,

Sophie

C/o C.E. Baber, Triple B Ranch
24 Rivers
PO Box. Vaalwater
South Africa

Dear Tamzin,

I'm sitting in the most lovely garden, under huge Jacaranda trees and doing nothing. It's strange. I was meant to be going to stay with friends who are running a big game ranch near Hoedspruit, which borders the Kruger, but my car, Fred's old *bakkie*, failed its Roadworthy (MOT). The man didn't like the rusty tailgate. Instead the Babers kindly invited me to stay on their farm, where I'm panel-beating in their workshop. It is a horrible job.

Xian, the sweet-natured Friesian Mum rode, died after a long struggle and then my own dear horse developed symptoms. It was agonising to watch. His neck blew up and he lay, unable to move, but battling away, in terrible pain. Walter was wonderful. He said he didn't want to put Sam down as he still could pull through, but I couldn't bear to see him suffer and, in the end, had to come away, tears streaming down my face. Sarah-Jane went on nursing him for me, rubbing ointment into his dreadfully swollen neck. I arrived here at the end of myself, so tired I was unable to speak but Mrs Baber was kind. She showed me to a little thatched cottage in her garden and let me sleep for a long time.

The Babers have about twenty horses on the farm, a breeding herd most of whom have never been ridden. Alan Dryden couldn't cope. He somehow managed to get a mare called Samantha stuck under a cattle lorry and disappeared in disgrace. Instead we sent the Babers a young couple who have experience in breaking unhandled horses. They're doing well. It's difficult training old brood mares, but Shane learnt how to handle wild horses in Australia and works quietly, gaining their trust. His girlfriend Laura has got me up on some of the newly broken ones and we've been riding across this beautiful cattle farm. It's a Bonsmara stud so they keep lots of bulls, which always seem to be wandering through the garden. Charles Baber said they're bred to be non-aggressive. Just as well. One bull caught sight of his own reflection in the glass doors of the dining room and would have been rampaging through the house if Nina hadn't shoo-ed him away.

The Bonsmara was developed by crossing *Bostaurus* with *Bosindicus* cattle, if that means anything to you. They're all a deep chestnut colour. 'We breed out any white markings,' Charles went on, 'but it does make them difficult to see on the road at night.' He told me the sign saying *Vier en Twintig Riviere* is an anathema as it should be written 24. 24 Rivers.

'There are a number of young people staying here,' Nina explained when I arrived, 'friends from Germany and Sweden, the Drakensberg and Pretoria.' In fact an incredible number of people of every race and colour seemed to come and go.

'It's so exciting to be able to entertain black South Africans properly,' Juliet said. 'During apartheid it was illegal for them to sleep overnight in a white person's house.' I hadn't known.

The Babers are all tall and flamboyant, glowing with energy. They never seem to stop moving unless they sit down to eat, or watch cricket. Juliet, who is about my age, spent four years in England - as a missionary, would you believe - before returning to teach at the secondary school in Vaalwater. She is nearly six foot tall, quite striking and never stops either smiling or organizing things to do. Her brother Rupert, who must be over six foot five, is over from Cambridge where he is a Rhodes scholar, finishing his MA in Agricultural Economics before launching on a PhD. Anthony is just back from his time in the Army, where he seemed to spend most of his time playing rugger. He is working with the cattle at the moment while entertaining hordes of friends, insisting we must all sleep out tonight, under the stars. Nina has a wonderful housekeeper called Marty who is not only packing supper for us but seems to keep the whole circus on the road. She is walking across the lawn right now with a loaded tea tray on her head. She said it's the easiest way to carry things, especially if they're hot, as it leaves your hands free. Miriam, who works in the garden, was moving furniture yesterday, carrying a wardrobe on her head. I return to Equus tomorrow, which is good as I'll see Sam, but frankly I could stay here forever.

Mum said you need to know about bird tables. I'd just use a tree but you could ring Alastair; he's an expert on them. He once made a series called *Bird Brain of Britain* featuring all sorts of designs including a mobile bird table on a milk float.

Must end as someone is off with the post, and they need me to ride one of the newly broken mares.

Lots of love to you all,

Sophie

CHAPTER EIGHT

Nottingham
May 1993

Darling Sib –

We are appalled to hear about your ghastly accident. I'm so sorry. I hope you're not in too much pain. Mum told me your horse had crashed into a tree and you broke your pelvis in two places, but that was all we know.

We're all fine apart from exhaustion. We've just been staying in London with Robert's mother for four days.

Hastings was up all night, because the house is under the flight path so I couldn't sleep either. Ahhh. So that was me, cross, tired and rat-baggish.

I was relishing the bliss of shopping in Peter Jones but had to take the dog with us. Well, no sooner had Robert taken Atalanta off to find a loo, arranging to meet me back in the Needlework Department, when Tadpole did an enormous poo right in the middle of the carpet. I was able to disguise it with the pushchair, but the trouble was that everyone kept coming up to admire Hastings, kneeling down right next to it. I was desperately fanning the smell with a shoulder pad. You can't imagine my agony; Robert couldn't find the loos and didn't come for a long ten minutes. I gave him one of Mum's gritting teeth looks across the room. Anyway, of course he couldn't stop laughing and had no sympathy but scooped it all up with a copy of *Private Eye* and put it in *my* bag. SO Embarrassing.

We went for lunch at your friend Leanda's house. She is expecting a third child any minute. Her two little boys looked well but she said she was all still a bit wobbly: The other day her au pair girl came to tell her that the children had locked themselves in the upstairs bathroom. She didn't think this a major urgency until she was outside in the garden and looked up to see her eighteen-month-old with his feet on the windowsill, hanging onto the bars *outside* the open bathroom window. This was three storeys up. She tried to persuade him to climb back in, but he was overexcited and just laughed, whooping with glee. The au pair was desperately trying to get the four-year-old to open the bathroom door. Leanda said they could have bashed it down, but she didn't want the toddler to take fright and let go of the bars.

'Ring 999,' she shouted, bringing sofa cushions out onto the tarmac drive beneath the window.

'Who do we need? Fire, Police or Ambulance?'

'All of them. And my husband; ring him at work.'

As it happened the emergency services all arrived together with sirens blaring and got rather jammed at the gate of the drive. While they were un-jamming, the little boy decided to let go of the bars. He fell, silently, dropping like a stone. Leanda, eight months pregnant, stretched out her arms, leapt over the sofa cushions and caught him.

    Blimey O'Riley, two minutes left before I collect Atalanta from nursery school. She's so pleased; she's been promoted up a table, so is now a squirrel instead of a duck, and bikes to and fro on her new birthday tricycle.

   Her party was a grrrreat success. Tamzin gave her a Prince Charming and we gave her a bride Sindy doll, which she adores. They snog together. Her cake was another Sindy doll, which was meant to be standing up with the cake being the skirt, but Sindy rather passed out and Atalanta was upset that the dolly had fallen into the cake, so that went down like a lead balloon.
Let us all know how you are; we are worried,
Lots of love
Perry, R, A, H & Tadpole

   Later: I was telling Mum about Leanda and Dad said that funnily enough the same sort of thing happened to him. When he was a little boy of eight he started playing with the door handle of his mother's car while she was driving along. The door suddenly burst open and he was flung out – at speed. He was caught by an R.A.C. man who just happened to be standing at the side of the road. He said he has been loyal to the organization ever since.

Gloucestershire
6th May 1993

Dear Sophie,

This is a quick note from me to send our love and sympathy for your rehabilitation. Your poor pelvis. It brought tears of anguish to hear of your accident, I do hope you recover soon.

April was a busy month for us. We spent a couple of days in Yorkshire with the otters and went down to Sherborne in Dorset.

I saw Tamzin and Hughie on my travels. He cries a lot. She has a large group of uninvited hippies camping on her doorstep and fears they'll stay for the whole summer; a stressful prospect.

We all visited Granny in Bedford after Easter. She was looking healthy. She says she enjoys doing nothing and obviously is thriving with the company at the Home. She had the air about her of a girl at boarding school.

Kamilla the cross Czech (Perry's new au pair) is extremely hard working, but doesn't speak a word of English, so they are hopping around like mime artists. Perry is extremely jealous of all her single friends who, when they come to stay, lie in bed until about 11.00am. She gets Atalanta knocking on her door at 5am each morning for an hour's activity.
Lots of love, thoughts and prayers, Dad

Triple B Ranch

Dear Perry and Robert,

    Yes, I remember flying through the air thinking, 'I'm going to hit that tree right between my legs.' And I did. I couldn't go to hospital right away because someone had assassinated the leader of the Communist Party and Pretoria wasn't a good place to be. [viii] But after the funeral Charles Baber put me, bed and all, into the back of a Landcruiser and his wife took me to see a Specialist who, after one look at my X-rays, confirmed that I have a double fracture exactly the same width as the tree trunk. Fortunately there are no complications and although I can't move I didn't have to stay in hospital. Instead I'm lying in Juliet's bedroom looking out over the lovely gardens.

    Walter the vet came to see me today. He'd been doing pregnancy tests on the cattle and was wearing a sleeveless green boilersuit covered in muck.

    'What are you doing sitting up?' He shouted, as he walked past the window. 'You must take the weight off those bones.'

    What still hurts are my poor bruised ribs, but only when I laugh. He says I can't do anything about that except not laugh.

    'Don't complain,' he said, cheerfully, 'You're lucky not to have ruptured your bladder.' He also told me that Sam has totally recovered from horse-sickness, which is a great relief.

    I'm just feeling woozy now and stiff from not being able to turn over at night. Juliet has lovely books, and I have my portfolio with me so I'm going to start painting from my sketches as soon as I can sit up. As it is I spend most of my time asleep, just trying to mend or lie in a daze listening to the turtledoves calling across Nina's garden.

When Laura gave me my first bath I fainted in the water, which was a bit alarming for her. And for me. What I find odd is that I seem to have swung from giving and giving, on the horse safaris, to not being able to do a thing but receive. When I first had the accident I couldn't feed myself or even clean my own teeth. Juliet slept on the floor at the bottom of the bed to get me through my first night as I was in quite a bad way. I've got to know the Babers rather well.

Although you have never met a busier man, Charles always seems to find time to drop in and chat. I'd always held romantic notions about having a farm in Africa, but the reality seems harsh. Today one of the main irrigators collapsed, a bull jumped into a field with his own daughters and some vile fungal epidemic is sweeping through a peanut field. Nina's old gardener had an argument with someone who hit him on the head with a galvanized bucket. She found him with a four-inch gash across his forehead. He'd been bleeding all night, too drunk to do anything about it.

My friend Andrew has written from Alaska. He said they have a horse that likes to lie down beside the campfire. They were having supper one night when it started to look uneasy and suddenly stood up. A grizzly bear was right on top of them. Andrew grabbed a burning branch from the fire and chased it away, but said the horse probably saved his life as he hadn't noticed a thing.

I hope you're all well and having fun. Mum wanted to fly out and nurse me, but I gather she's in a television series about pets and I would rather she was here when I can move about more. Love from your immobilized
but happy sister,
Sophie

Hardacre Farm

12th May 1993

Dear Sophie,

I do hope you're feeling a bit better. How Grim. I can only imagine the discomfort. You must feel so frustrated.

I've had the most irritating day. I thought it would be all right to ride Bodney to the blacksmith with Hughie in Perry's hippy sling. Alas, we did not make it. Bod went berserk about leaving his ugly orange girlfriend. He reared up like a stallion, with me clinging onto him, and Hughie clinging onto me. I managed to scream, and was saved by the lady who comes to clean the cottage opposite. Phew.

I'm afraid Johnty is wanting to know when your ugly orange tramp-wagon is going to be shifted. The eye-boggling plastic seats do glare at one.

He wants everything to look smart. We've painted all the windows of the house white. They used to be ugly orange too. And the Hindlesons are still repairing various things.

They're only a month behind schedule.

'I've been in the infirmary with me vein,' Mr Hindleson told me, on the last occasion when he had to be off for two weeks.

'What's wrong?'

'Oh, it's gone mouldy, Miss Tamzin,' he said cheerfully. 'I fell off a ladder, ye see, twenty-five years ago and it's never been quite the same since.' No.

Hughie is three months old, 12lbs 15oz and ~ if the vicar remembers, is going to be baptised on 13th June at 12.00. He smiles, laughs, splashes in the bath and has just found his thumb. Poor little scrap; he now has a bedtime around 7.30pm having been left to SCREAM for a week until he learnt. At one time I nearly thought I was going to have to employ a night nanny.

Mum has been in the Welsh valleys.

'All of Merthyr Tydfil want me,' she says, doing her annual ten-day lecture tour with the otters.

Crowds of people come to see them. I couldn't bear it, but Mum says she has a hand-sanitizer spray, and if undesirables come too close she squirts them with disinfectant.

Dad has been advising us on septic tanks. At length.

Lots of love,

Tamzin

Triple B Ranch
24 Rivers, Vaalwater
South Africa

Dear Tamzin,

I'm up on crutches having to learn how to walk again. The consultant said gravely that I must 'operate within the confines of the pain.'

'Oh, Goody Gumdrops,' I thought.

But it's OK; I have a trapeze rigged up so I can sit myself up in bed and I'm painting pictures of rhino from the sketches I did of Tracy. Walter stepped on one but he has been helping me get the conformation of the animals right. I can't bear it when drawings aren't anatomically correct, but have been using bright colours. You thirst for colour out here. It must be the demands of constant sunlight.

It looks as if I won't be able to ride for six months so I've decided to make a go of the artwork; I've always wanted to be a painter. When I went for my appointment with the surgeon in Pretoria, Shane and Laura drove me to a framing place where I'm getting about thirty watercolours mounted and ready to sell. I've already been given an enormous number of commissions, so must get cracking.

Being on the farm is wonderful. Just when I was starting to feel morose one evening, Juliet strode into my room and flung open the curtains. All the young people had come to sing for me;

Gospel choruses, sung in rousing harmony. One song seemed to be about *A new corrector*. I wasn't sure what this was.

'Actually they're celebrating the time that the vicar was given a car,' Juliet explained. 'The words are "New car Rector!"'

Life here is much like it must have been in the English countryside a hundred years ago. Everyone knows each other, grew up together.

'And have no secrets,' Charles assured me.

Sandy tracks lead from the main house up to a village of small, white cottages, each surrounded by a vegetable garden. The ones belonging to the older people are made in the traditional way from wattle and daub, plastered with cow dung, and painted with geometric patterns. Although many are roofed with flat, tin sheets now rather than thatch, they look beautiful.

About 200 agricultural workers live on the farm, bringing up huge families. Effie, the lovely lady who came to nurse me when I was first injured, looks after all the little children at a crèche beyond the tennis court.

Their playground includes three wrecked cars. These would no doubt be considered far too unsafe in England but the children love them, of course. They jump up and down on the roof of an old Humber while the tiny ones stand inside, waving out of the un-glazed windows.

Juliet took me up to meet her friends who teach at the Sotho primary school just beyond the cattle kraals. They have about 120 children up to the ages of sixteen or seventeen. I couldn't get over how old some of the pupils were but it's partly because they take time out.

'Teenage pregnancies have increased dramatically in rural areas.' Juliet told me. 'You don't start school until you're six in South Africa and only move up a grade when you pass the exams, no matter how old you are.'

They think it outrageous that you automatically go up a year in England, but she said it's not good to have adults in gymslips.

'I can understand why they had riots and unrest in the Soweto schools in the 1970s. A lot of pupils were over the age of eighteen with children of their own and wanted to be taught in English rather than Afrikaans.'

'Only three universities would take black people and they all taught in English.' The headmistress explained, 'We suffered. It is hard to find yourself in Higher Education, having to learn another language.'

I would never have been able to cope.

'Everyone still needs to pass in Afrikaans before they can matriculate.' Juliet told me later. 'Most of the older generation working on the farm can't read at all. They have to put a cross when they write their name.'

Laura said she even had to hold someone's hand while they made their cross.[ix]

Shane and Laura have decided to stay and start horse trails on Triple B Ranch, as the farm is called in the stud register, offering cattle mustering as an activity.

'If people can remain onboard,' Laura said.

They've had twenty falls to date, so I'm not the only one.

'That fat girl managed to defy gravity.' Shane said. 'How could she fall onto her head, when her bottom is so big?'

I think she probably just got tired. When a group of Laura's college friends came up for the weekend Anthony took them on a seven-hour ride, with nothing to eat or drink. Some of them had never been riding before. Ever. Ant had wanted to check the cattle; cattle ranging over about 100 square kilometres.

Charles Baber has suggested they call the venture Horizon Horse Trails and that they do up an old farmhouse by the big dam for people to stay in. I've been helping to hem the curtains. Laura has made a swimming pool by sinking a circular cattle trough into the lawn. It was rather effective until she had to drain it. A genet had managed to get stuck inside and could not be persuaded to stop running endlessly round and round.

Anthony on his 16-hand Anglo-Arab

I've always wanted to learn how to lasso, but it's not something you can do sitting in bed. Mind you, Shane can do it from a cantering horse; most impressive. He has a Western saddle with a knob on it and everything. Pommel, it's called a pommel.

I think you'd better come out and have a go. Effie could have Hughie at the crèche and Johnty could go farming with Charles. He has about 2,500 head of cattle and, with the rented grazing, runs about 9,000 acres, growing wheat and maize, peanuts and tobacco on the irrigated land. The calves are being weaned and the air is full of the sounds of lowing at the moment.

As Laura says, 'It's all a bit different from Pontefract,' where she comes from.

The only thing about South Africa that alarmed her was the length, or absolute non-length of the men's shorts.

'And you know,' Laura went on, 'They can wear 'em tight; it's enough to make your eyes water.'

Tamzin, you will be relieved to hear that I've told a reliable, Christian organization called *Youth With a Mission* that they can have my car. Juliet says they'll put it to good use and have a resident mechanic if anything goes wrong.

Shane looked at her, then at me and said, 'Jesus wants you for your Sunbeam'.

Could you let them have the registration papers when they come to pick it up? NB: I've been praying about you and the New Agers like mad. Let me know how things go.
Lots of love,
Sophie

Hardacre Farm
28th May 1993

Dear Sib –

Our New Age Travellers were moved on today. At last. A large Police presence accompanied them. A bulldozer had to be brought in to clear the filth they left behind them – burnt out buses, cars and revolting rubbish. Last Monday night they were playing their *thock, thock* music so loudly that even Raddy could hear it from her house. They did seem to enjoy upsetting everybody.

Hughie is sitting in his bouncy chair playing with his baby gym, which gives me approximately 2½ seconds to write to you. I do hope you're feeling better and getting over the shock of it all. Here the lilac is out and the grass is growing madly. Poor Johnty spends his entire life cutting it and Bod is so fat I can only just put a saddle on him; no room even for a numnah.

I've just returned from Hartney Whitney where I bought a hosta for Johnty and Morning Glory for £3.00. Thought of you in Africa where they must grow like weeds. It's for Mum. Sophie, she wants to buy a mule. Have you any idea why? I haven't told her about Thelma. You will be glad to hear she is better and the fur has grown back, but she'll never look like a cat again.

Do you like our new address stamp, or does it make my letters look like an M.O.T. certificate? A man is coming to move your car tomorrow. When I asked him how he was getting here he said, 'The Lord will make a way.' Couldn't resist asking if Jesus would need directions. Lots of love, T xxx

Equus Horse Safaris

one Sunday Afternoon

Dear Perry,

I'm back at Equus, sitting in my rondavel amidst piles of papers and stacked up pictures.

The kind, kind owner of the reserve has given me a great deal of commissions. He wants me to paint all the camps and lodges he has built. I go off on crutches and sit in the sun drawing what amounts to a great deal of trees and a few tents. I've also been asked to paint the church at 24 Rivers, someone's dog (that has just died) and a portrait of the Portuguese mechanic who helped mend my *bakkie*.

My bones have nearly mended but I can't carry anything and won't be riding for a while, which is boring, especially since Sam desperately needs schooling. Jez says he loves the cross-country course so much that if they ride past it he stops and won't go forward until he's been able to plop over a few jumps.

I've been helping Sarah-Jane with what she calls, 'An Ultra-luxury, Five Day Wilderness Trail' (ie: exhausting mobile safari, bounding miles over rocky roads).

Someone has to go ahead of the riders to set up camp for them and I'm the only one who knows how to get to where they should be.

Fortunately I have a strong, silent type called Brian to heave and lug for me. You can't imagine the amount of stuff you have to take; pots and pans, washstands and thunder boxes, jars of marmalade, ice cubes and saltcellars. Clonk, clonk, clonk.

To try and make life easier for ourselves we persuaded the clients, a British stockbroker and his wife who were on honeymoon, to spend their last night at our main camp as they were flying off the next afternoon.

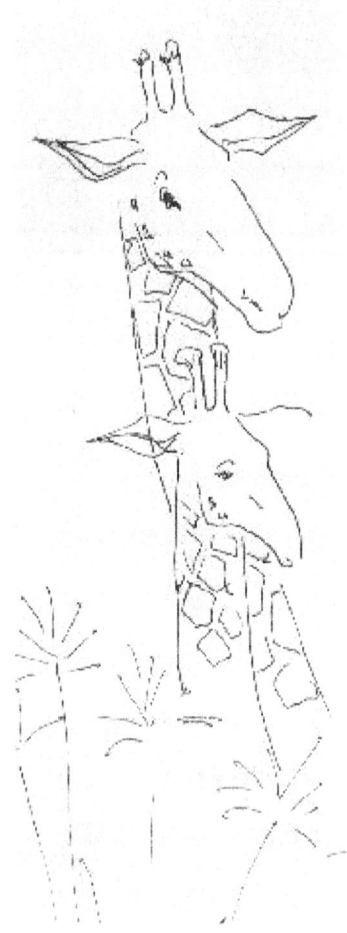

Of course the weekend guests, who poor Wendy was looking after, turned out to be excruciating – a kagooled, 'we are **serious** about the bush' family of four who kept arguing, two bitchy old ballet dancers (male) and a boring man who comes up here with a different girlfriend every other month. In an attempt to spare the honeymooners their company we decided to give them their own special lunch in the bush.

Brian and I left late and everything imaginable went wrong; I took the wrong track, we had a puncture and I set up the picnic much further south than Sarah-Jane expected. She'd told me to put the table 'under the big, flat-topped siringa tree' in a remote valley that I found was full of siringas.

Meanwhile she'd stopped for a break on the way to meet us and left the horses to graze without tying them up. Sam ran home → bride wandering around in the bush → husband charging round looking for me. In the end they found us and their lunch by chance.

However when I was driving them back to the camp I missed the first turning, became disorientated and got totally lost, for the first time ever. I felt chronically frustrated and was terrified I would make them late for their flight. Eventually we bounced into camp and they packed up.

Now, these poor people had hardly seen any game. As they were driving out in their hire car they met Brian coming towards them in my little blue *bakkie*.

He'd just seen two rhino bulls by the water pump and suggested they should hop on the back to come for a quick spin so they could get a good look. This they did, getting stuck in deep sand, while the bulls plodded towards them. There they were, sitting on the open back of my Nissan, newly married, totally vulnerable and already late for their flight.

There's still no sign of my runaway horse, and as Sarah-Jane is pacing about looking anguished, I'm beginning to get worried. Being in his saddle he could easily become caught up in a tree.

I can't look for him myself and can't think what has happened. Two of the other guests have broken down so Brian is still under their car in the yard and as it's Sunday afternoon there's no one to make up a search party.

Later: Brian will have to take the whole engine out of that car. The guests will never leave otherwise. I'm going to give them tea now and try to persuade them to buy some paintings. I need the dosh to spend on frames and paper for the next lot. There's still no sign of Sam but I'll drive around a bit until it gets too dark.

Dad is coming out here soon. We are off to stay with the Babers and then to visit Billy and my other friends in the Lowveld, if Fred's pick-up will get us there. Lots of trouble in the Homelands; our last clients were stoned driving down there.
Lots of love,
Sophie

Mthethomusha
Eastern Transvaal

Dear Tamzin,

    I thought I had lost my horse for good but Lazarus found him grazing in the bush. He came home looking most unrepentant. Dad arrived safely and we both managed to heave our creaking bones onto horses, me riding for the first time in three months, Dad lumbering along behind. I don't think he'd bargained on seeing any wild animals but we rode in silence and of course saw more game than other people do in days. We found an ostrich on the nest and were looking at a pair of secretary birds when a great buffalo cow came out of the bushes to see Dad, who started getting into quite a sweat. That same night the whole herd surrounded his tent.

We have now crossed the Drakensberg and are staying with Billy who has been made Warden of one of the most amazing reserves in the Eastern Transvaal. It is hilly tribal land and we've been sitting on high, rocky outcrops listening to the cry of crested eagles.

Reports kept coming through of a rogue lion that was taking cattle outside the reserve. Such animals can be dangerous. Billy headed off with his rifle, tense with excitement. I felt like a pioneer's wife, watching the languid setting of the sun, while I waited for the hunter's return. He woke me up in the middle of the night, eyes blazing, to tell me of the victory, describing every detail. In fact, I was given a full description of every twitch and movement with all the sound effects. This took a long time and I could hardly keep awake the next day.

We found a species of bird as yet unseen on the place. Billy was speechless. It was a white goose, a domestic one. He commanded his scouts to catch it, but they missed and I enraged him by adding it to the official bird list. It must be the result of a diet of beer and *biltong* whilst living with bilhartzia because Billy really has grown more eccentric. He was so annoyed when a helicopter had the audacity to fly over his game park that he took out his revolver and had to be persuaded not to shoot it down. Today he acquired (confiscated) a guitar made out of a 5 litre oil can. It's brilliantly made. You can tune it and everything. I found him sitting on his veranda playing it with a warthog looking on. I could make a documentary about Billy, but the resulting controversy might lead to civil war in South Africa.

Despite having a larney lodge for overseas tourists the park's main revenue comes from buffalo hunting, which Billy loves. 'I took Nelson Mandela hunting once but he was only after eland.' I don't feel at all bad about buffalo being shot but became quite tearful when Billy said he was going to 'take out' a giraffe. People do hunt them, but I don't know how they can feel good about it. One of Jez's friends has just made a documentary called *Some of my best friends are Afrikaners*. It was about barbequing a giraffe on a spit. He won an award for it.

My love to Johnty and whoever you might see,

Sophie

CHAPTER NINE

Hardacre Farm
9:VII: 93

Dear Sib –

An age since I last wrote. Poor Dad, what did you do to him? Luckily his tick-bite fever is much better but it was a bit of a worry as the doctor thought he had malaria. Whilst he was flying back we had a sad time. Bee the Otter died. Mum was totally shattered. She nursed her for ten days but the kidney stones took their toll and it was not to be. The story was on *The Ten O'clock News* and in all the national papers. *The Sun* ran the headline 'Otter way to go', which was a bit grizzly. Even I had to admit Bee had been a great ambassador for her species. Dad said that Mum must have given about fifteen hundred talks with her. Letters have flooded in.

While Bod is still the fattest horse in the world, Raddy has, on loan, the thinnest horse in the world. We do look odd together but are enthusiastic riders, please note. Raddy suggested that we should hack over to watch the filming of *Black Beauty* at Winterbottom Farm. She told the Production Manager that I might be able to help them if they were looking for a fat beauty. She is more embarrassing than Mum.

The hosta I bought in Hartley Witney never came up. I rang the garden centre to complain.

'Bring it back,' they said.

'But there's nothing to bring back.' I searched the pot after a while but found no evidence of life whatsoever. I had been watering it diligently for ages.

Your dear old car has gone to the Godly house – collected by some fresh-faced youths who were transfixed by the sight of Maudie gobbling up Hughie's sick. It was a miracle they found me as they came via Raddy's house, bouncing down her back drive.

We sold the Dick Dastardly Mobil to Johnty's best friend, what a relief, and have bought a proper estate car, good for growing boys and bad bullterriers.

Hughie is now six months old and what a wriggler he is… he can traverse a room on his tummy leaving a trail of snot and dribble like a large slug. He just adores Maudie. Affection is shown by a sharp tug of the tail or tweak of a nipple. I wish she could suckle him. I've almost given up, just a feed in the mornings. I'm not a good cow.

Hughie is, as I write, in the wolf cub's walker, using his vocal cords and puking. He is a wonder at this and pukes the whole time. It's usually projectile, ALWAYS an exceptional aim, and sometimes manages to hit the *Dry clean only* Chanel suit of some woman who fancies motherhood, which is always a good wheeze.

Sadly his sweet pelt of hair fell out and he is now bald. Raddy's baby has beautiful thick, blonde hair. They sit together in their prams squeaking at each other.

Hardacre Farm is so lovely. We had a good two weeks to make our hay – 2,600 bales of it but since have not had a sunny day all summer. One crop we did have was a family of little owls. They're gorgeous and I see at least two every day. The young are covered in such fluffy feathers. I've kept one for you.

With lots of love,

Tamzin, Johnty, Maudie, Bod, Thelma and Hughie xxx

EQUUS HORSE SAFARIS

Dear Tanzindia,

Oh, dear, yes poor Dad. He thinks he must have picked up a tick from an old Army sleeping bag that Billy took out on his lion hunt, but I'm not sure. My engine packed in (typical) and I had to get one of Billy's rangers to drive Dad back to the airport while my *bakkie* was fixed. I found a brilliant mechanic called Ronnie who needed to overhaul the brakes and the clutch as well as re-bore the engine. It was all painfully expensive but I could understand why when he showed me the worn-out parts. We had been pouring in as much oil as petrol. It sounds like an aeroplane now. I remember you used to call ladybirds 'Ronnies' when you were little. He was a nice smiley man with a big, fat tummy and looked just like one. He kept hens in his scrap-yard and showed me an egg that had been laid by a cockerel. It was small and round with no yolk.

I had to stay on with Billy, but he had a great big packet of Quality Street, so that was OK and I did a lot of painting. I'm back at Equus now. We are all reeling with shock because it rained today. It isn't meant to until October. Everything got wet, including Jez who was out on a camping trip with two Finns in smart jodhpurs. He left them in their tent, having a zizz and has just cantered back to collect more whisky and to have a hot bath without them knowing. He looked muddy and exhausted. 'I'm beginning to get jealous of these dogs. Tigger spends more time asleep on my bed than I do,' he said. 'I used to think, "When I'm in Africa life will be slower and I'll have more time to contemplate things of eternal value." Fat chance'.

While Tiger is in favour for locating a dung beetle in Jez's only pair of dry boots, PK is in disgrace. He has just eaten the end of the gear stick and pee-ed on the bed of our nice new cook, an erstwhile City broker called Kate. Some Italians arrived at the camp today (straight from Venice) to find PK asleep right in the middle of the dining-room table. They thought he must be made of china.

JIGSAW ABOUT TO BEAT HELL OUT OF A NEW COLT

Sam is now so well he has become impossibly competitive, prancing about and startling everyone. He frightened Wendy so much she wants to sell him. I think he is fun and that I'll never find such a talented horse again. The girl who came here on honeymoon could manage him but she was once a jillaroo and is now a steeplechase jockey. You don't get many of those. Having struggled to keep going, we now have so many bookings we are turning people away and have had to buy two new horses. Sarah-Jane went to collect the eggs and came back with Meisie's old white cattle pony. It's the sweetest little thing with a bushy mane and has been called Marshmallow. Wendy bought a chestnut Saddlebred called Red who is even hotter than Sam; I'm afraid I gave her one of Mum's little looks.

I wanted to get Brian to burn the muckheap today but greatly fear that I've already been too bossy. He has to sleep under the ironing board in the laundry room as it is and I'm worried that he's fed up of having to trundle round after me just to lift things. But there is no one else to help. I've just discovered Lindizwe unable to stand, clutching an empty box of white wine. My wine. She must have consumed five litres all in one go.

*****

Now it's tomorrow. The rain has gone but great clouds are filling the skies again. I'm having a mighty war with the rampant bougainvillea in the garden, getting the grooms to thwack it back. They stand on chairs and wallop it with knives they've tied to long poles, which is effective although I rather fear for the telephone line. My ears are ringing with their complaints but Sarah-Jane said, 'Don't listen to any groans; we've just had an Indaba about actually having to do a bit of work now and again.'

An Indaba is a problem or a meeting where things get thrashed out. The main difference between the white staff and the Sotho staff is that, whereas the white South Africans work at Equus for the experience despite the money, the Sothos work for the money despite the experience. There are always grievances when it comes to payday, which deflate and rile Sarah-Jane. This time she said she refused to pay for a doctor's bill since the treatment was for gonorrhoea. I'm not sympathetic about this either. I told everyone about the risk of AIDS before Christmas and they obviously took no notice.

'You have to respect people's confidentiality,' Kate muttered. She was shocked that the doctor had specified the diagnosis. I think that when it comes to HIV/AIDS the confidentiality clause is going to lead to millions of deaths, especially in Africa where women can't say No to their men. They get bashed up if they do. If AIDS was an outbreak of smallpox, or some lethal blood disease it would be notifiable and everyone's state of health would be a public issue. Tests would be compulsory.[x] You can't get into this country without a yellow fever vaccination certificate. No one makes a fuss about that. The Botswana government require horses to have veterinary inspections declaring them clear of venereal disease before they allow them into the country. Even the geldings.

I found that while the guests think I'm about twenty-three (someone once asked if I was in my gap year which was quite a thing) the Sotho people think I'm much older than I am. The latest guess on my age is fifty-eight. It must be because I'm such a tyrant. I've caught it from Billy.

Most of the time I behave like a nineteen-year-old. Except that teenagers tend to have all sorts of plans for the future and I have none. None at all. Sarah-Jane told me I should marry Billy, as if that would be a solution to life's problems, but somehow I can't see it and I'm afraid there's still no scandal re my love life. There is a Zimbabwean tobacco farmer who likes to sit next to me in church, but that's about it. I'm still furious with Jez for setting me up with a perfectly odious insurance assessor who came to stay with his whingeing, eight-year-old daughter. I had to have dinner with him and his saggy grey tracksuit, listening to constant dialogue about his Ferrari, helicopter and Lloyd's debt. He gave me a R2 tip when he left. What an insult. I said I'd put it in the church collection.

The Venetian lady has just ridden in saying she enjoys riding Sam, which is good but now PK has gone and dug up my cabbages. I bought a wonderful garden sprinkler but keep leaving it on by mistake and have drowned the parsley, which is all I seem to be able to grow well. We do have a promising mango tree about to produce out of season. The peaches are blooming four months early, which is odd too, so beware of global repercussions.

The ranch owner went to a game auction to bid for giraffe and bought fifty crocodiles instead. I've no idea why. Mind you I often go shopping and come back with something I don't need.

We are all wondering what he's going to do with them. The Palala is full of Red Data fish and I won't be able to swim if he puts them there. Critical aren't I?

It actually has nothing to do with me but having strictly banned any shooting on the reserve, to the extent that he went berserk when Sarah-Jane shot a puff-adder in her rondavel, he has let an American come and hunt Desmond. Desmond is a rhino bull. Andrew says you have to accept that it makes sense to let the hunters kill an old male that is going die any minute. This is indeed a game ranch and they're farming wildlife. But the day before the hunter arrived they hovered over Desmond in a helicopter and dart-gunned him to check that the horn was more than 52 inches long and would make it into the record books, which seemed slightly unsporting. The plan is to use the money to buy a herd of endangered roan antelope. I don't suppose there would be much wildlife left in Africa if people weren't keen on preserving it for the hunting. This does bring in substantial revenue. I just don't want to get shot in the bum.

Beautiful, golden evening light has broken under the dark clouds and is now flooding the landscape. I've started drawing wild animals again and tonight feel I must use the painting to make a contribution towards conservation. Not sure how. A gallery near Billy's house has twelve of my pictures, which is quite exciting. I have quite a few at two other shops and am selling them to clients. Well, I've sold four and have given five away. The only problem is that I can't exhibit them in our dining-tent. It has no walls.

Granny wrote to inform me that your son is 'on solids 3 x a day', which I'm afraid sounds quite revolting from this perspective. But my love to the solids-eater anyway. I'll keep your letters and read them out loud on his 21st birthday.

Lots of love,

Sophie

Big panic; Limpopo, one of the Friesian colts, has just torn his side open on a gate catch. It was such a huge wound that Walter had to come over and stitch him up. He said that he might as well attend to PK while he was at it, and we castrated him on the kitchen table.

Equus Horse Safaris

Dear Perry,

You would be stunned at the dedication. I've actually run out of art paper. I'm not all that brilliant yet, but plough on regardless, like a dung beetle. It's good to produce something with a lasting, visible result. I love working as a guide but you have nothing much to show for it at the end of the day. My map of the reserve is hanging next to the owner's Picasso.

People keep coming to Equus on honeymoon, which mystifies us. The last couple said that having done something of a tour before they reached us, ours was the only double bed they encountered in Africa. I put Dad in it. Poor Dad, he was surrounded by buffalo munching away all night long when he really wanted to pee. I suppose if you were on honeymoon buffalo might add another dimension.

I'm not riding yet, but have said I'll manage everything for Sarah-Jane when she goes to England with Jez in October, so I've advertised in *The Farmers Weekly* for a side-saddle. Charles Baber said I ought to ask for a husband while I'm at it and read me their Hitching Post page out aloud over Sunday lunch. One man was advertising for a wife:

'Anything under 95kgs considered.' That is the weight limit we have for male riders.

I saw an aardwolf as I was driving back from Triple B Ranch last night. They're members of the hyena family but have gracile jaws and, like aardvarks, exist almost entirely on termites. Imagine trying to survive on nothing but white ants. I've found large stones that, like the ones Dad found in England, have obviously been turned over so the insects can be accessed but am not sure whether aardvarks do this or if it could be a honey badger at work. Both species probably do it.

This is a drawing of a bushman painting of an aardvark:

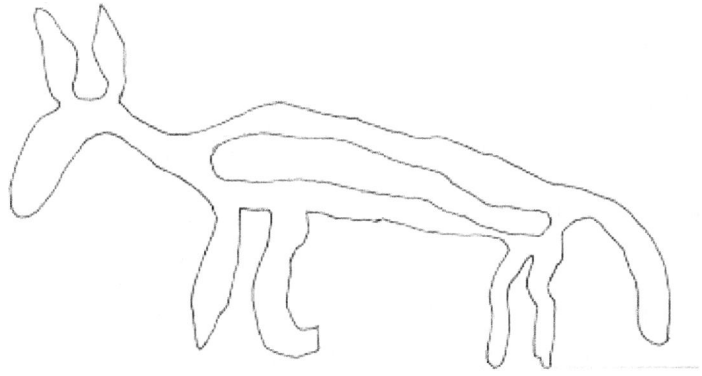

I took the clients on a night drive on Saturday night, with a spotlight, and saw a brown hyena, a solitary animal with a face like a hairy teddy bear. You tend to only find the spotted hyena where you have lion, although I saw a small pack up on the Nyika Plateau.

The Controller of BBC 1 has accepted my idea for a natural history series on people working with animals in the bush. Alastair wants to call it *Dawn to Dusk* and record each episode in an actual day, to capture the anticipation and excitement of the moment. I think this sounds a bit nerve-racking. One episode will be spent going down the Zambezi in a canoe, another flying over

Kenya, one will follow chimps through the rainforest on foot. This has always been Alastair's dream. I've been asked to do a couple of weeks' preliminary research for the southern Africa episodes, which I can do in September from Wendy's office in Johannesburg while she'll be on safari, travelling around the Savuti with Donald.

Give my love to your mwena (little ones). I think they would like it in Africa. Perhaps Robert might learn Zulu and become a game ranger. He would enjoy catching poachers. (100 rhino were taken from the Kruger Park last year – the official number was ten).

My love to you all,

Sophie

Hardacre Farm
1:9:93

Dear Sophie –

I can't remember when I wrote to you last.

Johnty has bought me an estate car, which makes my life so much easier. I now look like a real mother. Hughie is just divine; going white-blond.

He sits in the same pram as Raddy's baby now, playing Tug o'War with toys and laughing – it is so sweet. The Australian nanny took them for a walk together.

Disaster. The pram tipped over. Luckily neither of the babies were hurt.

Poor Raddy fell off her pony cart, and she was. Her four-year old daughter landed in some thistles and was fine, but Raddy was dragged along the road. She has deeply grazed her back, and her face hit a wheel. She has a nasty black eye with a purple-green cheek, rather like a prize boxer.

Hughie is very skinny. I had him weighed the other day, and was told he is **underweight**.

I felt as though I had failed as a mother; tears welled.

I should think he was the only thin baby in there that day – all the others were obese, like their mothers. They blobbed around the surgery dressed in vibrantly coloured, hand-knitted matinée jackets with dummies stuck in their faces. In the meantime, I was stuffing my poor child with sponge fingers in the hope of encouraging a growth spurt; food getting everywhere and setting rock solid within seconds.

Perry says you're after a sidesaddle. I would love to have one; they make jumping jittery horses a lot easier. I haven't ridden sidesaddle since I played Linda in *Love in a Cold Climate*, going over five-barred gates (which the stunt women were far too frightened to attempt).

Oh dear, my occupation as a mother seems to have put a stop to high-jinks like acting.

Raddy's cheekbone and jaw are, it turns out, both broken. She is left with a deep dimple, but is being brave.

Lots of love,

Tamzin x

EQUUS HORSE SAFARIS
PARK TOWN NORTH
JOHANNESBURG

Dear Tamzin,

I'm eating asparagus and strawberries and the streets are full of blossom. It's spring and I'm living in Johannesburg with a bullmastiff called Oliver. Wendy has an old colonial house but it has one of those exciting remote control gates we always wanted when we were little after spending Saturday afternoons watching *Doctor Who.* I found out that in reality these were moved by rotund prop men, which was a bit of an anti-climax, but this gate is opened by a snazzy gadget and has a notice on it saying *ARMED RESPONSE.* The real thing.

Everyone here is obsessed about security. The lovely, leafy suburban roads have been barricaded, every fence topped with razor wire. Paranoia lurks on every mother's face as they lurch round corners in huge four by fours with bull bars bolted to their bumpers. It is indeed like something from a mad, futuristic movie. On the other hand, living in South Africa is quite like being in the 1950's. I saw a man keeping a comb tucked into the top of his knee sock.

I'm doing all my own framing at a workshop down the road. It's absorbing when it works and completely infuriating when it doesn't. I'm not sure about accepting art commissions anymore. I have to draw an absurd picture of a chicken carrying a suitcase tonight and make signs about not putting inappropriate things down lavatories, yippee-oh-dandee. Billy kindly took more of my pictures to the wildlife art gallery near White River in the Eastern Transvaal. He said, 'You've got a wall,'

'A wall?'

'A wall. A Sophie Neville Wall.'

I don't imagine for a second that any of the paintings have sold, but still; I'm pleased to have a wall.

I've also been running the Equus bookings office, so life is busy but I do get out in the evenings. I go to cultural movies and have actually found a suitor – sweet but weedy with big glasses, so don't get too excited. He takes me out to dinner and all that. I sit making up funny stories about Oliver and the enquiries I get. Wendy thought it a brilliant idea to put brochures in tack-shops. It wasn't. We get loads of people ringing in, but they never book, they just want to talk endlessly about their own horses which all have names like Twinkle, Supreme and Strawberry Delight. Like ice-creams.

I'm longing to get back to the bush. We've been given another 12,000 acres to explore and the baby animals will be born soon. Must go and draw the chicken and find the gate-opening gadget, which I've now gone and lost.

Love,

Sophie

Nottingham

3rd October 1993

M'darling Sib,

This bears wishes for your birthday. Sunday night and I'm sitting at my desk, hot whisky toddy at my side and the fire blazing away. Today we were expecting a couple for lunch over which I toiled, even making two puddings, and they didn't turn up. Must've forgotten.

I was in a BBC 'Courtroom Drama'; a reconstruction of the trial of the Bridgewater Four, filmed in Nottingham. The location was so close I said I would drive, stupidly, because I then worried so much about where I was going to park I took the bus and had to come back on it wearing a ridiculous 1970's hair-do, a permanent with flicked sides. Everyone stared at me. Although I bet the style comes back into fashion it hasn't yet and I vowed I'd ask for a car to collect me next time.

Atalanta is terribly well and adoring nursery school. I'm the cookery teacher this Wednesday. Seriously. Except I'm not going to cook, exactly, as we are doing Chocolate Krispies. Atalanta is frightfully pleased about me being 'Miss Perry', but I could never be a real teacher. To impress you further I'm having my fourth of thirty German lessons tomorrow night. Yes. I know. It's such a brain strain, I can't tell you. I also made the mistake of telling the tutor I was going to live in Germany, so she has made it her mission to get me fluent. Well, I'd better not let on that I was stationed there quite happily for two-and-a-half years when I was first married, without speaking a word.

This is all in preparation for next year when, if you please, Robert drops me and the kinder in Osnabrück and goes off to the green line in Nicosia – salt to the wound, yes Cyprus – to sun himself on a six month unaccompanied (wives not welcome) tour. Well, I'll get a happy holiday at the end I suppose. So, a long way away, but what a bummer. I hate knowing so soon what we're going to be doing next because it makes you look to the future too much. And we love it here. I go every week to the auctions and flea market to fill our house with more rubbish; it's great fun. We have quite a few friends coming to stay including Lu Llewellyn. She's pleased with herself as she gets a car with her new job, so the Sunbeam wouldn't have lived happily ever after with her at all.

Loads of love,

PRAHT

EQUUS HORSE SAFARIS

21ˢᵗ October 1993

Dear Perry,

It's difficult, isn't it, getting the balance between planning for the future and living for the day, enjoying yourself in the here and now. Africans live so much in the present they're forever running out of sugar, but I used to spend my entire life making provision for a future, (which never happened) or worrying about the past, (which was stupid).

A Christmas present arrived from you today. Last year's. Thank you. It was a surprise. The insulated bottle cooler is hanging from my curtain rail looking willing. It contained a funny letter about Atalanta eating Christmas decorations.

I'm most upset; my car was squashed by an electric gate. It closed on it. Nicki thought this amusing but I'm having problems opening the door. She is back from America, roaring around complaining about the disgusting state of the tack shed. I knew she would, so I left it untidy especially.

Sarah-Jane is in England for a while but the business is growing. We now have a Camp Manager called Claudia, Kate the cook, two chambermaids and an enormous washing machine; the type you might find in a laundrette called a *Speed Queen de-lux*. Fred has returned and a new ranger called Grant has joined us. He drove up in a red Land Rover, towing a horsebox containing a typewriter, six fire arms and a stallion called Bovington. This has added to the variety of life. I'm glad he's arrived as we have twenty-five horses to look after now and I needed him to plumb in the Dream Queen or what-ever-it's-called.

Poor Grant. He's spent the last two years living by himself on the Transkei border growing oranges, and suddenly he's surrounded by girls. He said walking into the bathroom was a terrible shock. He didn't know which way to look and this was without anyone in it. Nicki flummoxed him; I don't think he's ever heard girls swear so rigorously, but then I haven't either. Right now she is guiding him through a copy of a South African publication of *Cosmopolitan*. He bought it - for my birthday - not knowing what else a girl would like. 'Oh, but I would have been happy with a penknife.'

'Would you?' he said looking crestfallen, 'I was agonising over what to buy you. But *Cosmopolitan's* a really nice magazine isn't it?'

'Solid sex,' Nicki said, flinging her head back and roaring with laughter.

'Oh, No.' Grant was dismayed. He'd no idea of the nature of the contents but Nicki grabbed it with glee. She has been getting full mileage, reading whole passages out aloud and made him fill out a questionnaire on *'Does your pantyhose satisfy you?'* (Nicki had to explain to both of us what pantyhose were; they're tights). One question asked, 'Was one leg longer than the other?'

After spending a month in Johannesburg I managed to get a lift in a Cessna flying up to Kasane on the Chobe River. The pilot was a sweet old boy who let me fly from Francistown to Nata. It was rather like riding a touchy horse. I loved it. He admitted that he was relieved that I don't weigh much.

'I agreed, over the radio, to give a lift to a young lady last week. Sight unseen; she must have weighed 22 stone. It was very difficult. We managed to take off, but I couldn't get her out.'

It was an under-wing plane and she was literally stuck inside.

I managed to get out, into a boat, and crossed the Chobe River to spend a week in Namibia to find out if we could run horse safaris in the Caprivi Strip. I saw incredible game, thousands of buffalo congregating on the floodplains and watched elephant swimming the river but decided that it might be just a bit dangerous to swim horses across. I've never seen so many crocodiles in my life.

I went riding around Victoria Falls before some clients of ours gave me a lift back through Zimbabwe. Just before we reached the border I found a prayer on the wall of a loo, which I liked and copied down. When I was re-writing it in my sketchbook later, out on a wilderness trail, I read it to Grant as I thought it described him well.

Take time to think, it is the source of power,
Take time to play, it is the secret of perpetual youth,
Take time to read, it is the fountain of wisdom,
Take time to pray, it is the greatest power on earth,
Take time to be friendly, it is the music of the soul,
Take time to give, it is too short a day to be selfish,
Take time to work, it is the price of success,
Take time to dream, it is hitching your wagon to a star,
Take time to love and be loved, it is a God given privilege,
Take time to look around.

When we returned he had a fax from his sister waiting for him, a brief one forwarding him this very same prayer. She'd just been sent it by their mother.

Isn't that amazing?
Lots of love, Sophie

CHAPTER TEN

Equus Horse Safaris
PO Box, Marken
Northern Transvaal
South Africa

Dear Perry,

You know, the worst thing about living in a round hut is that you can't sit up in bed properly; there's always a gap between the furniture and the curved wall. I'm surrounded by a clutter of books and painting stuff. It has been raining steadily and the air is full of the sounds of frogs and crickets.

I spent the day of my birthday[xi] riding through the hills thinking about life and love and happiness as we took a girl from France with a broken heart off on a three-day ride. We stopped for the night at a lodge by the river where we had a big fire and roasted marshmallows on sticks like children, singing late into the night. The next day was so hot we had to take a long break for lunch. Grant thought I was making a terrific fuss about crocodiles and insisted on swimming.

'I really don't want to be eaten.' I said, without trying to frighten the client, but he carefully took off my watch and then threw me in. The cheek. Then he told me I looked beautiful and picked me a bunch of knob thorn leaves. I think he does know a bit about girls after all.

Grant once had a pet baboon, or his friend had one. They used to take it with them to gymkhanas. You have to let them groom you to ensure they stay happy and relaxed. It does your relationship no end of good. I tried to cut Grant's hair with the nail scissors but he grabbed them and hacked away himself until he looked like Action Man, which is just too bad. He is also threatening to have SOUTH AFRICA tattooed on his ankle. I hope this is a joke; he is terribly proper about everything else. In fact he has better manners than anyone else I know. Mum would approve. When I asked him if he minded me being bossy he said, 'Anyone who does must have a problem with their pride.' He is open and honest and old fashioned and laughs a lot. Very impulsive. Not at all good for me.

I decided that since he's even told Meisie and Mrs Hennie that they look lovely, I would not let his compliments blow me away. Then Lindizwe, burst into my room and with a great sense of importance presented me with a matchbox. It was full of beautiful red, velvety insects. For me. From him.

It's all Sarah-Jane's fault. She put an advert in the *Farmers Weekly* not for a husband, but for someone to work at Equus. She turned down one applicant after another on the grounds that they were no fun and wouldn't be the kind who could hug us when we were miserable. Grant never thought he'd be able to get away from his oranges long enough to come for an interview. He'd wanted to join the Natal Parks Board anti-poaching squad but couldn't make it for the training. I'm so glad. It's one of those jobs you hear horror stories about; if the poachers catch the rangers they chop them up into bits and leave all their parts scattered along the road for the rest of the unit to find. To discourage them. Anyway, he drove up here and surprised us by wanting to be the manager, seeing the whole job in career terms, which no one else had. I haven't considered my own career for ages.

Grant once lived alone in the bush for about six months, surviving by hunting, fishing and eating wild spinach with his horses. He said he became an expert on guineafowl, which I suppose you would do if you were hungry. They have nineteen different calls. He is tri-lingual in Xhosa, English and Afrikaans (in that order) and claims to speak three other African languages. He has a deep love for the African people pointing out how much more talented they tend to be than Europeans when it comes to music, dance and design. At the same time he insists on travelling with a revolver. 'I can understand what the *munts* are saying in the streets,' he told me.

We went to call on one of the local farmers recently. I wore a pink, flowery Laura Ashley dress that I normally keep for wearing at border posts. Grant thought this was lovely. But I only have one. So I need your help. Please look in all your cupboards for pretty dresses, ask your friends for cast-offs and send SWIFT AIR.

Hoping all is well, and my love to Robert and the children,
Sophie

from the Rainbow Nation

Dear Tamzin,

I had to return to the Eastern Transvaal to get my engine serviced by Ronnie the mechanic, so as we had no visitors for a week, Grant and I took leave and went to visit Billy.

It was wonderful to get away. We found ourselves driving across the Highveld, swooping down Long Tom's Pass[xii] and then up to the old gold mining town of Pilgrim's Rest. I felt happier than I have ever, ever been.

We found Billy in a contemplative mood. He told us that when a small pair of elephant tusks had recently gone missing from the office safe, his assistant Warden, a Swazi called Victor, started cracking rather too jolly jokes.

'What did you do, Bill?'

'I said, "Don't tell anyone, but I'm going to call in the witch-doctor to show us who took them."'

The tusks were back in the safe the next day. Victor was the only person who knew about the threat.

'Billy would you really call a witchdoctor?' I asked him as he strode on through the bush.

'No, complete waste of money. They charge a fortune.'

He has to let them into the reserve to collect tree bark and pointed out a fat lady with dreadlocks in brightly coloured clothes wearing lots of beads, but said, 'Their *muthi* only works because they draw on occult power. I don't need demons to tell me that Victor is nicking ivory.'

The truth is that Billy has devoted his life to Nature Conservation and uncovering incompetence or corruption pains him. He could earn far more money working for himself or in the private sector and has certainly sacrificed his social life for the cause.

'I'm beginning to wonder why I should bother working for the Government anymore.'

'You're needed to train up others.'

'I know, and I enjoy that, but it only works if they want to learn. You keep finding rotten apples who let down the genuine trainees. Victor gained his position on the Affirmative Action Scheme.' Billy explained. 'I'm all for it. But it isn't going to work if he abuses the system and starts stealing ivory from the Parks Board. This is tribal land after all. He is robbing his own people.'

He said that although it is vital to move black people into administrative positions many of them don't have the background or experience to cope.

'They're inheriting a highly complicated, computerized system. The Afrikaans paymaster was replaced the other day. Well, no one received their pay checks. She was back on contract within two weeks.'

Grant loved meeting Billy and hearing all his stories but we left him to his work and spent our time exploring the Crocodile

River gorge while my car was in the garage. I've decided that Grant is exactly like Peter Pan - except that he is considerate. And he's never flown.

He keeps asking me to marry him but I'm dubious as to whether we both have a serious dose of bush fever.

I haven't actually said 'Yes' yet but I thought I'd go shopping for my trousseau anyway. I found a swimming costume in Woolworth's but no flowery dresses. The wedding list is going to have to include a rifle safe, two saddles, a martingale and a Massey Ferguson tractor.

He refuses point blank to come to England. Are you shocked? I'm amazed. He said he would build me a house on the Transkei Coast, grow our food and make me contraptions. I think you would need lots if you didn't have electricity. Everyone will have to bring pots of face cream for me when they come to stay. He wants four children. All the boys must grow up to be farmers or game rangers and all the girls must get married.

If you want to know, he is tall with one eyebrow, as Mary Dieu would say (two but they join in the middle), a straight nose, crocked teeth (from opening beer bottles), a strong jaw, and is a good driver.

He thinks there will be civil war in South Africa and that he'll have to fight. Your job is to break all this gently to Mum and Dad.

Lots of love,

Sophie

PS. Grant has just walked in looking unshaven, holding his revolver and a pink rose. He went fishing last night and the red Land Rover broke down leaving him to walk back nine miles, barefoot. He has discovered that the Sothos have called him Rainbow. I thought this was rather apt; he's like a rainbow but he said, it's because 'he came after Fred'. Fred was called *Rapula*, rain man, because whenever he went on leave last year it rained and they reckoned he went to the coast to turn the pump on. Josie was called *Maru*, which means rain cloud, as the rain came through her.

Nottingham

25th November 1993

Dear Sib,

What a terribly exciting letter about the man who knows more about guineafowl than girls. Robs said he wasn't even the tiniest bit surprised because you've always said you would marry someone in the *boosh* accompanied by the sound of bongo drums.

We will miss you enormously if you stay out there forever – but on the other hand we could come and visit, which would be fun. I can't see how you could envisage coming back to London Town, especially after living such a different life. You would also find the people limited and frustrating.

Now, I'm going to send you some eyelash dye. You can dye everyone's eyelashes at Equus, but I think you would frighten Grant forever if you did his, so don't. A make-up girl at the BBC told me that they used to dye one of the male newscasters' eyelashes and eyebrows so that his face would be well defined on the screen, only they started chatting and muddled up the two colours. While they dyed his eyelashes brown, his eyebrows turned jet black. There was no time to rectify it and he had to read *The News* looking like a clown.

Robs and I are off to London tonight for a Charity Ball. I've had a new party dress made, ever-so-nice. We all went to a terrible and therefore terribly funny pantomime on Friday. The best bit was a poor little pixie wetting its leotard. I've had two

small Canadian boys staying for the last three days. DON'T have four children. Having them to stay was the most powerful contraceptive in the world AND I still have my au pair. Oh glory; they're making hairclips, nay bowties, out of cardboard and sticky-back plastic on *Blue Peter*. What will they think of next?
Lots of love,
PRAHT

PS: I've been collecting vouchers from the supermarket and can fly up to five people out to S.Africa, cheap.

PPS: Don't, I repeat *don't* go and get married between 8-15th June. We are booked to go to Fuerta Ventura then.

Hardacre Farm
6:1:1994

Dear Sophie –

Is this news true? Everyone is in a high state of excitement – wedding dresses are being collected by the hundred and seem to be much easier to find than Laura Ashley ones – you can have one for every day of the year if you like and, I imagine, wear your chaps underneath.

Mum nearly burst into tears at the news of a strong jaw.

'Nice, large, kind ears, I expect,' and 'What a lucky man to find such a super girl; he could not have found a better one in the entire world,' and so on and so on. She had to have at least ten of Johnty's mince pies and one and-a-half cups of tea to calm herself down.

I do hope you're nice to Grant and do *not* tease him – the poor fellow.

I stink of sick. Edam cheese. Hughie, who is so curious we now call him The Spy, has just thrown-up everywhere and has a nasty ear infection not unlike Granny's. (She went into great detail about how the doctor has to deal with hers – disgusting). So, Spy is on antibiotics and is not happy.

Progress report: Standing up in cot, crawling on all fours rapidly, screaming 'Mumma' and 'Dadda', opening cupboards, trapping fingers… He has an inquisitive index finger, which due to mischief, has only half a nail left. This finger is very wicked. It has just shot up my nose and succeeded in twisting and probing so violently blood poured and I thought, in my agony, I would have to go to Casualty to be stitched up. He now has six teeth, which can be as effective as the finger. Poor Maudie wishes she was an only child so badly. He bit straight through her ear.

Christmas and New Year are now over and as it's Twelfth Night we've removed all the drooping ivy and holly. The house looks bare.

Whilst I was standing in the field, galvanized buckets in hand, a massive Middle Earth hail storm erupted through a black and red sky. I expected an Orc to come running at me; very odd.

Dad keeps getting attacked by the natives in Gloucestershire for opening his sluice gates and flooding the valley. He tells them to talk to God about it.

I want to hear more about keeping a baboon as a pet. Wouldn't they become rather a liability?

Lots of love,

Tamzin

Equus Horse Safaris

Dear Perry,

An ex-Rhodesian policeman tried to bash down the door of my rondavel at 3.00am this morning. He was drunk, ended up smashing my window with his hand, gaining twenty-five stitches for his efforts and hasn't apologised for disturbing me. He was convinced that we were hiding his girlfriend. We managed to convince him that we weren't, only to find her squatting, petrified, in the vegetable garden. I don't suppose she envisaged this fate on first meeting him.

Because the window was broken my rondavel is full of insects now and I've been bitten to pieces. Grant snapped a leaf off an aloe plant and put the juice on the bites to soothe them but this has turned me yellow.

It's raining like you wouldn't believe. Did you know that a raindrop falls at 7mph? Let me tell you that this is hard enough to make its way through a thatched roof. We've just had 10% of the annual rainfall in the last hour and the feed room is flooded. All my vegetables have been flattened, completely. I'm feeling pretty flattened too but it is lovely lying in bed when the rain is heavy. We have ten overseas guests getting wet at the camp with Grant. They keep finding frogs in their shoes. He has to remove them, checking the tents for 'bugs and little critters', which he was amused to discover meant insects. Nicki told him that he must take the clients seriously when they complain about weirdo creatures in their tents. Andy once had a tourist complaining that a lizard was sleeping on his bed. He thought they were making a fuss about a little gecko but it turned out to be a monitor lizard the size of a crocodile.

Grant has given himself another dreadful hair cut with the horse clippers and I can't help laughing whenever I see him. He doesn't mind, he loves being teased and just keeps hugging me.

'Why don't you give Nicki a hug?'

'What do you mean? Do you want to get me into trouble?'

She just roars with laughter and strides off in the direction of the yard to swear at the horses, singing *'Girls just wanna have fun, ermph. Girls just wanna have… they just wanna have fun.'*

With all the rain the bush is looking beautiful, quite different from last year, with trees in bloom and young animals being born all the time.

Summer has come to South Africa and suddenly there are swallows everywhere and the hills are clad in waving grasses. We are hoping that if the dams fill we will be able to swim the horses. We have a paradise flycatcher nesting right outside the kitchen door and an injured Marsh Owl living in a cardboard box. It's a young one that Kate is trying to rehabilitate since it flew into the game fence. Now when we need them we can't find any mice or snakes. We did see a black mamba but it was eight-foot long, a bit big for feeding to a young owl. It reared up at me but Grant bravely charged at it on his horse, swinging a scythe that he'd been using to cut a trail and it disappeared.

We had a group of sixteen schoolgirls up for a camp over the long summer holidays. Wendy made Fred give them a vaulting display. Poor Fred. The horse took fright, careering off from under him and he went flying over the lunging arena fence.

'I don't know what hurt most,' he said later. 'The fall, the humiliation or the paperbark thorns in my underpants.'

Grant and I went to Botswana for a week, where we were asked by the owners of two different lodges to set up horse safaris, but in flat dry country so hot, we are thinking of looking at a reserve in Namibia instead. It'll probably be even hotter there. It's a long way to drive. I'll return to England on the 26th February, as my ticket expires the next day. Grant thinks I ought to stay a while as the South African elections will be on and he is sure there will be violence.[xiii]

Someone filled the mess tent at camp with hideous decorations but otherwise we had a good Christmas with lots of people staying, only we all went down with 'flu. Grant was so ill he didn't want to have anything to do with anything, so we went off to 24 Rivers without him. So many people arrived at the Babers' little thatched church that we had to sit outside under trees. It dawned upon me that I was a spinster of this parish and that Desmond Tutu must be my Archbishop.

Sarah-Jane has returned from England with lots of energy and new plans. Nicki is off to ride in Wyoming, 'Yee ha!' she says, and I leave Equus next week to stay at Triple B Ranch with the Babers to concentrate on painting for a while. I've had a vile head cold for days and have started snapping at everybody, which is very bad of me since we've been so busy and no one has had much sleep. We start working with the horses at 4.00am and often don't get to bed until 11.00pm, so it's no good if you're sickly. Sitting up to see New Year in with the guests complaining about frogs nearly killed me off. I don't know how you cope with the constant job of mothering.

Lots of love,

Sophie

Triple B Ranch
24 Rivers, Vaalwater

Dear Tamzin,

The lady we were meant to go and see in Namibia died in a car crash, so Grant and I drove to the coast where his parents have a house right by the shore.

I spent most of my time talking to his father about the economics of farming ostriches and whether it's a good idea to eat them. He has called his house Duntillin (I didn't get it, but he has retired from farming) and had converted the greenhouse, potting shed and other garden huts into bedrooms for their guests.

Grant's room was under a water reservoir. We did eat an ostrich egg. You drill a hole in the top and shake out the yolk. It made a giant omelette, the equivalent of about twelve hens' eggs. It didn't taste quite as nice. The texture was grainy, almost like semolina.

We had driven down through the Stormberg where Grant grew up, and walked around his old farm. It was so isolated that he had to go to boarding school when he was six; to an Afrikaans one, which must have been tough. We drove back taking the Swartberge Pass through the Karoo, so it was a long trip, a journey of about 4,000kms but heavenly. It was lovely seeing the country with Grant. We camped under towering cliffs in the Free State, walked behind waterfalls in the Drakensberg mountains, and swam in the sparkling ocean. He took me down into a cave system where we had to squeeze up tunnels and through small gaps, like a journey to the centre of the Earth.

I'm sitting beneath a frangipani tree now among a sea of agapanthus in Nina's beautiful garden, painting a great map of the Baber's farm while working on other commissions. A sweet and enthusiastic German lady gave me 1,000 marks for five paintings, which is an enormous relief as I was running out of money.

When I was driving back from her house I saw clusters of bleeding hearts had been painted on the signboards to my friends' farms. The doctor's gate had been daubed in red paint. This was not a romantic gesture; it's done to label them *kaffir boeties* –

kaffir brothers. Someone had stencilled FW on the bottom of a street sign saying STOP, so that in effect it said Stop FW (de Klerk). It's just Rightwing intimidation, but Grant insists that it is time for me to get out of the way for a while.

Juliet has just returned from her school declaring that all the teachers, most of whom are happily married and strict Calvinists, have been given a full demonstration on how to avoid catching AIDS.

'No detail was spared; nothing whatsoever was left to the imagination,' she assured us, 'but I couldn't help asking the guidance teacher why he wasn't taking precautions himself.'

'How do you know?' Charles asked, looking quizzical.

'Well, he has managed to get two schoolgirls pregnant while being engaged to someone else. He told me that he's not particularly worried about catching AIDS himself since he is convinced we are all going to die in the forthcoming elections.'

'This educated individual,' Charles informed us, 'is the ANC candidate for our local town council.'

I asked my Sotho friend Johanna if she wouldn't consider standing for election in local government but she answered obliquely saying that not all Citizens were members of the same political party.

I'm going to be helping at Horizon until I fly home. Shane is bringing on a number of new horses. They've all been given rather alarming names like Crash and The Hellbitch. They already have a Thunderhead. It will be Crash, Bang and Wallop soon. The Hellbitch is actually quite a nice Arab. So many big, heavy men have been booking in that Laura has had to find a Percheron carthorse to carry them. She has called him Massey, short for Massey Ferguson. After putting on a Western Games weekend for a group of cowboy fanatics, Shane was presented with a gangly quarter-horse cross called Jack.

I think he looks like a camel but Laura said, 'Just you wait, he'll make a champion one day.'

I've been riding round on a black stallion called Bismarck that Nina bought to cover the mares. The only problem with him is that he seems to fancy donkeys and zebra instead of horses. Ant rode him on the game reserve he is starting up and said he ended up charging through the bushes, whinnying frantically with zebra running about in all directions.

'He must be a Liberal,' Charles decided.

'He must be confused.'

You can think of me riding in a snazzy pair of buckskin chaps with lots of thongs. I made them out of two springbok skins and look outrageous, but I am convinced everyone will want a pair. (They're a bit hairy).

I made a whole outfit; a pair of chaps and a waistcoat, for Solly, the local pop star (and waiter at the lodge). Quite dashing but he did get a bit hot during his performance.

See you very soon,

Lots of love,

Sophie

19th June 1993

Nottingham

Darling Sib,

I can't tell you how long I've been meaning to write – I've had me 39p stamps sitting waiting, but y'know how it is.

I had an awful fright today. Atalanta lost control of her tricycle going down a hill just as a truck came roaring around the corner. I watched terrified. She swung to the left, riding up onto the grass instead of under the lorry, which missed her by inches. The bike crashed into a tree. She flew over the handlebars and hit her head but she seems to be fine now.

It was a near thing. Meanwhile Robert was nearly blown up by the Territorial Army. I've decided that being a wife and mother can be a stressful occupation.

Hastings is two tomorrow so I'm savouring the last few hours of having a one-year-old baby. Atalanta is the one who benefits most – she's giving H. her bashed tricycle (which thankfully is blue rather than pink) and therefore gets a brand, spanking new bike with stabilisers, doesn't she. Mum and Dad acquired it as a free gift for attending a time-share sales talk.

We've just returned from the auction rooms – der, der, der… We bought THE most enormous dining-room table with five leaves. Well, we assumed you could take some of the leaves out if you wanted to but had it transported home on a low-loader only to discover you can't. At all. It fits in the dining-room but only when jammed between one wall and the other. Guests have to go underneath the table to sit on the far side. Once there, they can't exactly be Mummy's Little Helper either. In fact they're stuck. So much for the smart Army dinner parties I'm supposed to give.

I left a bid for another lot, which I thought was a freestanding towel rail, but I must have written down the wrong number. When Robert went to collect it found we'd acquired... another table. It's surprisingly nice, but dear, oh dear.

We are having a non-existent summer. I've made a headboard for our bed; home improvements where 'er the eye can see, but I've no more news so just send our love,

Perry x

In the mountains near Tzaneen

Dear Tamzin,

They have biscuits here called EET SUM MOR. And you do; you cram your face with them until the whole packet is gone.

I've been back in South Africa a month but seemed to have achieved little. I painted a suburban house for a glamorous South African television personality, a portrait of the local millionaire's pigs and made a desperately bad attempt of drawing someone's dog. I should have known it would be disastrous when he rang to make the arrangements.

I could hear him saying, 'Down Brutus. Down!'

Brutus was a hound and completely uncontrollable. The only way I could get it to stay still for a moment was to draw it lying down on his master's unmade bed.

'This is when your wife comes home unexpectedly, isn't it?' I told the man, 'And I have to try and explain that actually what I'm doing is drawing a picture, as a surprise for her birthday.'

Otherwise I've just ridden and ridden and ridden. And then ridden out again.

The idea was that I would live at Equus and work four hours a day in exchange for my keep but they've been short-staffed and busy. Most of the horses have conked out in revolt. Seven are lame for no reason other than chance and they're the ones that are smiling. We are all missing Nicki's infectious laugh.

Grant hadn't had a day off in two months so I've dragged him away and up to the mountains around Tzaneen for a week.

We've been lent a little cottage, which comes with a funny old man called Joseph and his extensive family who live opposite. There's no electricity so we are sitting by candlelight, listening to the African chatter outside. We drove up here, rather coldly, in Grant's open Land Rover, through endless tea plantations. I look rather odd and hill-billyish, clad in scarves and a hat with dark glasses, but it's all sun and wind and cold at once. You have to 'wrap up well', as Granny would say, but it is lovely driving through a rainforest with the windscreen down. (This hinges back so that it can be laid flat across the bonnet). The people up here take our appearance as normal. They seem to lead a funny existence themselves, growing bananas and avocados.

When he was driving down to collect me from the airport Grant drove my little car into a herd of cows. Someone had left the gate to their field open and they were crossing the main road in the twilight.

Although he is a good driver and wasn't going fast, Grant didn't see them in the headlights until it was too late. Three cows were killed, and my car was completely written off. The cattle belonged to my friends the Babers, who were on their way down to deal with them. They found Grant wandering around with a bleeding hand and brought both wrecks back to their farm for the night. He woke up early, borrowed one of their vehicles and met me at 7.15 the next morning looking shaky.

I've been trundling round looking for another *bakkie*. Grant's Land Rover seemed to get jealous about my return, promptly discarded its exhaust pipe and has spent days in various garages too. It seems to thrive on the attention while I'm now quite revolted by second hand car salesmen.

I don't have much money to spend; in fact I've hardly any and was beginning to feel wobbly about it until I thought of Granny. She managed to live in Africa before she was married, with no money at all. She told me the only income she ever made was from selling her paintings but that she'd a horse called Strawberry and used to ride around northern Tanzania quite happily.

After searching the back of beyond myself, I've been asked to run the horse trails on Triple B Ranch. Shane and Laura, who set it up a year ago, have had enough. Laura assured me it's not losing money.

'But then again it only made R3.40 profit (about 75p) last year,' she said gaily.

I think it's splendid they made anything at all but am not sure about taking it on; the idea is that tourists get to go cattle mustering and I've only done this once. It would be lovely to have my own house where I could paint but that isn't exactly the right reason to take on the partnership and I've been flung into a quandary. It's being out in the wild with game that I enjoy. I'm hoping to take a group to ride in the Okavango Delta in August, which would mean riding in wild country with lion and should be spectacular. Do you know anyone who would be interested in coming with me? Mum would love it.

Grant was quite amazed that the elections and handover of power to the ANC went so peacefully. I watched the inauguration of Nelson Mandela on television at the Babers' with a crowd of farm workers.[xiv] Juliet, who was holding the new South African flag, said with her eyes glowing, that it was a near thing as Zulu Inkatha Party only agreed to be included in the election at the last minute. I was intrigued to hear that while I've been riding round the Waterberg, a massively important reconciliation project was being held on Lapalala Wilderness, the private game reserve near us.[xv]

'It was all top secret.' Juliet told me. 'My Godfather, Michael Cassidy, who has an organization called African Enterprise, arranged it. They would ask eight to twelve senior politicians and party officials up for a weekend. Once at Kolobe Lodge,' she explained 'each person would tell the story of their life to the group, share their vision for South Africa and outline what steps they thought needed to be taken to achieve their goals. Michael told me it was wonderful because politicians from different backgrounds were at last able to understand what others had suffered or been through. Many of the black delegates, having spent chunks of their lives in prison or exile, had never been in the bush before and found themselves on game drives, seeing kudu and giraffe for the first time.

'Later, in the run-up to the General Election in April, Michael organized prayer chains involving four million people round the country. Things looked bad when Inkatha refused to take part in the election but Michael brought a Kenyan negotiator called Washington Okumu in to mediate. While Lord Carrington and Kissinger failed to get anywhere in negotiations, he found an honourable way of including Inkatha in the ballots at the last minute.'[lvi]

Meanwhile, in Marken you wouldn't know that anything had happened. They have a lot of lemons there; sacks full. I wish I could send you some.

Joseph, the old caretaker, has just wandered in unannounced, looking for dog food.

'Did you have a nice day?' I asked.

'YES,' he said. 'I got drunk.' He isn't really, but his wife thinks so. We laughed.

Thank you for having me to stay at Hardacre Farm; it was lovely to see you all.

Lots of love to everyone, especially the Spy. Hope the weather isn't too grotty.

Love, Sophie

Hardacre Farm

Dear Sib –

Blissful weather here. We've just cut this year's hay; 3,200 bales and the men are stacking it now. It smells wonderful. Hughie adores the tractors and jumps up and down, waving his arms frantically behind our new child/stock proof fence.

I've been looking after my ill boys. The Spy acquired 'Infantile Hand, Foot and Mouth', a highly contagious viral infection with blistering skin rashes. It's more common than you'd think. And Johnty, who always seems to be getting into scrapes, has done so again, tearing the ligaments from both sides of his ankle.

Why is he so disaster prone? When he first started working with grain, he was walking along the top of a goods train one day, peering into the grain holds to check they were dry. The train was moving forward towards the automatic hopper, which was filling each wagon up. He tripped and fell through the small round opening into the empty steel hold. This could have killed him, except that his fall was broken by a pile of old wheat – but he realised that if the wagon filled with wheat he would drown.

There was no one around and all the time the train was jerking towards the main silo. I think he was so desperate he managed to jump high enough to catch the lip of the round opening with his fingertips, but although he'd fallen in, the width of his shoulders made it nearly impossible for him to get out in time.

Luckily the hole he fell into in the garden only came up to his knees. He'd dug it himself.

Hughie can now walk behind the trolley-dog we gave him. He goes along with bandy legs like a monkey. Last night I met him in the corridor having mastered the art of climbing out of his cot.

Yesterday I thought there was a funny smell. Maudie had rolled in fox droppings. Looking down, I saw to my horror that Hughie was LICKING it off. Mr Dan, the farmer who came to set the mole traps, said I really ought to call the doctor, even though it was 7.00pm on Monday night. The doctor hooted with laughter, said what a revolting child I had, and that I had quite made his day.

Thelma is still alive and catching my darling baby doves whilst their mummies watch. Hughie roars at her and grabs her coat until she roars back. Bodney is v. well, v. lazy, v. out of control. I went riding with a friend, who said,

'Oh yes, I forgot Bod only has two strides; walk and flat-out gallop.'

Dad has just dropped in on his way to play Queen Victoria's butler in a film called *Mrs Brown* starring Billy Connolly. Do you think it's a farce? He said Mum is currently getting mauled by the new generation of otters, one of which she has sleeping in their bed; nothing changes. I made him ride Johnty's bike, which he said was by far the most painful experience of his life.

Lots of love,

Tamzin xxxooo

PS: The man who cut and baled our hay also cut three of his toes off. They managed to sew on his big toe and now, after a week he can wiggle it. Quite amazing.

CHAPTER ELEVEN

PARK TOWN NORTH
JOHANNESBURG
THE NEW SOUTH AFRICA
(No one actually knows what this is)

Dear Perry,

I've spent all day trying to finish a picture of Grant hunting with his horse for an article he has written for *Magnum*, a magazine on shooting and guns (his favourite reading). He was upset when I drew him peering from behind a termite hill in the distance, 'I do know how to stalk you know,' and even crosser when I drew him 'too close' to the reedbuck being hunted.

'I'm a better shot than that.'

His latest horror is that we use bay leaves in cooking; thinks it's unbelievably stupid to put leaves in food.

'And what's this rubber stuff?' he asked, holding up a slice of Mozzarella.

He generally loathes 'civilization', isn't comfortable in Johannesburg and makes a terrible fuss if we go to a restaurant that doesn't have meat with two vegetables on the menu. He is more used to towns like Vaalwater where they serve chicken giblets at the hotel. (Truly they do).

I calmed him down by taking him to a cowboy film. Wendy thought it would be a good publicity stunt if we wore our hats and stood outside after the film, handing out brochures to members of the audience. We did this but none of them looked as if they would or could ride a real horse.

We need people who can stay on at the moment. A scraggy old buffalo has been on the rampage. It chased Jez - who was riding my horse - and a client called John Sobey down a track for nearly two kilometres and is still lurking near the camp.

John, whose father stayed at Equus last year, is mad keen on photography. Having not seen the rhino much we found a young male standing peacefully on the plain in front of our house at sunset. It was quite far away and as the situation looked safe, I suggested John could use a tree for cover and get off his horse to take a steady photograph. The rhinoceros came trotting towards him.

'Climb the tree.' I yelled.

Slowly, with great umm-ing and ahh-ing John heaved himself and his long lens up into the tree. I had to ride at the rhino, yelling, and chase it away. All this is keeping me in work as a cartoonist.

On Lapalala Wilderness the Warden's wife, Conita Walker, has an orphaned black rhino called Bwana. We go and feed him his bottle and scratch his back.

'He was found abandoned when only a few hours old.' Conita told us, laughing. 'He tried to charge the ranger who found him.'

Black rhino are much more dangerous animals than the white rhino we've been riding with. They're browsers and live solitary lives in thick bush, myopically charging at those who intrude on their privacy. I learnt they used to occur all over Africa. In the research I've been doing for the BBC, I found that at the turn of the century black rhino were such a menace the Government contracted hunters 'to kill the vermin'. When they wanted to clear an area for tribal land, they shot 996 in one year. Now there are less that 3,000 left. Twenty years ago you could buy a license to kill black rhino for £5.00. It cost £20 to shoot an elephant. Since markets for rhinoceros horn opened up in the Yemen and Far East they've been heavily poached and black rhino are now registered as 'vulnerable' on the Endangered Species list. They have corrosive spit, rhinos. My fingernails have gone all ridgy from being sucked by Bwana.

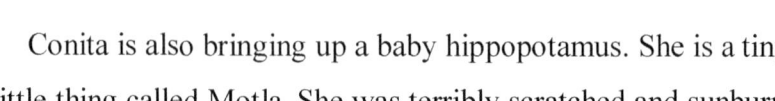

Conita is also bringing up a baby hippopotamus. She is a tiny little thing called Motla. She was terribly scratched and sunburnt when the scouts found her but she is recovering and has rather taken to human beings. I would happily spend all my time with her.

Instead I went to find the wreck of my car, to see what could be salvaged. I took one look and burst into tears. It was so squashed I couldn't see how Grant could possibly have emerged alive. It is a miracle. A cow must have somersaulted over the roof. Only Grant and the tyres survived. I've bought another old but less rusty *bakkie* and am getting extra headlights fitted.

The wildlife series I suggested to Alastair has been scheduled for a primetime slot on *BBC One*, which is good news. I'm going to set up the three episodes to be filmed in southern Africa, and leave for Botswana soon to see if we can film wild dogs in

Moremi. I'm back in Johannesburg investigating this and setting up another recce to Namibia where I want to see if we can film penguins.

I've also had to frame and deliver a picture of a house I painted for a well-known newsreader. I'm extremely surprised she commissioned me. I met her at Equus, when she came for dinner with her boyfriend, a filmmaker called John Varty who owns Londolozi, the reserve where Andy worked. We don't have a television, so although she was introduced to me as Gillian I didn't know her from a marigold, and for some reason re-introduced her to all the South Africans sitting round the fire as Adrian. Well, this girl is famous. They all knew exactly who she was and just stared at me as if I was mad. Then her boyfriend, who is equally famous, asked me if I was drunk. I looked at him as if he was mad, because I still didn't realise I was making a mistake.

We are looking for a cook, if you know anyone who would be interested. We had an American chef called Sherman for a while. Sherman, like the tank. He was most professional, but some boys came to Equus on a stag night and that was that.

The stags were very naughty. I should have known that they would over-estimate their riding ability. As all the horses played up to the general hilarity things became quite chaotic; Nicki and I, with men all over the place.

They did like my fancy chaps, 'Yee ha. Follow the springbok, guys.'

Predictably, they set out to become drunk on the Saturday night and we were worried they would get done in by the mad buffalo that was still around.

Sherman gallantly offered to stay up with them, only he left afterwards in a bad way. Emotionally.

We didn't know why until we read through the Visitor's Book. The best man had written, "Rode the horse, climbed the mountain, roped, tagged and branded the Californian."

Lots of love to everyone,

Sophie

PS: Would you or Tamzin know anyone who would like to come riding in the Okavango in July? Off to ride on elephants there next week.

Hardacre Farm

25th August 1994

Dearest Sib,

It's *pouring* with rain, the first for a long time and Hughie is outside dancing in it. He refuses to be locked inside. In March, Johnty and I will be having another man-cub. How am I going to cope with two Spies? You will have to come home and look after me.

Dad said that Judi Dench was playing Queen Victoria in *Mrs Brown* and that it was all very formal and serious, only Billy Connolly went and winked at him in the middle of the longest scene which was somewhat de-stabilizing.

Just for the sake of contrast Mum appeared with her otters on *That's Life*, wearing a baggy sweatshirt covered in paw prints. She would do. Poor Johnty didn't know how he was going to face walking into the office on Monday morning.

The cousins have been staying in force. Perry bought Atalanta a crash helmet from the local tack shop so that she can wear it on her bike and when riding. I topped it off with a pink silk.

Everything here is ticking along. Usual dramas. Raddy forgot that she said *Yes* to having two 'deprived children' from London to stay for ten days.

They arrived: Asa (male) aged 5 and Amber (female) aged 7, who normally exist on a diet of Coca-cola, highly flavoured crisps and video games. The ten days have been traumatic. Being stuck in the country was not the children's idea of a holiday and Raddy couldn't always understand either their Cockney accents or their vocabulary.

'Caws, everywhere. Loads of em.' Asa said one afternoon, running down to the duck pond where Raddy was giving everyone picnic tea.

'There can't be,' Raddy said firmly, thinking the child was talking about cars. 'There's no reason for cars to come up our drive.'

In fact there was a herd of black bullocks all over the lawn, trampling the flowerbeds.

'The pigs are 'er.' Amber said, looking towards the lane.

'Pigs?'

It was the Police. In a panda car. They had been chasing the cattle for three days.

It all sounded rather hard work. Raddy said if the pearly gates are not open for her she'll have a few things to say to the angels. She has no flowers left and looks totally shattered but then they're all off to Tresco for their holiday so I've no sympathy really.

A feature film is being made on King Arthur and his round table at Quewell Park just across the main road from us. They had the most dreadful accident filming after dark. The director wanted the knights to ride armoured horses, at full gallop, holding blazing torches. One of the poor horses had molten wax poured onto its shoulders. It panicked and bolted onto the dual carriageway where it was killed by a milk lorry. The truck driver must have thought it was an apparition.

We are off to, not one, but two agricultural shows this weekend. Johnty is judging the corn so the Spy will see lots and lots of tractors, the loves of his life. I did try to give him a doll but it didn't work. He called her Wild Thing and was so abusive to the girl I had to take her away.

I can't think of anyone rich enough or babyless enough who wants to come riding in the Okavango. Aunt Hermione would be on for it but she is busy sailing across the Pacific. Is this safe?
Lots and lots of love from me,
Tamzin
PS We're off to Pembrokeshire soon. Can't wait.

Homemade postcard of Hastings on his second birthday – June 1994

Both sproglins are well. Atalanta now cycles around in her new helmet looking like Penelope Pitstop.

Hastings has fallen in love with Thelma and spent his whole time at Hardacre Farm seeking her out. Unreciprocated love. I think he is handsome.

Robert away on courses, so went to visit Granny. She is worried about you doing things with wild elephants saying, 'They can be most tiresome' and that you 'will be squashed until you turn into strawberry jam.' I said you would be riding horses, not elephants.

She gave me a bottle of Chanel №5.

'But Granny. It's your favourite,' I said.

'Yes,' she said matter-of-factly, 'And it will be YOUR favourite too.'

Tadpole was ticked off for knocking old ladies off their Zimmer frames at the home and we left in disgrace.

Lots of love from us all,

PRAHT

Equus Horse Safaris

Dear Perry,

Thank you for your card. I'm sitting up in bed listening to the jackals howl. It's cold. The trees are golden now and Sarah-Jane is dyeing her hair red to match. Grant is digging little trenches all over the place. I've no idea why. He keeps talking about the house he is going to build me, but I'm not so sure. I asked him to make a laundry rail to hang the ironed shirts on. After hours and a great deal of swearing, he proudly showed me an enormous triangular erection made of gum poles, painted a shiny green colour. You could, conceivably, use it to hang clothes from, but we couldn't get it into the house. It wouldn't fit through any door. Or window.

I'm just back from a fantastic trip to Botswana. I did ride an African elephant. It was extraordinary. There was a family of sixteen led by a magnificent male called Abu. 'Most of them,' I was told, 'were originally from the Kruger Park, spared as infants from being culled, although the oldest female, who is fifty-two, is an African elephant who had been kept in a zoo in Ceylon. The three other adults had been shipped to America when they were young, trained and kept in captivity.' Randall Moore, who was working with circus elephants there, found Abu in a bad state. 'He was lying in his own muck in a freezing cold barn. I decided to bring him and two others back to Africa.' Having brought them as far as Kenya he found that, because they had been tamed, the authorities wouldn't let him release them into the wild. So now they live and work from a safari camp in the Okavango Delta with an assortment of young elephants that are also kept in training.

Abu's Camp is lovely. I walked out along a jetty over the lagoon and saw spotted-necked otters diving for fish in the early light. There were flocks of pygmy geese and whistling duck filling the morning with their calls. It was exciting making my way from my tent, along the windy path 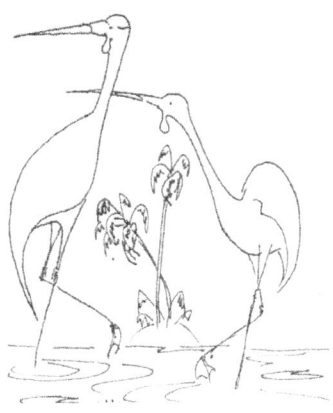 through the bush to the Elephants' compound. I could hear them trumpeting. They're awesome; so big you have to be quite careful not to get in the way when Mahouts are saddling the adults.

You climb into the saddle when the elephants are down on their haunches then, *Wumph!* They're up, and you find yourself three metres high, looking around into the tops of trees. With a small group of American tourists and one skinny English girl loaded, they set off, walking through the bush with all the small elephants following of their own accord. The babies nudge your feet with their trunks and run around seeing what they can find in the bush. It was funny sitting so high. You sway around a lot, a bit like you would in a boat or sitting on a sideways rocking chair. The mahout sits in front, on the elephant's neck with his legs tucked behind the ears.

It became quite cold up on top of Abu. Windy. The elephants seemed highly motivated by food and headed for clumps of palms, eating whenever they could. If anything foreign is seen in the bush, like a matchbox, the elephants will pick it up and hand it to their mahout in disgust. Abu had just given Randall a valuable pair of Zeiss binoculars.

After walking along for about two hours the baby elephants came running out of a group of trees trumpeting madly. They'd come across two lions that shot past us looking terrified. The older elephants totally ignored them, walking on, across floodplains, past herds of grazing antelope and under a dead tree with vultures sitting in the branches, until I felt as if I was living in *The Jungle Book*.

Walking alongside the elephants was even more delightful than riding them. It was so interesting. Their skin is incredibly sensitive; they get outraged if you tickle them with a grass stalk. At one point a squirrel ran up the leg of one elephant, thinking it was a tree. When he reached the top the squirrel realised he'd climbed an elephant, looked deeply shocked and ran down the other side. The little elephant went all wriggly, as if he needed to get something out of his trousers.

The Elephant Back Safari Company is very well organized. When I was following the elephants on foot we came to a river and I found a dugout canoe waiting to take me onwards. As the river became deeper the baby elephants continued walking until they completely submerged. They just reached up, using their trunks as snorkels, so they could keep breathing underwater. I was poled downstream, alongside the wading adults.

'You must know,' said the guide, 'that Okavango water is the purest in the world.'

At this point a big, round poo fell from above us and floated past. The Americans looked on, their serious expressions unaltered.

I was collected from Abu's Camp by a wildlife documentary producer called Tim Liversage, who was once Warden of the

Okavango. He was busy making a 35mm film on hippo and had a camp nearby with aquariums full of small crocodiles. A tame Pel's fishing owl was sitting outside the tent where he'd been editing; a great brown bird that surprised me by landing quite silently above my chair. I'd met another cameraman in Maun called Ken Oake who said I must come and meet his wife. She was lying in bed with a tawny eagle sitting on her legs and had a kitchen full of tame monkeys.

Tim flew me north in his own plane. We looked down on the dazzling river system beneath us.

'The Okavango River,' he told me 'comes down from the Angolan mountains, cuts through Namibia but then goes nowhere. It used to cross Botswana on its way to the sea but seismic activity tilted the level of the land so the Okavango River now drains into the Kalahari where it spreads out, forming an inland delta.'

Although I think it starts to rain in Angola from October or November, the effect isn't felt until June when the floodwaters attract large numbers of game. Alastair calls the Okavango Delta a swamp, but although there are vast areas of dense reed beds it's more like a series of water meadows and lily ponds with low islands and quite extensive plains of dry land between the river systems. It's completely flat but with tall trees; Illala Palms and colossal ebonies, sausage trees and baobabs. Tim flew low over deeper water choked with papyrus, pointing out a sitatunga – a rare aquatic antelope.

We landed at Mombo, a camp on the western tip of Moremi National Park where I had come to see wild dog. Alastair wants one of the episodes to record what it would be like to spend a night in the bush, from dusk to dawn. Well, it would be exciting at Mombo. We drove right up to the wild dogs' den in an open vehicle. Vultures were hopping around and before long a few, lanky spotted dogs emerged from the ground. They had five little puppies, which the bitches were jealously guarding. After moseying around for a bit the dogs suddenly left to go hunting. We raced after them, crashing through the undergrowth, but they were impossible to follow. We did find them on a kill but not until the next morning. They had pulled down a lechwe and were gobbling it up voraciously. When they've eaten all they can they leave the carcass to the hyena and jackals, returning to their den where they regurgitate food for the nursing mothers. What struck me about them was how dog-like and playful they are. I took wonderful shots of them wagging their tails and leaping about just for fun. But they're killers all the same. Tim told me that wild dog became such a menace to stock farmers they were shot as vermin and are now endangered, with only about 5,000 around.

I also saw leopard, a pair of cheetah and lions drinking after their night on the tiles. But what I wanted to include in the documentary were the nocturnal animals that are not usually filmed; porcupine and aardwolf, bushbabies as they leap through the trees and springhares; large rodents with long bushy tails that bound around on their back legs like small kangaroos. The nights were cold and by the early morning it was freezing. I'll send you a picture of a lion with me in a great army jacket, wearing a balaclava helmet and gloves. It's clear why the animals have such thick coats.

I've been drawing up storyboards and sequence lists to send back to the Natural History Unit. It's going to be quite a series. I'm excited about the next recce, which will be to Damaraland in Namibia this October.

The little trenches, it turns out, are for solar electricity, which Grant is installing at the camp. I couldn't work out why solar electricity required trenches, but then he explained that he is running the cables underground.
Tell Penelope Pitstop I love her.
Thinking of you all, Sophie

St Andrew's Road,
Bedford

Beloved Sophie,

Thank you so much for the lovely postcards, which I'm always delighted to get. They arrive on my breakfast tray in the morning. An elephant safari sounds dangerous. Do take care. I don't want you to die.

One of the old ladies has died. They die all the time. This one had a fall; broke her arm in two places and her leg. The shock and pain were too much for her. I'm going to the funeral service on Weds.

<u>Please don't go</u> to Madagascar. Your cousin Jamie has had malaria four times. I hate him going but he says his heart is there. There is no transport and he has to walk 25 miles to the next village. I know they have a funeral once a fortnight. You have had such illness and now you are so well. You must look after your health.

If you do go to Madagascar they will put a makeshift bed in Jamie's room where he sleeps with several children. Take sheets, a towel and a rug. It is in the rainforest and they get a lot of rain. Wear gumboots, rain gear and take lots of vests in case you have a malarial sweating turn. You mustn't let your wet vest get cold. It's what kills you when you get malaria. You catch pneumonia and die.

Your mother says if she doesn't get a part in a pantomime she is thinking of going to Mombasa to stay with Reinhild for a week and then come out to you. That's a much better idea.

You can see Jamie when he gets married in Scotland in the spring. His fiancée is a very beautiful girl, 5'11" tall with bright red hair. She was a model and worked in New York, Paris, London and Milan - and then came home to help with the family hotel in Argyll. It has one of the best seafood restaurants in Scotland and has won a prize. Jamie is going to France to buy Champagne for the wedding. I do not think this is a good idea. I am worried he will get ambushed.

I had a card from Hermione saying they had sailed 3,000 miles in seventeen days. It does sound tiring.

Your parents are going to Ireland for a fortnight to be in a Walt Disney film of The Old Curiosity Shop. We've been having glorious weather. I hope it keeps like this for them.

I have been watching and enjoying Wimbledon. How well they all play.

God bless you and keep you Darling,
with very much love,
Granny.

Handmade postcard of little girl in school uniform from Nottingham, 8th September.

Dear Sophie,

Atalanta is at her second morning of school and Hastings has started at playschool a whole year early, as there are so many spaces and everyone else is still wetting their knickers.

We WERE going to Wales this weekend but drizzly rain is forecast and the car is dickey delvet.

I've been given four days' work at Central Television; a part, amazing grace, playing a teacher. Ha, ha, ha. It was a bit embarrassing. I had to go and tell the security guard on the gate, who of course only knows me by my married name, that a chauffeur-driven car was coming for Perry Neville, and that I **was** in fact called Perry Neville. I'm sure he thinks I'm onto something dodgy.

Hastings is dying for a walk so I'll take him to the post box. Hope all is fine with you.

Tons of love from us all,

Perry

Hardacre Farm
15: 9: 94

Darling Sib,

   We have a new puppy, seven weeks old called Harry; sweet and good and nothing like a bullterrier. No wonder people have Labradors. I'm being strict. He sleeps in the old machinery house, which has been done up with Thelma's heat lamp and a fenced run; quite the smartest kennel in Hampshire. He sits with his rolls of fat looking through the chain link and does not cry. Maudie, having been thrilled at first, is jealous and gets into a terrific fury when put into the kennel too. This morning she was sick on the kitchen floor three times to show me how unhappy she is.

   Our front meadow is being ploughed up – most odd looking out onto plough instead of grass. It had never been turned before and the poor tractor driver was buffeted about. The Spy and I went in the cab too – v. exciting and quite illegal.

   My horse has pulled a hamstring in the rear offside. He has odd movement and a huge vet bill. I'm fed up with spending so much money on these ridiculous injuries. I stood in the field and, like a spoilt Pony Club child, stamped my foot and cried. I had 3½ months left to ride before I grow too fat and now the only thing to do is turn him away and let nature take its course. Maddening. I met a girl the other day who was having a baby. When she was expecting her first child she completed the cross-country course at Gatcombe, despite being 4½ months pregnant. By that stage you can feel the baby move and look like a barrel, but she didn't tell her husband, as he wouldn't have let her compete if he'd known she was expecting a child. I have to say she did look a bit like a horse and trotted rather than walked.

I bought the Spy his second pair of grown-up shoes, still an exciting occasion for his mother, although the stupid shop girl didn't measure him correctly and kept us waiting for hours. Unbeknown to her he left his old, scuffed ones on a shelf in the shop. The trials of being a housewife. The trials of being a wife. We went down to Dorset to visit Johnty's parents – It was terrible, their eleven-year-old dog suddenly started having fits and then dropped down dead. Johnty's poor mother was devastated. I tried to cheer her up by telling a slightly earthy story about Maureen Winterman's terrier and it was a disaster. Maureen has a dreadful little dog, which jumps about and runs off the entire time. I was riding past with Amanda Quellington, of all people, and we noticed this animal had a white lampshade on its head.

'Do tell me, Maureen,' Lady Quellington asked, 'What is the lampshade on your dog for?'

'Well, Lady Quellington,' said Maureen. 'It's to stop him from licking his scrotum.' My parents-in-law did not think this quite so highly amusing as Mum did.

I'm going to be thirty soon. *Zut alors.* As a birthday treat, Johnty and I are dumping the animals and Hughie on Perry for a long weekend in the Bath, which we thought would be good fun. I mean a long weekend in Bath.
Are you still wanting a wedding dress?
Must go, lots of love, Tamzin xxx

Nottingham
October 1994

M'darling Sophie,

A Very Happy Birthday.

I hope the parcel arrived safely. I'm afraid downtown Nottingham is not inspiring.

Tamzin got six vases for her birthday and I got food poisoning – a rogue prawn at her birthday lunch. The publican offered me a free dinner but I'm far too embarrassed to accept as I'd given him such a personal description of my colonic variations.

Both children are exceedingly well. H always cries when I leave him at playschool but actually loves it and comes home bearing great works of art – cereal boxes with pasta glued on.

Your birthday is the deciding day on whether Britain pulls out of Bosnia or not. If not, Robs goes there for six months in May. Oh dread. He would love to go and I'm not worried about the dangers out there; it's the *s e p a r a t i o n*. If he doesn't come home for lunch the children get upset. It would still mean having to move to Germany, where we'll also be separated from Tadpole, as I couldn't bear for her to have to go into quarantine when we eventually return to England. Aunt Tamzin has kindly said she'll have her to stay again.

I saw James Money-Kyrle who said he nearly died of food poisoning after Alastair Fothergill's wedding. He was due to fly to China the day after, as he is making a film about exotic palaces, and ended up in Beijing Hospital, where they put him on opium. It made him very, very ill but he says that working for bitchy American power women has been an even more grizzly experience.

'They change their minds constantly.'

'Oh but James, women do.'

Granny says you're painting and painting. I want you to paint the children please.

Lots of love from us all,

P xxxxx

Hardacre Farm
20:10:94

Dear Sophie.

Everyone has been v. worried about your emotions. I just can't bear it for you. I do hope you're not feeling too bruised and unhappy. Never mind, you can go round singing songs like: *'I'm gonna wash that man right outta my hair'* and not shave your armpits.

I hope you had a happy birthday none-the-less and enclose a late present… I have now joined you in the 30 stakes; what a thought.

Did I tell you about my day?? Two surprise parties – one lunch and then dinner for twelve, given by Raddy – very shocking but very, very nice. Bath was super – such a treat, although only one night at a smart hotel (loo paper folded into a point etc).

We looked round the baths – I was rather disappointed, as they don't smell. I was expecting a whiff of sulphur.

Mum and Dad came to stay the night before. Were they here to look after their beloved grandson? No. You're totally right, Mum is mad; they were off to be in a Sly Stallone movie called '*Judge Dredd*', which involved a night shoot at Shepperton Studios, joining 500 extras to play hobos - bag people. Mum wore her normal clothes. They started filming at 8.00pm and ended at 6.00am. I should think you would have to go straight to bed for three days to recover.

Hughie adores the new puppy and calls him Harrreeeee. Harry was a christening present from Raddy. An active one.

Thelma Carole has not been well. Last week I noticed a bald and scabby patch on her shoulder and took her to the vet. He winced and said it was a hideous abscess, and then, Sophie – then he picked the largest scab off with a fingernail. ****! I told him how brave he was. He removed the other scab, commenting on how interesting it was and that I should come closer. He picked up a pair of scissors and (with Thelma standing stock still) trimmed back the raw flesh. It was a rat bite. My £20 spending limit (before having her put down) was not waivered. The bill came to £19.95.

Thelma is now eighteen. Another of her lives used up.

Bod's hamstring is much better but I've given up riding. My girth is now 35 inches. It's the same as Perry was when she was nine months pregnant. I'm six months. Far fatter than the puppy. I suppose I look better in my elf costume.

We are going to Dorset for Christmas as Mum and Dad declared they're going to Osnabrück for some reason.

I bought Dad the **most fantastic** canoe from the Basingstoke dump. It's a double-seater with a frame hand built in mahogany ~ quite stunning. Five quid. All Dad has to do is put a new skin on it and, as Raddy's husband says, put stacks of buoyancy bags in it to keep Daphne afloat. I collected it in their vintage Land Rover. The dump men thought this vehicle was great, but as I stalled all the way home with the canoe sticking out of the back, nobody else on the road thought so.

I think my next baby is going to be another wicked boy – it wakes up in the morning and kicks me <u>all</u> day long. Already. I'm so bruised inside it makes me reel at times. When I have a bath it kicks and moves about so much tidal waves are caused. It's virtually impossible to get out of the tub. I have had to tie a rope to the taps so I can pull myself out.

Must fly,

With all our love,

Tamzin, Johnty

and

The Spy

Back from Neverneverland

Dear Tamzin,

Yes, right out of my hair, but I'm very sad. The rainbow has evaporated, as rainbows do.

I'd been away for ten days, framing pictures in Johannesburg and returned to find he had changed his mind about quite a lot of things, for one reason or other.

I had a car accident on the way back, destroying my white *bakkie*, the *Wit Bliksem*, (or White Lightning) as Fred called it, which somehow went into the back of an AA van.

Don't laugh. It was quite jarring. I was going through double traffic lights at an intersection running beneath the motorway near Alexandria, the township where vehicle hijacking occurs every twenty minutes. The local Police were not able to understand that I was underneath a road. I can still drive my car but the bodywork was so crumpled that it's technically written-off. A bit like me.

I didn't quite know what to do but Nick Archer came out, on leave from the Foreign Office, and we drove back up to Botswana where I was happy. Nick is a complete contrast to Grant; sophisticated and urbane with a dry sense of humour.

'I hope you're not too intent on single-handedly re-vitalizing the South African car industry,' he said, climbing into the Wit Bliksem, which I had persuaded a farm mechanic to re-build for me.

We drove north and spent four days at an elegant camp in the Makgadikgadi Pans with a rather dashing guide called Ralph. He was very enthusiastic about the area. It was once a vast inland lake and although the floods still arrive once a year the water evaporates, forming huge salt pans. The biggest in the world or something. Ralph took the two of us out into nowhere on quad bikes and we walked around looking for flint tools left by Stone Age hunters. In some areas the surface of the pan has gone all bobbly like a giant poppadum.

In the end we were driving across the flat surface in the moonlight. I saw a fire in the distance and pointed it out to Ralph, who I was riding with.

'Ostrich poachers.' he yelled. 'Let's go and buzz them.'

It wasn't. It turned out to be a fire made especially for us. A drinks table was set up with ice and little slices of lemon. The diplomat was delighted, made gin and tonics and offered me a peanut. I could see something in the gloom beyond, and walked over to find a beautifully laid table, with silver and linen napkins. They had brought dinner out for us too; delicious chicken tikka with a great brass tray of syambals, my favourite, favourite thing. I felt so flattered.

The night was cold by the time we ate but Ralph took a spade and shovelled hot coals from the fire under my canvas chair to keep me warm, which was lovely. I didn't want to move and was rather hoping I could stay out there, instead of having to find our way back to the camp in the dark.

We didn't go far. Our beds had been brought out to us, and were standing on the pan, fully made up. Nick snores, so they had set them apart and we had to call to each other across the emptiness. I snuggled down and lay, surrounded by stars which filled my whole field of vision, then woke just before dawn with the sky around me going red as the sun flooded over the lip of the flat world I found myself in.

We ate bacon and eggs, fried up for us on a big fire. I sat close to it with a huge cup of steaming tea in my hands feeling like one of the early explorers who had had to make their way across these wastelands on their way north. We found a great baobab tree with seven trunks growing on the edge of the grassland like some monstrous plant from another era. A cross once carved by David Livingstone was cut into the bark.

Nick and I treated Ralph to beer and chips in an African bar and then drove on to Maun, the dusty supply town on the edge of the Okavango. I had arranged to meet three South African friends of mine who were joining us to ride in the delta. I had been trying to find a selection of girls for Nick, seeing as Fiona had gone and married someone else last year.

'They are ladies aren't they?' he asked me seriously.

'Nick. They are. They are, it has to be said… The Galloping Grannies.'

Gales of laughter were coming from a thatched hut we were walking towards in the hotel garden. Three ladies in jodhpurs were beside themselves laughing, and we laughed with them, on and on over the next seven days. It was good medicine. They looked at me and sang:

There's been a load of compromising
On the road to my horizon,
But I'm gonna go where the lights are shining on me -
Like a rhinestone cowboy
Riding out on a horse in a star spangled rodeo
Like a rhinestone cowboy,
Getting cards and letters from people I don't even know…

And how we rode. Poor Nick. He was the one who was charged by an elephant and was the one whose horse wanted to roll in the mud, but I was the one who was rescued by the cheerfulness surrounding me.

Well I really don't mind the rain,
And a smile can hide all the pain…

I did find someone for Nick; a pretty Scots girl called Rowena McIntosh, who was working at the fishing camp on the Okavango River where we went to spend our last two nights.

She took us out bird watching in a dugout canoe, through channels bordered by tall reeds that wound their way into secret lagoons.

We saw African Skimmers breeding and went Tiger fishing, which was rather thrilling. Tiger Fish fishing. I caught lots.

And I dream of the things I'll do…

Rowena managed to convince Nick that we were going out to a restaurant on the river run by an eccentric, gay Frenchman called Pierre. Nick put on his linen jacket and we roared off in a speedboat into the night.

I thought, 'There can't possibly be a restaurant out here,' but didn't say anything.

Beyond rather a cronky, homemade sign saying *Pierre's*, a three-course dinner with candles and champagne was waiting for us on a little island.

Rowena had sent the camp waiters on ahead to set up the dinner with tables and chairs, as a surprise for us.

So, I'm feeling much better now and am staying at Horizon. No. I'm still upset. We were such good friends. Had so many laughs, such great chats, had so much in common. I feel desolate; but that's what you get for falling in love with cowboys.

Laura was great. She came up behind me and held my head in her hands for a long time. She is funny; she was interviewed about the horse trails, live on the Radio yesterday. It's meant to be good publicity.

The male presenter's opening line was, 'I hear horses bite at one end, kick at the other and are uncomfortable in between.'

Quick as a flash, Laura said,

'I hear the same can be said of some men.'

While Shane and Laura decided to persevere with the horse trails here after all, Sarah-Jane arrived with Jigsaw, seven stallions and Kalahari highlights in her hair. She has uprooted. After many tears she has sold her share of Equus to Wendy and is off to set up horse safaris in Botswana with Jez. They want to ride there with the wildebeest migration.

Jez is off to build a barn on the Makgadikgadi Pans and the new horses will be trucked up as soon as she can organize export permits, or that's the idea. It all sounds rather brave to me. The stallions are extremely vocal. Shane thinks they'll fight, but they haven't yet. Sarah-Jane said she wanted to try something new and that the clients will find riding them exciting. Well, yes.

Rowena managed to persuade Nick to lug an incredibly heavy wooden giraffe back to London for her. He was a bit grumbly about that. But he didn't mind taking this letter.

Lots of love,

Sophie

Christmas Card -
C/o BFPO London, England

Sibethy, here is another school photo for you.

We move on 14th December for further adventures - in Germany. Mum and Dad say they'll fly out to help us move, which is fantastic.

I'm excited about going as lots of friends will be there, but it means Christmas amid packing cases.

R is definitely off to Bosnia. No more thoughts of Cyprus for him.

Write to me often when I'm on my lonesome.
A Very Merry Christmas
with lots and lots of love from
Robert, Perry, Atalanta and Hastings.

Triple B Ranch
24 Rivers
Vaalwater, South Africa

Dear Perry,

Rot schnabel maden hacker. This is a redbilled oxpecker in German. I thought you would like to know that.

The children must be so excited about being abroad; I hope you're in an interesting area. Wasn't there a concentration camp at Osnabrück? Namibia is quite Germanic, or rather the cities are, but everything works, which is quite unusual in Africa.

I went to see Blythe Loutit, the Director of *Save the Rhino Trust* who lives in Damaraland, one of the last true wildernesses; a great desert of red rocks with flat-topped mountains stretching on forever and ever. You would think nothing could survive there but I kept seeing zebra, springbok and even giraffe. At one point a huge kori bustard strutted alongside the road munching away on a scorpion. The country is big and peaceful, except I was nearly run over by a black rhinoceros.

I was on foot, stumbling after Blythe's trackers across a boulder-strewn plateau. We dropped down into a dry riverbed where they pointed out a rhino cow with a small calf. She was some distance away, but spotted us and came hurtling over the rocks.

There was only one tree of any size nearby. The scouts zipped up it but although my pelvis has mended I'm still not that agile and can't jump. I had to wait until the Blythe's mechanic was able to climb high enough to pull me up. Rita, the rhino cow hit a low branch. *Whack*. At 35 mph. The two trackers were standing on it. Her horn made contact in the space right between the two of them. If she'd felt like coming round the other side she could have speared me in the bum, but she stormed off in a huff. I felt a bit shaky after that.

Blythe is incredible. She is married to a chap called Rudi Loutit, Chief Warden of the whole area. I was warned that he has become like a character from *Monty Python's Flying Circus*, since like Billy, he fights a constant war against ignorance and vice.

'I found him biting his car tyres once,' someone told me. 'He'd had two punctures within ten minutes. It left him stranded, nine hours from anywhere, which he found aggravating at the time.'

After tracking a number of rhinoceroses, we came across a herd of the rare desert elephant Rudi is monitoring. Unlike most elephant, which don't hesitate to fell mature trees, the elephants in Damaraland and the Kaokoveld to the north only ever prune plants that regenerate quickly, as if caring for their fragile environment.

We were driving past great green, blobby euphorbia bushes. They're so poisonous that although kudu nibble at the small flowers, nothing much eats them.

'Look,' said Blythe. 'There's a squashed one. Elephants use them as sofas and take the weight off their feet by lying on the springy bushes.'

I couldn't work out how so much game could survive in such an arid environment, but she explained that black rhinos can exist for four or five days without water and that the plants and bushes that do grow there, *boscias* and strange looking *commiphoras*, are particularly nutritious.

She stopped beside a heap of rhinoceros dung, a midden established as a territorial marker, and tore apart a ball of poo, which she put under my nose. It smelt aromatic, herby like thyme.

Mum says that wild otter spraint smells of violets and used to be collected, kept in snuffboxes by the otter hunters of old.

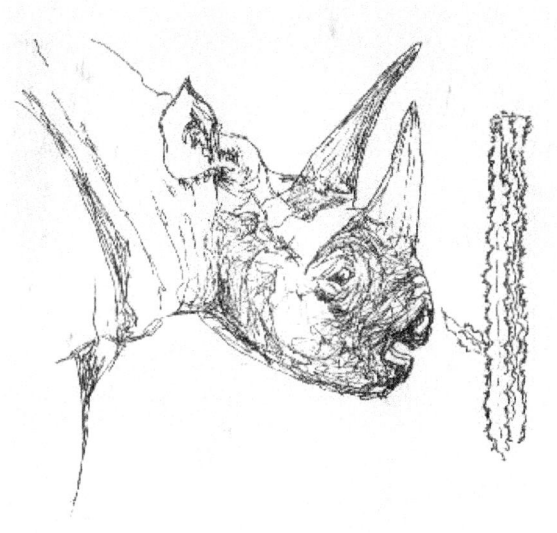

EUROPEAN PERCHA

The desert was amazing. 'We'll start by finding a waterhole and follow fresh rhino tracks into the hills.' Blythe told me. 'The scouts can easily walk thirty kilometres before finding the animals deep in the mountains.'

I didn't know if I would be able to keep up but it was beautiful. Bottletrees were in flower and we saw great flocks of sandgrouse flying into the sunset.

'In the breeding season thousands of these birds flock around waterholes,' Blythe explained, 'filling their breast feathers with water like a sponge, before flying back to their thirsty chicks who wait, trying to imitate stones on the desert floor.'

Pied crows would come to see us and there were quirky birds like spotted dikkops or Damara korhaans walking around.

I was taken to see a prehistoric forest made up of fossilised trees and on to a place called Twefelfontein, where there are hundreds of engravings in the rocks, carved by Bushmen long ago.

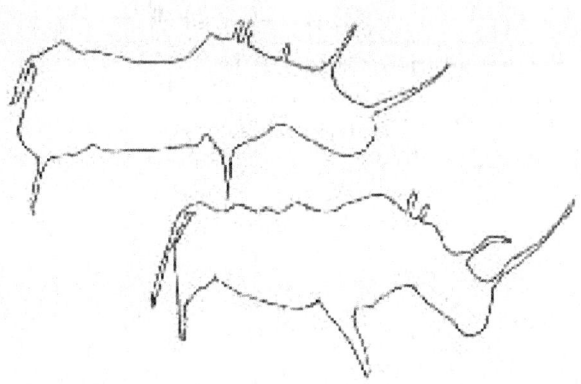

Rudi and Blythe spent ten years living in a hut on the Skeleton Coast, where they kept horses who grazed on reeds growing around the mouths of rivers. Blythe said she loved it by the sea and filled her time painting, sending weekly nature notes to the *Cape Times*.

'Things changed when war with Angola broke out, as the South African Defence Force occupied the whole area. What with guns and bored soldiers, the wildlife took a hammering.'

One year a botanist took Blythe to a waterhole where seven black rhino lay dead, their horns hacked off.

'There were only about forty rhinos left in the Damaraland. I decided things had gone too far and went off to see the Minister for the Environment.'

He took her concern seriously but mysteriously 'committed suicide' soon after.

Undaunted, she formed *Save the Rhino Trust* to bring control to the situation and now, twelve years later, cares for 115 animals. The soldiers have gone but poaching remains a threat. Rhinoceros horn is worth more than its weight in gold.

But it isn't just that. Rhinos are still regarded as dangerous pests; last year a baby rhino was stoned to death by a group of yobs, just for fun. Andrew's right; the local community need to see their wildlife as an asset to be valued and cherished rather than as vicious beasts. Showing our documentary at schools might help.

Blythe spends three weeks of every month sleeping out in the desert, as she ranges 40,000km/sq with her scouts. She lent me a bedroll and took me over the great stony plains, down the dry Hoanib River where we found giraffe browsing, and on until, after two days, we reached the Skeleton Coast National Park.

Rudi had arranged for his rangers to meet us at the boundary. It was so exciting. They drove us over the enormous Namibian sand dunes, miles and miles of them. You only climb the dunes by roaring up, as fast as possible in four-wheel drive, hitting the crest and then hurtling down the other side, using the momentum gained to take you up the next dune. It was terrifying. I couldn't believe it possible.

At one stage Jan, the outrageous ranger whose Land Rover I was clinging to, skidded sideways and came to a halt on the crest of a high dune.

I stepped out and walked around for a while. There were dunes for as far as you could see. It was magnificent.

We dropped down into the Hoanib River mouth and found a gemsbok, or oryx – a big desert antelope with sword-like horns, with what looked like a small pack of wolves running behind.

Jan said that some tourists had recently reported that they had seen lions chasing gemsbok, but the fact is that these antelope crèche their young who, with their darker colouring and almost fluffy manes, look so unlike the adults you would think them a completely different kind of animal. They appear to be chasing the female, when of course they're just following her.

The Skeleton Coast itself, *The Burning Shore* that Wilbur (Smith) wrote about, is bleak. Pelagic currents scoot up from the Antarctic, changing the African climate into something rather

Welsh. It's odd. The cold sea air hits the desert forming mists or fog while the sea rages away. It's notoriously rough and icy cold but so rich in fish that you find prolific marine life.

Hundreds of seals were resting on the shore, and while gulls circled above us, cormorants looked on sardonically from the rocks. It was very, very smelly. There had been an inexplicable die-off of seals. Scavengers such as black-backed jackal and brown hyena, were picking at washed-up carcases. An old lion was once spotted strolling along the beach.

Blythe loved it all. We walked along the shoreline, hunched up in our jackets, clutching hankies over our noses. She showed me patches of glowing, burgundy coloured sand made up of hundreds of tiny garnets; garnet sand. It's an indication of diamonds.

There was one rusty wreck of a ship that had been stranded on the coast, and a morose collection of rhino skulls from poached animals found by rangers over the years.

After staying the night at an old whaling station we moved on down the coast. I was startled to see flamingos, but they feed on salt pans, with avocet and other waders. I saw flocks of pelicans and they have penguins further south. Ones that bray like donkeys. They're faithful creatures and mating pairs have been known to stay together for as long as fifteen years.

Jan told me about a penguin he rehabilitated once. It was found dying on a beach and was given to him covered in oil. He didn't know if it was a girl or a boy penguin but it became quite tame, demanding to get in his bath, and insisted on sleeping either in his bed or on top of the family dog. Jan would take it everywhere, out shopping or to the cinema, where the penguin would sit in his own chair, watching the screen intently.

'The only problem,' Jan said, 'was that he was attracted to fat people. He would wait at the garden gate, sneak out and follow them excitedly down the pavement, wings flapping. My mother would have to run after him and put him under the garden sprinkler until he calmed down.'

Every evening Jan would take his penguin to the sea where it would swim, diving through the waves ecstatically, but always waddled up the beach and jumped inside the Land Rover before Jan could bear to drive away.

'He was eating up to nine pilchards a day, and finding a source of fresh fish was becoming difficult. I realised I would have to send him further south to be released near an established penguin colony.'

Jan made all the arrangements with Nature Conservation and put his beloved penguin in a wooden crate, with careful instructions given to all involved in his transportation.

But the crate was moved and forgotten about. Jan returned after working in the north to find his penguin had died, abandoned in the wooden box.

I left Blythe alone in her desert and flew back to write my report for the BBC.

I don't think we will be able to broadcast the really interesting stories...

I'd been driven around by a fascinating man; an Afrikaans geologist who had worked as a prospector in the area for years. His labourers disclosed all sorts of hidden secrets about poaching syndicates and double-dealing; tales of murder and intrigue.

He'd witnessed the extent of SAADF poaching when those in command, quite illegally, went off to hunt elephant until every waterhole in the Koakoveld was surrounded by their carcasses. Two of his friends who were working as botanists, saw a helicopter with a net of rare black-faced impala slung beneath it.

'They took a photograph just as the enraged face of PW Botha, then President of South Africa, was peering out of the open door,' he told me. 'They knew they would be arrested for this but the helicopter couldn't land with the net beneath, so the botanists took out the film, hid it under a rock and when their camera was confiscated all the authorities found were pictures of plants.'

All I know is that I want to go back and ride across the Namib Desert. Come too. Rowena said she would.

I found her at Horizon, battling with the new horses. She is going to work for Sarah-Jane and made me promise to come up to the Kalahari for Christmas.

I'm busy seeing who I can persuade to join me in the hottest place on earth, so have been contacting my most eccentric friends. You never know, I've told them we might just spot Wilbur.

As it is, I fly to Cape Town on Friday in search of yet more smelly seals on a recce with a BBC producer, to see where he can set up a live broadcast for New Year's Day called *Global Sunrise*. I met Robin twenty-one years ago when he was sent to direct his first film. It was for *Animal Magic.* Can you remember? It was about us. I had to row up the lake with the parrot on my shoulder. This time it's going to be a gannet; or that is what it looks like.

Think of me. We have to go out to sea and I'm worried I'll chunder all over the poor man.

Lots of love,

Sophie

Osnabrück
Germany Jan. 1995

Darling Sib,

The wonderful land of Oz is so wet and windy that the television won't work, so I'm catching up with letters, which is high time.

Osnabrück is a friendly place and there's a beautiful old part of town with lots of character. But once you have finished sightseeing the reality bites in, and it's cold. Our quarter is quite well laid out but is moth ridden and mouldy.

They have rules for everything in Germany. It's dreadful. You're not allowed to mow your lawn or hang out your washing on a Sunday. You're not allowed to wash your car, except at a carwash. A bonfire? Absolutely NOT. You must put your recyclable rubbish in transparent yellow bin liners but if the rubbish men spy a non-recyclable baked bean contaminating a tin you get a huge neon REJECT sticker on the sack for public humiliation.

And you must keep the pavement and an area 6 foot (sorry, 2 metres) outside your garden fence, clean and clear. If someone slips and injures themselves on ice or unswept snow in this area they can sue you. In my case they're much more likely to slip on dog poo.

There's a big housing estate behind us. Do the Germans take their dogs (which MUST be kept on leads) to the woods on the opposite side of the road for their morning constitutions? No. They take them on the verge bordering my garden. Atalanta fell in some. It got all over her little pink lunchbox and her new shoes. I'm afraid I couldn't face cleaning them, so threw them away. They couldn't go in the re-cycling bin.

The next morning, I was coming back from the school run (which I wish I could do in your Chrysler Sunbeam as everyone thinks Norma Major is turning up when I appear in Robert's Jag), when I saw a girl allowing her dog to do a Scooby Doo-doo right where Atalanta had met the last one. I YELLED at her. Now, my German course had taught me how to buy train tickets and book hotel bedrooms but not how to yell at people.

'Nicht hier. Meine garten. Meine kinder.'

She scampered off, dog in tow. In the meantime my Canadian friend, Val was rolling around laughing.

'Well, actually Val, it's not funny.'

'No, no, Perry... it's not that... She was ENGLISH.'

Atalanta has not settled at all well at the Army school on the base and leaves the house each morning in floods of tears, which breaks my heart. The crux of the matter is that she isn't making any friends in her class.

I've been to the teacher (myself in tears) begging them to move her to be with the children who live in our street but they won't do anything. She is also leaps ahead, and it's frustrating as they refuse to build on what she already knows, taking her right back to the beginning.

Hastings, on the other hand, loves his playgroup and is picked up and returned each morning by bus, cheerily singing his nursery rhymes. His favourite expression is, 'Excuse me, *Frauline?*'

I've been collecting clothes and toys for Robert to take to Bosnia. He is going to pack his tanks full of aid supplies to be distributed at orphanages and schools. He can't wait to get going. *Boys Own* stuff.

Guess What? My darling husband has bought me a 'going away present' of extravaganza. A new (tax free) Volkswagen. My first car. The only vehicle I've ever owned before was the 50cc moped.

I'm having to invent 500 ways to cook bread and water. I did, in fact, emigrate with a large quantity of groceries; a year's supply of pasta and toothpaste, as this country is expensive. I'm afraid I rather resent having to pay £8 for a packet of Fish Fingers. It's five times the price of any shop in England.

I'm missing Tadpole terribly. Tamzin put the phone next to her when she was lapping up water and I collapsed in tears. What am I going to do when it's Robert who is away?

You are a lucky girl; I'm yearning for the sun. It has been absolutely icy here, flipping freezing.

Lots of love,

Frau Perry xxxx

Triple B Ranch

Dear Alastair,

A Christmas letter – I must write and tell you about my recce with Robin; it was quite something.

I arrived at Johannesburg Airport early, only to be 'approached' by, guess what, a contract car thief. There I was, alone in the underground car park, with my money belt dangling around my neck, bags lying on the ground, struggling with the gorilla lock for my steering wheel, when along comes the jolly thief.

Luckily security officers do exist and I was able to get myself together in order to sort out Robin's flights.

He was hours late flying in from Hluhluwe. I ended up getting him off one plane and on to another in about ten minutes. It was pouring with rain.

I went down onto the tarmac, grabbed him saying, 'Robin. QUICK – run.' and we just made it onto the last flight to Cape Town.

It was the first time he'd seen me in twenty years. He'd travelled from Natal in a terrible storm, which had bounced the light aircraft about until his head hit the roof.

But the real action started the next morning when we were due to visit a bird colony on an island off the coast.

I had been told to meet a boat at a small harbour called Kleinbaai – so Robin and I duly arrived in our Corolla hire car clutching permits, cameras and binoculars looking, as you can imagine, thoroughly English. Around us on the quay were a number of dour Afrikaans fishermen, wandering round scowling at the state of the sea.

The place is called the Cape of Storms; it's where the Indian Ocean meets the Atlantic. And it is rough. Can you remember that scene in *Local Hero* when the Russians come? Well, the South African version was, in reality, far more bizarre.

I was trying to gather information off the fishermen in my halting Afrikaans:

'*Cremora, Oom.*' (Good morning, Uncle) I was saying to a fat one in a bobble hat with yellow, insulated dungarees strapped up under his armpits, when a tiny white boat appeared. It seemed to be leaping over the waves that were slamming against the harbour entrance.

'*Die mol Americano.*' (The mad American) he declared.

And he was right.

Vroom, vroom, the engine revved. Standing in the stern, holding onto the bow rope was a short, dark Californian, wearing nothing but a rolled down wetsuit and numerous thongs, off which hung sharks' teeth. He had a ponytail. These features don't make sense to Afrikaans fishermen. Neither does only having one outboard motor; not in that sea.

Well, out leaped the Californian.

'Hi. Mark Marks, Great White Shark Research,' he said grabbing my hand. '…and this is Derek.'

Derek was a green looking ecologist, still sitting in the dinghy. Mark leapt back into the boat and flipped open a red box, which was all that was inside once Derek was out. In the box was nothing except a cell phone, which Mark started dialling.

'Effing not answering – I'm trying to get a weather report.'

The Afrikaners looked on in total disbelief.

'Are we going in this boat?' Robin asked politely.

'Yup, just keep your hands inside. The sharks get attitudinal (sic).'

Like complete fools, Robin and I sat down on the red box and went off, out to sea – whack, whack, whack over the waves – for seven kilometres, with Mark Marks standing behind us like a surfer. I couldn't see where we were going; there was nothing ahead but ENORMOUS waves.

After about half an hour of this we started seeing seabirds, then a long, flat island with a few white sheds at one end. Waves were breaking around it. At the southern end was another, smaller, rocky island.

'It's called Geyser Rock, because the waves shoot up so high between the two islands,' Mark yelled at us.

He then took us there; right into the channel. It was not wide.

'Now this is one hell-luva-groovy seal colony.'

It was. Extraordinary. Seals were everywhere, about 50,000 of them. Cape fur seals. There were seals in the water – right by us, sticking their tails in the air.

'Look, look, look.' Mark shouted, 'Shark bites.'

They all had scars.

'I've just found one bitten clean in two,' Mark went on.

Well, I started looking for sharks. And at the rocks. I kept thinking we'd crash against them. There we were, right in front of the colony, almost too terrified to take photographs. Robin couldn't even get his camera out of the red box.

It has to be said that Mark was an expert with the boat. He made it back to the main island where we pulled up at a jetty. It's an old sealing station and the various houses there now belong to the Department of Nature Conservation.

We sat in Mark's room for a while before venturing out to see the birds. They covered the entire island. The smell was overpowering even with the high wind. About thirteen large groups of breeding Cape Cormorants were holding onto their land claims amidst numerous shuffle gangs of Jackass Penguins. A few Crowned Cormorants had nests on higher rocks and I saw Whitebreasted Cormorants on Geyser Rock.

Along the shore were Oyster Catchers, Swift Terns and Hartlaub's Gulls. You should find lots of migrants in January. Mark said they have Arctic Skua. 'Groovy ones,' if you can get your brain round that.

It's all go. Kelp gulls swoop about looking for eggs to snatch, the seals predate on penguins and sharks are after the seals. No shortage of stuff to film. On top of everything else there's a colony of sixty-five tortoises living there. And Mark Marks. He would make a brilliant presenter for any U.S. co-production; so enthusiastic and such a character.

'Hi there, little guy,' he said picking up a lost looking penguin and laughing when it tried to peck his eyes out.

The island is quite historic. You can still see iron vats where they used to boil up dead seals to extract fat from their blubber. The whole place used to be covered in fur seals, culled for their skins, but the caretakers now make sure they keep to Geyser Rock, as they want to preserve the penguin colony. There are 75% fewer penguins than in 1900 and they're on the endangered list, vulnerable not only to oil spillage, but suffer if ships swill out their tanks at sea, as detergent damages their feathers' natural waterproofing. I read that 'many were killed by underwater blasting during the construction of the ore-loading facility at Saldanha Bay'[lxvii] and could get hold of recent pollution stories if you want.

I had taken sleeping bags and sausage rolls in case Robin and I found ourselves trapped on the island, but as it was bright and sunny we thought the weather was improving. It wasn't. The way back was nearly the end of us. Robin was awfully brave. He sat on the box, keeping a lookout as the waves crashed around us. Mark stood in the back swearing all the way,

Whack. Crash. We were caught by one wave, which sent him flying and were nearly flipped over. I just sat on the floor, prayed, and prayed and prayed. I didn't want to be bitten in half.

I don't know how we reached land. No other boats were out. Derek was standing on the quay alone with his binoculars, laughing with relief. Robin looked at me, dripping wet and said,

'You know, I never even filled out a BBC Safety Report Form.'

So the only problem with Going Live from Dyer Island would be getting out there. You couldn't land in a helicopter because it's almost completely covered in nesting birds. Massive rubber ducks might be the answer. Perhaps I could ask the Navy to help.

By using my best Afrikaans, I managed to get permission from a Colonel Ekestein at the Department of Correctional Services to take Robin to visit Robben Island. It's still a high security prison. Beyond the trendy shops on the Cape Town Waterfront there's a square brick building. You go there, get screened by security (bodily searched), walk through rather intimidating steel doors but then leave on a purpose built ferry with plastic seats and an assortment of people who, I suppose, work at the prison. This time we whizzed out over the sea in comfort, safety and a fug of cigarette smoke.

A taciturn old warder showed us around the island. It was all slightly unreal. We found ostrich strutting along the seashore and bontebok grazing placidly whilst great waves were breaking on the beach beyond. You can find flightless Chukar Partridge that were introduced by Cecil Rhodes at the turn of the century and there's a colony of about 13,000 penguins that have returned recently after an absence of about 200 years.

The warder told us that after an oil slick hit the Cape he trained prisoners to help clean up the birds and the penguins are now happy nesting there. I suppose it's quite peaceful breeding next to a maximum-security installation. Table Mountain rises up in the hazy distance behind the colony and Robin agreed that it would be quite cool and rather surprising for a presenter to declare:

'Here we are, broadcasting live from Robben Island… where penguin chicks have just hatched.'

But I wouldn't want to spend my life there. It must be cold in winter. We went round to see the old lighthouse and the infamous limestone quarry where Nelson Mandela was forced to work for thirteen years. The white stone was indeed garish. He wrote in 1964 'Robben Island was without question the harshest, most iron-fisted outpost in the South African penal system.' He was imprisoned for 10,000 days. Imagine.

I took Robin to a few other possible locations on the mainland including the Cape of Good Hope where we saw whale, and Lambert's Bay, a working fishing harbour on the west coast, which could be useful. It's famous for the hordes of gannets, which nest alongside groups of cormorants demonstrating strict apartheid. As you'll read in the report, filming there would be easy-peasy, 100% reliability for a live broadcast.

Come out when you can for a holiday. You can think of me bobbling round with Diana and Lucy who are flying out for Christmas. I'm not sure how much they'll enjoy camping without tents, but still.

Much love to all,

Sophie

Triple B Ranch
24 Rivers
Vaalwater

Dear Tamzin,

Fred is here and I have Sarah-Jane and Rowena staying in my bedroom. They're collecting the horses they bought to take to Botswana. One had the tip of a crossbow arrow imbedded in his bottom. Walter cut it out, saying the colt must have been used for target practise. Poor thing. No wonder it was nervy. Sarah-Jane is in a rage about the abuse of hunting regulations.

Jez rang from Maun, asking if he could bring two hitchhikers to stay when he drove down. I was imagining a couple of miserable hippies in droopy ethnic garments but they turned out to be pretty girls of about twenty-three, with long blonde hair and long brown legs.

'Ant is going to think Christmas has come early,' Fred said laconically.

Fred was quite right. Ant returned from a dance in Pretoria early the next morning and fell instantly in love with the pretty girl from the Kenyan coast called Tessa, who was lying asleep on my veranda, her curly blonde hair falling towards the floor. He is currently showing both girls round his game farm with Fred, and has been doing so for the last five days.

Since then, my friends Lucy and Diana flew in from England and collapsed beside the swimming pool.

'Ant and Bee,' Lucy commented as she watched Ant carefully showing Tessa a South African road map. 'Note: attentive girl.' Lucy went on. 'I'm afraid, Diana, that I just cannot be that adoring.'

'Yes, it's probably the reason why none of us are married.' Diana declared loudly.

'Too choosey, you mean,' Lucy said. She's right. No one is more attractive or more eligible than Lucy. She is still single at thirty-seven and fed up with people asking her why she's not married.

'So nosey, asking that,' Diana said.

'They could be trying to flatter you.' I pointed out.

'Do you think?' Lucy said screwing up her nose. 'No. It's a stupid question. Marriage isn't exclusive to the beautiful and interesting, they're just nosey-parkers. As far as I can see all sorts of dull, ugly people manage to get married when they're twenty-two.'

'I don't know anyone who married that young.' Diana retorted. I had to tell them that both you and Perry were.

I took my dauntingly single friends off to see Conita's orphaned rhino but have to say Diana had Fred chatting her up in the back of my *bakkie* all the way there. We arrived in such a rainstorm that we couldn't get out of the car, so I drove on to see everyone at Equus, where Lucy and Diana instantly managed to find two most marriageable Englishmen. The sun emerged after tea and I took them out to see impala grazing on the plain beyond the house, in the kind of dazzling gold light you get after rain, only to get covered in ticks. The shrieks.

I dread to think what will happen when I get them on horses, for that is the plan. Girls on tour: *Sophie's Safaris for Spinsters*. Guess what we are off to do? Ride the stallions across the Kalahari.

With Ant's help I collected my horse Sam from Equus, so am riding him around the farm, which is fun although Diana couldn't see the point of being on a horse with quite such a frantic buck. His tail does hit you on the head. And I still don't own a saddle.

If you see Nick Archer, please tell him a letter is on its way. Knowing Diana and Lucy well, he is demanding a full report on their doings.

Lots of love,

Sophie

Triple B Ranch

Dear Nick,

I don't know why Diana and Lucy should attract disaster but they did. The first drama was a snake in their bedroom. I found Diana in her nightdress, standing on the bed, telling me she'd taken out her contact lenses but was sure there was a snake and could I get rid of it. I didn't believe her but she was right. It was a night adder and quite poisonous. I hammered it to death with a polo stick, which I thought brave of me.

OK; then a contact lens was lost in a tree. I had forgotten that Bismarck, the horse Diana was riding at Horizon, is enamoured by zebra and they ended up going through the bush quite literally. Shane rigged up what he called 'a tarp' for us to sleep under at night. It wasn't a long one. Rain poured down while our sleeping bags got wetter and wetter.

Elephant don't normally walk out into the main road, but they did when Lucy started to drive my car. We ended up canoeing down the Zambezi; well, you can just imagine. Hippo decided to attack Diana and Lucy's canoe. I was all right. I was with the guide.

You can actually canoe right to the edge of Victoria Falls without being sucked over, but Diana was not ready to believe this. We somehow made it to Livingstone Island and spent the night camping there in the middle of Victoria Falls. It was quite wet-making. From all the spray. 'Do you think,' Lucy asked with dripping wet hair, 'that there might be an outside possibility of meeting Mr Adequate tonight? If not, I don't think I'll change for dinner, if it's all the same with you.'

We spent Christmas with Sarah-Jane, riding her horses on the Makgadikigadi Pans. They did all sorts of un-nerving things between the acacia bushes but everyone clung on. It was unbelievably hot. We had to go out early and then lay in our tents under the palm trees, quite unable to move from eleven o'clock until about five, spraying our dehydrating bodies with Lucy's cucumber foot spray.

Rowena said we were jolly lucky to have a lovely big tent and not be sleeping in the horse barn. Sarah-Jane has an iron bed in one of the stalls where she makes her groom sleep in case lion come for the horses in the night.

'He is called Manuel,' she explained. 'It's just like *Fawlty Towers*.'

It was; the car bringing us Christmas dinner from Francistown broke down and we didn't eat until 11.30pm.

'It doesn't matter,' Lucy said. 'More time to drink and so blissful not having little children around.'

As it was they went off with Jez to look for brown hyena and got lost in the dark, which I thought immensely worrying, but Diana came back saying it had all been terribly exciting. Nothing that worried me (ie: that was dangerous) concerned her a bit.

The last time I went white water rafting down the Zambezi, I fell out of the boat at the first rapid after being hit in the face by an oar and was underwater for about two minutes, spinning around in what felt like a giant washing machine. I was injured quite badly but couldn't get out of the deep river gorge, so I had to bounce down all the other rapids with my face swollen and throbbing.

Diana and Lucy went down about fourteen rapids roaring with laughter and said the only risk seemed to be the danger of falling in love with their Zambian oarsman. They loyally took the ferry over the Chobe River and drove back down with me to Johannesburg, when they could have flown. It took two days and, like you, they nearly missed their flight back.

Could you find out if Alastair is really cross with me for going to see the penguins without wearing a life jacket? Being able to survive for a long time in the water didn't seem to be the issue. Lots of love, think of us gasping in the heat.

Sophie

Triple B Ranch

Dear Perry,

Some man standing in the Bank, whom I had never met before, called me his Fraukie. '*Mei Fraukie*'. I thought of you. It has been hot and sultry with thunderstorms passing through. The bush is emerald green with vibrant pink and orange sunsets. I nearly saw my own sunset this month. Twice.

The back wheel came flying off my car. It could have been disastrous if I had been going full pelt along the tar road, but I gave a lift to some brightly dressed ladies and with the added weight on the rear axle the loose wheel spun off on the sandy drive. As I looked at the groove my wheel hub had cut in the track goose bumps rose as if full stops had been typed all over my arms. *Hoender vleis*, the Afrikaners call it. Chicken flesh. The ladies weren't a bit perturbed, just furious that their lift hadn't come to anything.

Then I was nearly struck by lightning. I was running across the garden as it was beginning to rain when everything went white. I heard Tessa scream. She said lightning struck the earth two-foot away from me. Charles Baber said that what with my adventures at sea and being unable to climb trees in a hurry, I must have been spared for a purpose. Aunt Vera was struck by lightning in Kenya when she was sitting on her veranda. The little dog lying on her lap was killed. She survived but was crippled for life.

We had a tragic death in Vaalwater.

'The policemen,' Effie told me, 'they shot a man they were thinking was a thief.'

'It was tragic.' Charles added. 'He was only collecting his laundry.'

Then someone murdered an old Afrikaans lady. It was considered to be political; racist retaliation, but a good Sotho friend of mine told me the farmer's wife had been kind to her when she was a student and had given her Afrikaans lessons free of charge. Effie didn't know what had happened but Miriam did.

'No, Sophie. The man who shot the Mrs cut off the ear. The ear,' she explained 'of the policeman who was wanting to arrest him before he ran away.' The other officer shot him in the back.

Otherwise things are quiet. I've been playing my flute in church, which must be painful for everyone, but I do stop eventually.

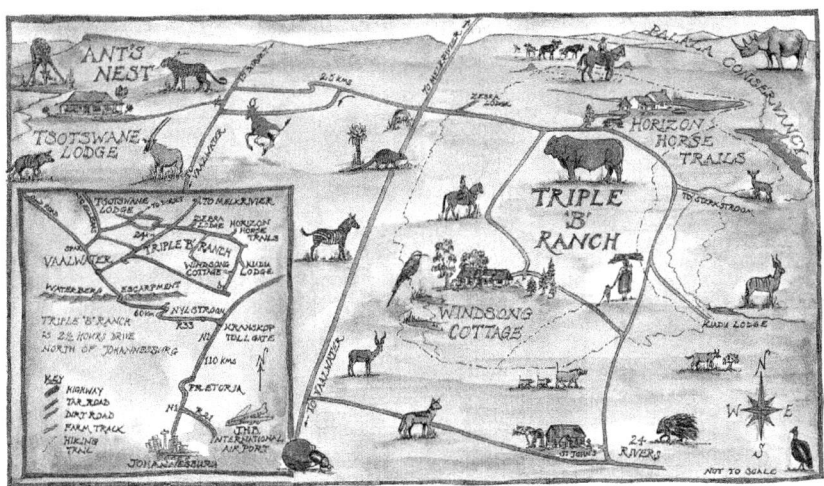

Charles Baber thought it would be a good idea to do up a couple of dilapidated farmhouses and mark a trail to attract hikers. It thrilled him that people would be happy to pay to walk around his farm.

It has been jolly hard work organizing this. You need bunk beds and loos, maps and marketing, with nearly a hundred little signs made (by me) to mark the way.

Instead of painting wildlife I've been sketching the hiking trail lodges and putting a brochure together. This was not exactly strenuous but I kept conking out and found myself sleeping a lot during the day.

Nina made me go for a Bilharzia test, and guess what, it came back labelled:

'*Level 4: Chrrronic*'. (The Afrikaans doctor rolls his R's).

This indicates that I've got it quite seriously and probably caught it ages ago from swimming in Lake Malawi. You will be delighted to hear that I have nematodes in my blood; little worms swimming about in it. I had to take a tablet the size of a conker in order to do them in.

Shane is just back from Botswana where he went to a place in back of beyond called Ghanzi to help Jez and Rowena look for new horses.

'We stayed with one farmer who wanted Jez to try his endurance horse,' he told me with an uncomfortable look on his face. 'I could tell something was going on: it took two of them to lead the thing out of the stable.'

Jez gamely climbed onto the horse's back. It shot off, jerking him backwards and bucking like fury.

'They have washing lines made of fencing wire up there,' Shane said. 'He was nearly decapitated. Rowena just managed to warn him in time. Then they opened the gate. Jez was gone for a long time. All we could see was a puff of dust on the horizon as he disappeared into the desert. Endurance rides can be anything up to 160 miles and it didn't look as if he was managing to turn round. I stood there with clenched fists hidden in my pockets thinking, How am I going to get back to Vaalwater?'

Jez didn't buy the horse. When I asked Rowena about it she told me that the farmer was about to appear in court on a charge of gang rape. He had been molesting children of the Bushmen. Back to England soon, since T seems about to pop.
Very much love to all and my love to you,
from Sophie and the nematodes.

CHAPTER TWELVE

Hardacre Farm
16th March 1995

Dear Perry,

I now know what it means to be a lady in-waiting. The baby is late. OH. NO. IT IS NOT, IT IS COMING. As I write it's coming.

Off Tamzin went, contracting away at 10.30pm. I was left with Hughie and a list of babies' names that Granny had sent. Her suggestions included: Tristram, Oberon and Kestrel. Mary-Dieu said that she called Oscar 'Oscar' just to annoy Granny. Not a bit of it; she loves unusual names. She called Mum 'Daphne' after all.

Johnty was back for breakfast, telling me that, 'It was quick and easy and he is called Guy.' Tamzin rang at 7.30am to say that they're letting her straight out, that she's amazed at how fast and well it all went, but could I go and catch the horses who have escaped from Raddy's field and are heading towards the main road? Just when I was going to instruct Tadpole on the art of ratting. And I couldn't find them. In the end we had a call from an irate woman who had seen three ponies galloping down the lane and herded them into her yard just before they joined the commuters on the A303. I went off with Raddy's New Zealand nanny, Tracy, and trotted Bod back in the rain, while Johnty collected the Queen Bee from hospital before going straight on to the office. I had been given the impression that having a baby was a specially romantic experience for a couple but Tamzin said, 'Not exactly' and that I could have come to observe. I would have loved to; I've only ever seen a wildebeest give birth.

I flew back from South Africa on a Greek plane with Shane. It not only stopped in Athens but in Thessalonica. For six hours. I took a photo for Laura. They gave us a hotel room, so I had a tepid Greek bath and a Greek breakfast. Dad collected me with a tree in the back of the car, so I sat between the branches until we reached Hampshire. He wanted to plant it in celebration of the birth. I found the two bullterriers lying end to end by the Aga like one black sausage. Tamzin's spare room is as lovely as ever, with cool linen sheets and piles of smart glossy magazines, although Hughie has been kindly bringing me commercial catalogues advertising bulldozers to read instead. He seems quite unchanged since I last saw him and still runs around naked all evening, refusing point blank to being put into his babygrow. It has to be worn back to front so that he can't get out. He has a gruff voice and sings a lot; funny little boy.

Saturday: Tamzin is lying on her bed, steadily deflating with the baby alternately guzzling and gazing. I've been prancing around trying on all her clothes, staggered at what is now considered fashionable. Sling-back shoes. I can't wait to tell Laura that flares are coming back in. Mum pitched up last night with a bottle of Champagne and a bunch of daffodils. She gave Johnty a lecture and then delivered the ultimatum: 'Either Sophie stays here or I do – Tamzin MUST be looked after.' NB: my opinion, my plans didn't enter into the equation. Johnty went off 'to fill the lawnmower with petrol' and hasn't returned.

I have to say that being a monthly nurse is not that complicated. I function mainly as a receiver of gifts and arranger of flowers, making Tamzin the odd plate of scrambled eggs and being idiotic about the sterilizer so that she doesn't give up on the breastfeeding, which she loathes. I do scrub the kitchen floor. The only thing I can't stand is having to make polite conversation with the Health Visitor, so I take Hughie off to play in the hay as soon as she comes round. There's a nice girl from the Czech Republic who does the laundry, and Johnty is quite a dynamic man at night.

Let me know if you have any more babies and I'll drop round,

Lots of love,

Sophie

Triple B Ranch
24 Rivers
Vaalwater 0530

Dear Perry,

Spring in England was beautiful this year with crisp, sunlit days. It was lovely being with Tamzin, lovely being at home, but after five weeks I was staggering about wheezing and ended up returning to South Africa with acute Bronchitis. It seems I'm just going to have to accept life as a health exile.

I spend my weekends hiker hunting. It's Charles' new hobby. We drive around in his 1950s Chevy trying to find them and nailing little signs to trees in case they're still behind us. The front seat of the Chev is so wide that when Diana and Lucy came to stay Charles managed to get all three of us, sitting in a row, on the front seat beside him. With Lucy wearing her summer dress and a wide-brimmed straw hat. 'What about the gear-stick?' she asked.

'Relax.' Charles shouted jamming the Chev into reverse. We bounded off to see how his cattle were doing. 'I'm a grass farmer,' he declared to their surprise.

But I'm beginning to digest this. You need to plant and promote, manage and maintain the right kind of grasses to succeed as a stock farmer – or indeed as a game rancher. He is teaching me about the different varieties. One is called *panicum maximum*.

Since Juliet has started publishing a school newspaper there has been a murder featured in every edition. She said, what was a bit scary was that her cub reporter actually knew the last murderer; he used to play soccer with him.

This month a farmer was shot in an organized armed robbery so we are being very cautious. Anthony supervises payment of the wages armed with a Commando regulation semi-automatic, but you have to be careful and double-check everything.

My friend Jez got dangerously lost on the Makgadikgadi pans recently. When he took friends out on the quad bikes, one ran out of petrol. The camp staff hadn't bothered to refuel.

They had no matches, no water, no radios. Jez left the two men on the pans and went off with the girl to fetch more petrol, only they broke down too. She was his old girlfriend. They waited for fourteen hours but no one came to their rescue so they decided to walk.

He said they ended up trudging on, without food or water for twelve hours, navigating by the sun and stars. After a while they started going a bit crazy and tried drinking contact lens fluid, which only made things worse. *Panicum maximum.* The girl had a little instamatic camera. They held it above their heads taking endless photos of the darkness to let off the flash.

Eventually, someone saw the tiny light from the camp and came to meet them. The two other men ended up walking for thirty hours. At least our hikers won't die of thirst; they can drink out of the cattle troughs.

Jez and Sarah-Jane have actually had to pull their horses out of the Makgadikgadi. As I thought; it's just too hot and dry. Not for the horses, but for the clients.

Jez is going to work for a big safari company while Sarah-Jane tries to find a camp they can operate from in the Okavango. I expect they could probably do with Charles' Chev, but then *'You'll never get to heaven in a Chevrolet.'*

Do you want to know why? *'Because God's got shares in Ford Coupé'.*

My work for the BBC took a turn. I was suddenly told I will not be required for the filming of *Dawn to Dusk*. It seems that by sending the crews to well organized safari camps I've made myself redundant, which is sad as I did want to see Randall's elephants again.

But as that door closed another opened. Of all the television programmes made on earth I'm working on *Blue Peter,* setting up their Summer Holiday to South Africa. They're coming in July; dead of winter here.

Isn't it funny? It's something I must have wanted to do when I was eleven and now it's all happening. I went to Television Centre the day before I flew out, armed with a list of exciting things I thought they could do.

I said they must go to a vulture restaurant, meet Conita's orphaned hippopotamus and spend a day with Walter, the vet. He was called out to remove a tractor tyre that an elephant had managed to get stuck round its neck recently.

The *Blue Peter* production office is far more intimidating than facing an enraged wild animal. They weren't at all impressed with my ideas.

'Have you seen *Blue Peter* recently?' the producer asked abruptly. 'The style has changed radically, you know.'

'Well,' I said, 'The presenters' hairdos have but when I watched it (with my nephew Hughie) they had an item on pets, an Indonesian dance troupe and *How to make a patio suite for your Sindy doll*, and I thought, How amazing, it hasn't changed a bit.'

This was true, but not exactly the right thing to say. They must have been desperate though, as they gave me a contract and I've come out with this laptop. I expect the only other South African Facilitators (this is my new job title) are taking News crews round Soweto.

Blue Peter want me to find child heroes. 'Like surfing experts.' It's turning my brain inside out. I rang a journalist who once came riding at Equus, who put me onto a story about a Gerald Durrell-like boy of thirteen who breeds silkworms. I always wanted a silkworm.

Anyway, last July the silkworms stopped spinning. The boy found out that an untested chemical spray being used in orange orchards was annihilating butterflies and moths for miles around and organized a Public Enquiry. Executives from a large international drugs company had to fly from Switzerland and were required to withdraw their insecticide from the market. Pets, privet hedges (silkworms eat privet), pollution: the BBC bought the story. And one of Nina's old boyfriends owns the orange orchards in question, so I managed to get permission for them to film the Outspan harvest, despite the fact that they'll probably slag him off.

The producer also liked the idea of a Wild Dog survey in the Kruger, because the puppies will be learning to walk in July, and guess what? It involves ordinary children sending their photos of the dogs to the Parks Board: there's a **competition** involved. Then they wanted to meet Nelson Mandela.

'Let's try,' I said boldly. 'What about meeting his grandchildren?'

(He has twenty-one). Yes, they liked that, so I'm currently trying to get hold of the ANC in a quest to interview Zidwa and Wolbo.

The BBC could have made a feature on bush fires this weekend. It was Sunday afternoon when the alert came through. Charles and Nina were in Pretoria collecting spare parts with Juliet, and Ant was the other side of the Waterberg with two Dutch air hostesses. There's no fire brigade in Vaalwater. You must fight yourself. I drove up to the Sotho village but found most of the men were drunk and that all the equipment normally used for fire fighting was locked up. I had to go with the few girls I could persuade to join me.

We found the fire had spread fast. By the time we arrived, flames were tearing over the stubble and leaping up into the gum trees. About seventy acres had already gone. The girls tore green branches from gwarie trees and started whacking the fire out. It's unbelievable how it travels and snakes around you. At one stage I had the farm vehicle the wrong side of the flames and had to drive, blindly through black smoke, nearly running over some bewildered dogs sitting the other side.

Shane came along in the end and showed me that the best way to fight a fire is with a box of matches. We back-burnt from a track, managing to save Charles' pump house, although R8,000 worth of electric cable was lost.

The Springboks beat the Australians. Even I watched the Rugby World Cup. It's the first time S.Africa could compete in world anything for 27 years ~ so you can imagine what it has meant for this country.

Most of the people on the farm were crammed into Nina's drawing room. Towards the end of the match a man walked in pointing into his open mouth in an agitated sort of way. He'd been mending his shoes and, using his teeth to pull the thread, had swallowed his needle. It had stuck to the back of his throat. He'd not chosen a good time to ask to be driven to the surgery.

I hope the boy in Bosnia is doing well. While we are hiker hunting, he'll be sniper hunting.

Lots of love, Sophie

Picture of a 1970's Ford Coupé with the words:
'Do you really think so?' written across it.

Germany
27th May 1995

M'darling Sophie –

I'm waiting for paint to dry. I've just started my costume for the 1960's party we're having. Since Robert won't be around I'm going as a wallflower in a cardboard box. The box is the wall; I'm meant to be the flower. Mum sent me her wig (it boasts 'top quality human hair' on the label) that is attached to a black velvet hair band so I can try to make a beehive. I still need accessories like false eyelashes...

Well, Robs has been gone a month now and is having a pretty Hairy-Mary time. Day 3: they were fired at with guns. Day 5: a round from a tank went right into the school where they were living, seriously injuring six men. The man sleeping next to Robert had to have a leg amputated. So, they moved into an old taverna, which they call the Spotty Dog and have engineers sandbagging them in. He's in charge of 250 men. They all have to eat with plastic cutlery and do their business in plastic bags.

And today's headline news is, '*Over 200 UN hostages taken and two French UN killed*'. But if they pull out there'll be a bloodbath. My only comfort is that Robert will, of course, be loving every minute. And he'll be livid if they get brought back before his boys are entitled to their gongs.

It's bloomin' hard work being a single mother in a foreign country when they miss their Daddy. I'm a bit hacked off with Tamzin, who hasn't even sent a postcard since I've been on my own, but I don't suppose people who are detached from it realise how straining it is for me, the worry et al.

I have to keep looking after the other wives too. Today we had an Open Day in the camp to raise money for 'Wives' Entertainment'. I made thirty bags of candyfloss (which is horrid stuff like hairspray and gets absolutely everywhere) and painted the faces of endless children; spiders, tigers, princesses... quite exhausting. A + H were brilliant and kept themselves busy decorating their own bodies.

Atalanta is still miserable at school but they've been having a pretty spoiling time since Half Term started – swimming and going to the zoo. (That was enough to make you weep actually; I won't go again. Some of the cages were so small and dull).

The rest of the regiment get back from Cyprus next week, finishing their six months away. The worst they can get there is a suntan and a hangover but it doesn't stop six months being a long time for the wives. Anyway, life ticks along for us all. Robert's address is: Grapple 6, BFPO XXXX. Do write to him. Mum sent him a large photo of her, Princess Michael and an otter. He is very lucky.

Keep safe and well,

lots of love,

Perry.

Osnabrück

22nd June 1995

Darling Sib,

My bout of gastric 'flu has gone and I'm better now, but I lost all the weight I gained after pleurisy and look like the regimental motto.

Robert is fine – still ducking and diving (bullets). He works incredibly hard, 18 hour-long days and spends any free time writing his Open University essays.

I was driving along the autobahn, feeling gloomy about him being away, when I looked up and there was Mum, smiling down at me from a billboard, dressed as a policewoman in a terribly tight skirt. It was such a shock I burst out laughing, and laughed on and on, with tears gushing out of my eyes all the way home. I had totally forgotten about the day she'd had cold feet. Did she know the ad was for an AIDS campaign?

The next saga of my life is the fumigation of this moth-infested house. It's a six-week operation, I'll have you know, during which we are forced to move out. The problem is so bad that I can collect a teaspoonful of maggots while I'm making a phone call. They creep out of the carpets. The last occupants reported them, but the house lay empty for four months before we moved in, and **nothing** was done about it, so the moths kept breeding in the carpets and have since been munching away at all my clothes and everything, including all Robert's incredibly expensive uniforms. (Not battledress – he's wearing that).

I've written to Alastair, enclosing a sample moth, asking him to send me information on their life-cycle, as I am sure one spray is not adequate. I want the fumigation job done properly. Alastair will probably think I'm barking as this is the first time I've been in touch since he came to our wedding.

I do miss Tadpole. Tamzin wrote to say that she'd had to leave both bullterriers with her mother-in-law over the weekend.

'Poor wee mites had to endure a thunderstorm and spent all night sitting on her knee, shaking like wobbly, black jellies.'

Well, I presume it was the dogs she was talking about and not the children.

Thank you for Hastings's book on the Goanna. Hope you're having fun. Tell me about the loveliness of it all, not the horrors. Love from us all,

Perry xxx

Triple B Ranch
24 Rivers, Vaalwater

Dear Tamzin,

I was determined that *Blue Peter* should feature Horizon Horse Trails and persuaded Bill the director to come up on a recce by laying on a Gospel Choir Competition.

When he arrived Laura, who has become the farm secretary, was lying on Charles and Nina's double bed in an old rugger shirt, with her hair in a top-knot, busy on the telephone. Our phones have wind-up handles, which you spin to get hold of the operator. The more modern ones have buttons so you can use Morse code to reach each other on the farm lines, but you often have to wait ages for an external connection.

'Is this how you all work?' Bill asked in disbelief.

'Hello, Tunnie,' Laura was saying to the operator. 'Do you know where Oom Charles is? …No, well if he makes a call tell him to ring home urgently, someone's been squashed by a trailer of tobacco leaves.'

I don't think they have daily problems quite like this in the *Blue Peter* office.

The other thing that struck Bill was that one of the Triple B Drum Majorettes turned out to be a boy, quite prepared to dress as a girl in white knee socks and a little gold mini-skirt.

'Sotho children would never make a fuss about something trivial like that,' Juliet said. 'They don't have the luxury of hang-ups.'

She'd been gathering the young people together for the competition but was having a problem with transport.

'Do you know,' she said, swallowing hard, 'Oom Bossie Bosman, who is an overtly Rightwing farmer, has spent all night repairing his diesel lorry so he could bring a choir up here. My liberal friends said they were too busy to help.' She leapt into her father's truck to collect another group herself. 'I need to hear through the songs quickly,' she said. 'Last time the choir from 24 Rivers insisted on singing, "When the Lord *satisfied* me" instead of "When the Lord *sanctified* me".'

The next day I took Bill on a donkey cart through the African village where he was impressed by the wire toy cars the children make themselves. He didn't think tobacco sorting was quite the thing for Children's Television though. Although the choir competition worked well, it's something endemic to South Africa so I doubt if they'll come to the Northern Province after all but Bill has booked into Horizon for his hols after the filming ends.

Then, '*Ping*. Thank you for playing,' as Andrew would say. 'That's all sports lovers.'

I am not required by *Blue Peter* anymore. Their research budget is all spent. My contract ended when I was still in the middle of getting together a story about micro-chipping penguins – computer-chips are inserted into the birds so they can be counted like supermarket items and studied easily. I've started sending stories to the BBC Newsroom, conservation stuff like the elephant culling debate, but nothing has developed. Shane and I thought we would be providing the horses for an epic drama to be made on the life of Cecil Rhodes, but they stood us up too. Probably just as well. We've all been so busy.

Juliet's secondary school was 'infiltrated by PAC activists', as they put it on *The SABC News*. In fact they were a collection of teenagers who started thumping the (white) teachers' cars with fence posts and casting spells on any of the pupils unwilling to join them. The manager simply closed the school and Juliet is teaching the farm kids at home.

Meanwhile Horizon Horse Trails has been inundated with KLM air hostesses. Flight *attendants*, you're meant to say. They come up and ride between flights. Ant is in seventh heaven. Shane asked if he would mind helping this last weekend as they had four 'flight attendants' wanting to come on a wilderness trail. He agreed eagerly and went along in Indiana Jones mode, only to find they were all men. It rained and his matches got wet.

'Everything got wet.' Laura has just told me.

I've been asked to look after the other visitors and the self-catering clients, who are staying up at the main farm in the old house that I helped Nina renovate. There are sixteen coming this weekend and I have thirty-two hikers, or did have. Frankly, they're proving more than a liability. They promptly get lost now. We've marked what Charles calls 'A Braille Trail'; you could feel your way round. But no, they insist on following cattle paths, which as Juliet pointed out, take them to a trough. But no further. There's not exactly anyone around to ask for directions.

The farm workers think the hikers must be loopy to pay good money to walk round here with a great pack on their back and keep away from them. When I asked one old boy if he'd seen, '*Die mens van Jo'burg wie loop*' ('The people from Johannesburg who walk,') he looked at me in disgust and said:

'*Huh. Almal dronk.*' He thinks they must be drunk and probably dangerous.

It the midst of all this someone stole the telephone lines going to 24 Rivers. They can make money selling the copper wire for scrap. It was maddening, the third time this has happened and must have lost Charles a great deal of business.

When the operator finally got through, I said 'If it happens again, please ring the Police straight away.'

'How will I know that the lines have been stolen?'

'Because you won't be able to get through to us.'

'But it would mean that I would have to pay for the call to the Police,' she said.

'But you're the Operator!' Local calls cost 50 cents.

'I'll pay.' Charles called out from the other side of the room.

'But *Tannie*,' I said, patiently, 'The wire that gets stolen belongs to you; to your employers.'

This had not occurred to her.

Once all the visitors go I can sit peacefully in my room, drawing while Sam grazes outside on the lawn. The only problem about painting is that I think about myself too much. I didn't mean to, but when I look back at last year I find that I had put people, time, work, etc before God, gradually letting Grant have priority, which was disastrous. I read this morning, 'Putting any person before God in our lives results in false expectations, disappointment and hurt and finally alienation.' Umm.

But I've nothing to moan about at all. In fact all the cups continuously overflow. Sunlight is streaming through the trees and I'm off to ride my pony across the most beautiful land on earth. If I go fast this can be quite relaxing as the speed seems to block out any thoughts at all.

Lots of love,

Sophie

CHAPTER THIRTEEN

Hardacre Farm

Dear Sib –

Great pangs of guilt for not writing. I haven't even thanked you for looking after us all in March. V. tired. Fattie Guy is demanding and gives me only four-hour sleeps before he wakes to consume more grub.

Hope you're feeling in the pink. Johnty is on holiday. He spent the first few days in bed with a bug – typical, but since then we've been having fun.

We all went to Marwell Zoo - saw white rhino, and a zebra doing a wee-wee. Thought of you. Then went into the Tapir House. Right on cue the Brazilian tapir did a huge poo in the water. The shell-suited woman next to me nearly fainted, but I was fascinated. Tapirs get terribly constipated if they can't go in running water.

Hughie was, I'm afraid, much more interested in the diggers on the construction site at the zoo than he was in the animals, until a Vietnamese pig ate a piece of his Lego.

Mum dropped in having been working flat out doing otterish things. She peered at Guy and said: 'He looks peculiar.'

Raddy, who happened to be riding by said 'But, Daphne that is not in the "Be A Good Granny Handbook".'

To which Mum replied 'I never follow handbooks.'

To which Raddy said 'Well, I think he looks just like you.'

Quite a fight broke out. Raddy had the advantage of being up on a horse and after a while was able to toss her head and trot off.

I rang Perry who is unwell again. She cried and cried. It's all my fault for not having written to her, Oh dear. Her Army house in Germany is infested with moths - which eat everything she has so lovingly made over the years. She'd had to take up the carpets and have everything sprayed.

On top of this she has to be ill, look after the children and miss Robert all alone, so we must all write like mad. I've been feeling so dreadful about not contacting her I've promised to write to all these wives I hardly know. (Well not quite).

My animals are driving me potty. We have new next-door neighbours with two rampant dogs who have, in the short time they've been here, serviced every bitch within a ten mile radius.

The people themselves are nice though. Bod is well, Thelma is still alive. I want to bring Leonard the donkey over for Hughie - but don't think Johnty does.

Lots of love – do, do write to P.

T xxx

Dear P,

Did you know that Aunt Vera was once kidnapped by brigands in Crete and held for ransom? Her husband came up with the dosh but she was having such fun gadding about in the mountains with her captors that she didn't want to leave.

I too am embracing life as a good time girl, riding through the Okavango with six flamboyant Italians. We came across a herd of buffalo today, so large it seemed to stretch from one horizon to the other. Found we were inadvertently pushing them down onto our one, small, Neapolitan Marchesa who didn't ride and was sitting in a dugout canoe, a hollowed tree known as a mokoro. It didn't exactly give her much protection from the most dangerous animals on earth, but she returned glowing.

Am taking them to stay with my friend Jez who is managing a camp on the Borro River and has promised to take us out on foot to watch lion. Thinking of you, in my wanderings.

Love, Sophie

Dear P,

Do you know about rain trees? Their leaves get eaten by froghopper beetles who, after extracting nutrients from the sap, literally pee the water out onto anyone sitting beneath in such quantity you would think it had started to rain.

I've been staying with Jez, the Botswana equivalent of a forsaken Army wife, having long, long chats. Sarah-Jane has given him the boot.

Just as he was at his most gloomy, Jez was called to inspect the cook, Whitey, whose testicles were expanding at an alarming rate. Do you get this happening in Germany? They grew so big that he had to be evacuated in the middle of the night. All the staff were clutching themselves the next morning, looking quite worried.

Jez just said, 'It's a pity Whitey had to go – selfish of me really but I'd just got him making Chipping Norton cinnamon doughnuts.'

I made Jez give me a lesson in how to pole a mokoro – rather precarious, no spare pole and you should see the size of the crocodiles just downstream.

Love,

Sophie

Maun, Botswana

Dear Juliet,

Maun is as dry and dirty as ever; the place where goats walk the streets and donkeys seem to come to die. They have three swearwords here: Jesus, Christ and Jesus Christ, otherwise conversation is dull and basic. Life on a bar stool. I find them quite uncomfortable.

No sooner had Sarah-Jane managed to get all her horses into the Okavango ~ a long, two-day ride of some 100kms ~ than they all decided to run back to their dustbowl of a paddock in town. Jigsaw got lost in the process, which threw her completely. There are lion everywhere. Jez went off to look for 'lost pieces of Jigsaw'. He hired a helicopter at great expense and managed to spot him from the air, but then lost Sarah-Jane amidst the angst. By the time I managed to get to her camp, she'd brought all the horses back with the help of a hunter called Peter. He's good-looking, laughs readily and is confident about coping with predators. How does she do it? When my car ground to a halt in the middle of the only roundabout in Maun and I found (miracle of miracles) a competent man to look after me, the relationship didn't go two inches. It ended with me saying, 'Thank you very much' on the roundabout.

I'm pleased because the local Police Commissioner promised me he would deal with any cases of cruelty to animals. It's rife. One donkey, which must have been hit by a lorry, was left injured and dying by the roadside for three days, dehydrating visibly in the terrible heat. No one was prepared to put it out of its misery because it's illegal to touch other people's animals. The Commissioner, who was in all his gold-corded finery when I met him, agreed that this was absurd and that I must tell the white community to report any further problems to him personally. Mum would have been so proud of me, but I have to admit I was only at the Police Station to pay a speeding fine. Now I learn that the reason you can't touch other people's livestock is because bestiality is so prevalent.

So, please pray for Sarah-Jane and the donkeys and me; I'll be in the Okavango for a while, then have to drive a long way by myself, through country where I fear my old car and few possessions would be considered rather more valuable than my life. And where I'm going I doubt if mechanics will be easy to find.

I hope the political activists have developed a better sense of direction. Naughty boys. Thinking of you all on the farm,
Lots of love,
Sophie

Dear P,

Sarah-Jane was excited about showing me her new camp, Macateer's. It's simple and elegant, looking out over a lagoon where lechwe come to graze. Little monkeys live in the trees above the tents and come to see me in the morning as if to show off their babies. I lay in bed last night listening to elephant shaking nuts from the palm trees, while lion roared in the distance. It's wild and remote with animals everywhere. The riding is incredible: marrrr-vellous, as the Italians would say. While SJ has gone to buy more horses, I'm staying here with Tigger, Rowena and a GPS gadget, attempting to map the area. We ride past herds of tsessebe and zebra while great flocks of birds rise up as we cross the floodplains. You're going to have to think of a way of joining me sometime.

Love,

Sophie

> Deutschland, and shocking autumnal leaves everywhere
>
> 27th August 1995

Darling Sib,

We've just spent four days in Trendleburg, three hours to the south – famed for its castles. The children were fed so much drivel about *Beauty and the Beast* I need my tongue cut out, but it was tremendous fun. The German food is as filthy as ever though, all fried and greasy. It's quite normal not to have a vegetable on the plate, apart from chips.

I haven't heard from Robs for almost two weeks, which is an odd feeling. And it's scary because he is on the Confrontation Zone, right in the thick of it. I was so lonely I phoned Lucinda, who now lives happily in Ireland and always makes me laugh. Atalanta confided in her all about her boyfriend who she'd kissed on the lips and described as 'an enchantment'. I had no idea she was in a relationship at all.

3rd September and still no news from Robert. I went to the NAAFI to buy loo paper today and picked up news that there have been heavy casualties. Now I can't block out the awful imaginings. The waiting is horrid, horrid, horrid. I keep bursting into tears – rushing out of the room as I don't want the children to see.

4th September. I was convinced that Robert was dead this morning. Gone forever.

5th September. Sophie, there's still no news of Robert. I've been told I must try to be patient but it is unendurable. I wish Tadpole could be here; I need someone solid to hold. I'm going to ring Tamzin now and ask how she is. I'll write again soon; do I keep sending letters to Maun or South Africa?

I had just put down the phone to Tamzin when it rang, quite startling me. Unbelievably, it was Robert, ringing from some UN base. He is alive and rather enjoying himself. They were just out of communication for a while.

Tamzin said the dogs have been a great embarrassment. They went to spend a weekend with some very smart, well organized people who said, 'Do bring the dogs if they don't mind sleeping in the kitchen.' The sleeping wasn't a problem. But there was a hatch between the kitchen and dining room. When Tadpole heard Tamzin coming down for dinner she leapt completely through the open hatch. Maud tried to follow her. However, she is much heavier than Tadpole and did a belly-flop, landing in a lemon meringue pie. There was a second pie but she trod in it as she was struggling back onto her feet. Sticky, yellow goo was then ground into the Persian carpet.

Having spent my time tirelessly raising funds for the 'Wives Entertainment' I thought I'd go along. It turned out to be men on stage doing *The Full Monty*.

Love,

Perry

FAX: From Sophie Neville,
C/o African Horseback Safaris,
Maun

Dear Perry,

Thank you for your letter, which somehow reached me before I left Botswana. I had no idea you had been ill. Mum said that on top of everything else you had pleurisy. Isn't that when your lung tissue starts sticking together? How dreadful. If you want me to come to Germany do say. I could fly Maun-Windhoek and take a Lufthansa flight from Windhoek but what airport in Germany do I need a ticket for? I'm here in Maun until 27/10/95 then C/o this Rhino Trust FAX number until 15th November.

Thinking of you,

Lots of love,

Sophie

FAX TO: Sophie Neville, C/o African Horseback Safaris, Maun

DATE: 22:10: 95

Dear Sophie,

Dad is in hospital. He collapsed when he was busy standing as Governor at some school in North Wales. He had three days of tests, having his heart monitored. He is absolutely fine, thank God. It's a bit frightening as I always imagine him as unchanged in the last ten years, which is ridiculous. They do have to remove an inflamed gall bladder. He says he feels much better and will be out in two days. So, no: no need to fly back. Johnty and Tamzin drove out to see us, which was wonderful. They got me out and about and laughing again. One lunchtime I said, 'I do think you do need to wipe Guy's nose.' A bit of white stuff was hanging out. Tamzin took hold of it with a tissue, tweaked and pulled. And pulled. And pulled some more. It was extraordinary; a long strand of spaghetti came out, perfectly intact. Do you want metric or imperial measurements? It was 10½ inches: 26½ cms long.

Robs is back in a fortnight's time. I can't wait. It's been a long old haul. But it never stops; in January he's probably doing a six-week course in England and then has five weeks in Canada next June. And he's actually losing money being away. Adds insult to injury.

Lucinda has just had a second baby called Flora, at the risk of being known as 'Marg'.

Tons of love, P xxx

Hardacre Farm

1:9:95

Dearest Sib –

Happy birthday to you. Thank you for the Madonna bra-shaped earrings; they're a mite dangerous but who cares? I'm feeling old and worn out by these boys. Guy is crawling for England, forehead covered in bruises. He has discovered dogs' water-bowls and that eating leaves makes you choke and that this results in a wizard reaction from Mummy (me). I'll send a pic of the church where Guy and Hughie were christened. Hot News: Lu Llewellyn has just become engaged; Peewee will fill you in on the details.

Lots of love,

T xxx

Dear T,

Les Adventures de Sophie en Afrique cont… I am, to my amazement, in Etosha where I've just had breakfast with a herd of springbok. It took ages and ages to get here, 1,200km from Maun in searing heat that melted me, my *bakkie* and the very road. My guardian angel came in the guise of a large Herero woman needing a lift. She was dressed traditionally in a long, Victorian frock, huge horn-like headdress and a dour expression. I feel quite elated and am as happy, as happy as happy, driving out across the pans by myself to spend hours drawing animals. I'm on my way to join the Rhino Trust in Damaraland where I've been invited to take part in a wildlife census. And to paint.
Lots of love, Sophie

FAX TO: Sophie Neville

C/o Save the Rhino Trust,

Khorxias,

Namibia.

DATE: 12:11:95

Dear Sophie,

What lovely desert postcards…. But have you seen any gerbils? All very dull here by comparison; I'm simply nurturing my babies, but thought you would like a fax. Johnty said he'd send this from the office.

Perry and Robert are together at last and are in (or going to be in) Florida. What bliss. They're coming by on their way home. I do hope cousin Tadpole, who has just had a dreadful cat-scrap with Maudie, will be looking less scared.

Mum is being a Fairy Godmother in a pantomime near Cardiff this year. You have to admire the energy – but why can't it be channelled in conventional directions? (Like baby-sitting).

Dad is being left to fend for himself so is coming to Hampshire for Christmas with his friend Albert. It will be such fun. Hughie is getting a farmyard. Can't wait. Johnty is a bit worried about Albert and Dad sharing a bedroom (ie: what people might think about this). But Albert says he'll bring his blue Tardis caravan. It looks exactly like a portable toilet. Johnty doesn't know about this.

Meanwhile life goes on in Hampshire… the shooting season is in full swing. I'm still playing tennis and riding regularly.

Ian T……….. was spotted kissing a woman (not his wife) on Raddy's drive and Hughie keeps seeing an imaginary man standing on the wall.

We have a new Swedish *au pair* who is possibly the most selfish person I've ever met in my life. Her self-centredness did not pay off when she tried it on Raddy. The poor girl was subjected to one of her BEST rages and ended up crying for about twenty-four hours. She has been working rather hard ever since. I don't think she'll either forget it or put a foot wrong again. What a joy.

I wish I had Tracy here, can you remember? She was Raddy's nanny who helped you retrieve Bod the day Guy was born. She wants to travel around Africa. Do any of your friends need someone good with horses to help out on the safaris? I attach a letter from her with a CV.

Lots of love,

Tamzin

Dear Perry,

I am in Namibia. The gemsbok I learn, can let its body temperature rise to 113° F (45°C). I can't. This little snow kaffir, as Billy calls all English girls, has finally begun to melt. I sit painting the mountainous landscape until it simply gets too hot, when I stagger off for breakfast at a nearby lodge made almost entirely of reeds. The restaurant at the end of the world. A tall German called Hoffy and a girl with emerald, snake-like eyes seem to take it in turns to stand behind the bar and do nothing.

Blythe Loutit has lent me the use of a hut about a mile down the valley, which acts as a base for the Rhino Trust, but I arrived to find no one here; no sign of a census team and no way of contacting them. I thought, 'What is a girl to do?' but was happy painting while I waited to see what would happen.

Sitting in the desert is more eventful than you might imagine. I was sketching away from a rock on the hillside, when I saw a Land Rover come out of the lodge, go down the road for a while and then drive round and round in tight circles. Hoffy told me later that an Egyptian cobra had wound itself around his drive shaft and they were trying to get rid of it.

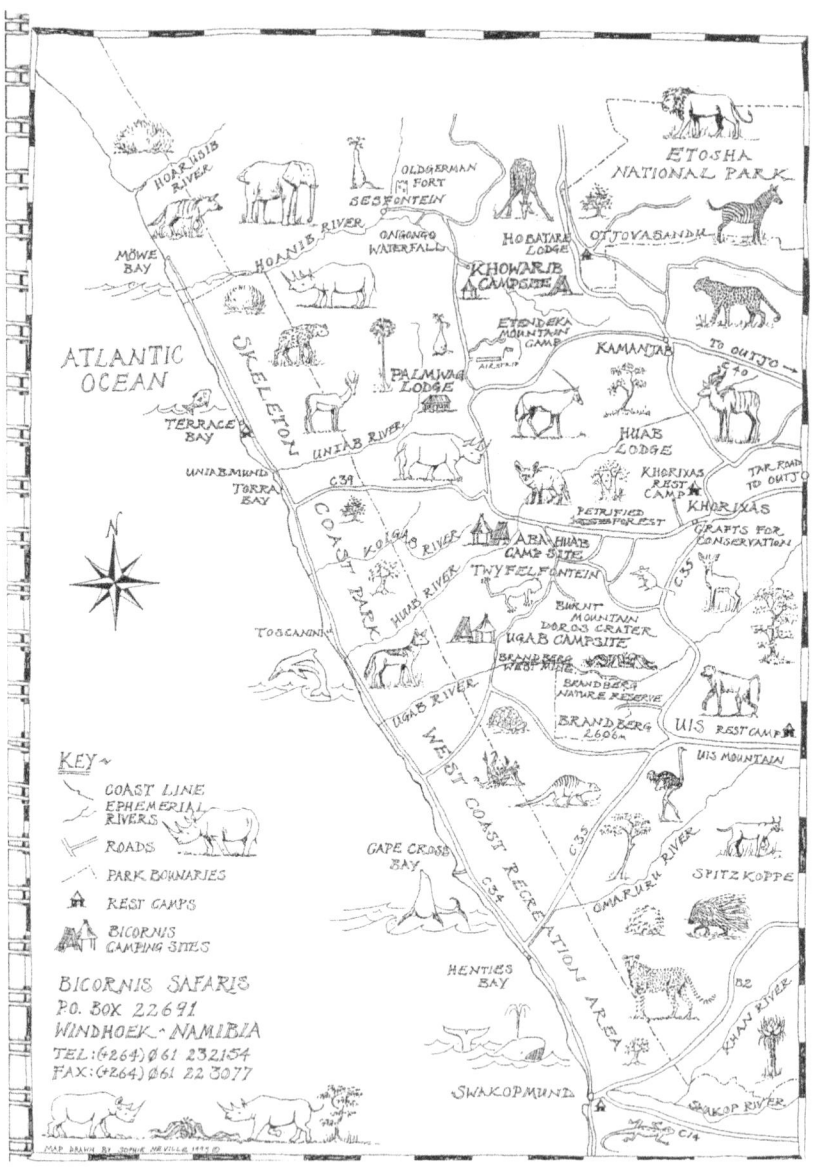

After ten nights alone, living off baked beans and potatoes, I was so hungry I staggered up to the lodge for supper but found it packed full.

I had to ask if I could squeeze onto a small table with a young couple I thought must be foreign tourists.

'No, no, we're not. We're Namibian.' the chap said. 'My father is a fisherman so I grew up in Walvis Bay, but my wife is originally from Sweden.'

They had met when they were working as international models but now have a landscaping business, making little deserts in people's gardens with river stones and aloes. They said I should come and see them if I was ever by the coast.

'Do you know my cousin's wife Julia….?' I started to ask them.

'Oh, Yes. The girl from Argyll who can play the saxophone standing in a boat…' They told me that Jamie has just made his brother-in-law water-ski across the Corryvreckan, an infamous Scottish whirlpool, dressed as a lemur. He tucked the tail into his life jacket but the hairy suit got so heavy when it was wet he thought he might sink.

The wildlife census, I discovered, had been postponed. Instead I found myself driving over the mountains, looking for desert elephants with Blythe, Rudi, all their dogs and an Australian film crew.

The rather brash female producer spent her time in the back of an open vehicle, rolling up the sleeves of her pink T-shirt and splaying her legs to tan the insides of her thighs. She flicked back her hair aggressively, making me feel somewhat surplus to requirements.

Rudi, who was shuddering at the sight of her, whispered, 'You're our guest; you just keep on painting, Sausage.'

We found a large herd of elephant almost immediately, browsing calmly in a ravine, which made it possible for Rudi to be interviewed sitting on a fallen mopane tree with the animals in the background.

I sketched away from the Land Rover while Blythe was speaking to her scouts on the radio.

'The problem is,' she said, dropping the mouthpiece to her lap, 'that the Australians are now going to expect it to be just as easy to interview me standing in front of a rhino and the trackers haven't been able to pick up anything yet.'

'Has one ever charged you?'

'Oh yes,' she said. 'The worst time was when I was caught out on an open gravel plain, with my dog barking at my heels. I had to stand stock still until the rhino was nearly on me and then step to the side like a bullfighter. But you can't do that with a film crew dithering around.'

No one could find the rhinoceros.

'Do you know,' Blythe said, 'Once upon a time I used to sell cosmetics. Believe it or not, it was less aggravating than this.'

As we made our way over the rocky mountains things began to get increasingly strained. Blythe and Rudi got fed up with the producer nagging them. She was in a different vehicle with the crew but we said all sorts of regrettable things before realising that Blythe was wearing a radio-mike and I had to disconnect the battery before Rudi said something rude on purpose.

Towards the end of the long hot day, the scouts' vehicle developed problems and kept stalling. We'd go 50 yards and it would stall, 100 yards and it would stop and not start again. Neither Blythe's mechanic nor the television technicians could work out why. By now the Australian producer was getting tetchy.

'I think I might know what the problem is,' I said, joining the others under the bonnet.

I had a funny feeling the air filter must have clogged up with dust, so unclipped the casing and shook it out. It was full of gunk.

'You see,' the Sausage said to the producer. 'I once had a Chrysler Sunbeam that was prone to exactly the same condition.'

The scouts found a lone bull standing on a hillside next to a bottle tree in the glowing evening light.

'They'll get excellent footage,' Rudi said. 'That Rhino isn't going anywhere. Those trackers have been running after him for 35 kilometres.'

I took a photograph of the sound recordist walking towards him with his tape recorder on his head.

After ten days in Damaraland I left Blythe and Rudi in the rather bleak desert town of Khorixas, where they're based, and drove on south alone. The roads seemed to be made of rubble.

All I had for supper was the remains of a tinned fruitcake that Nick had brought me from *Fortnum and Mason* but I was determined to camp off the main track.

This was a mistake.

After passing the great Brandeberg Mountain, I went about two kilometres up a rough track and parked into the wind. It was coming across the moon-like landscape at 70mph. As I started to get camping things out of the back of my car the hatchback door slammed down hard on my head.

I sat, dazed and disorientated, thinking, 'You stupid, stupid girl. You could be lying with your neck cut open by the glass and no one would ever find you.'

I went and slept right next to the road. As it was I saw no one at all until I reached the coast a day later.

One of Rudi's rangers had invited me to stay in Walvis Bay but he was out of town. I was driving slowly down his street, wondering what to do next when I recognised John, the chap who had once been an international model, unloading his Landcruiser. He invited me in for tea.

'Where are you staying?'

I took a deep breath and said casually, 'Oh, I was going to see if I could rent a self-catering cottage on the lagoon,' even though I couldn't afford to.

'OK. Would you like me to book one for you?'

'Yes, please.' John went off and made a call.

'We would have asked you to stay,' his wife Maria said, 'But we have a chap called Benedict Allen and his photographer here for the week and they have an awful lot of equipment. Camel saddles and stuff.'

'All organized,' John said coming back from the phone. 'I'll take you down there. It's not far.'

I quite wanted to see the camels but followed him through town and alongside the sparkling lagoon. Avocet and flamingos were standing against the sunset. John pulled up outside an impressive house on the esplanade.

'Here we are,' he said. 'My mother has a guest cottage where you can stay for free. Those self-catering cottages are far too expensive and this will be more secure.'

It was my birthday and being able to completely relax was the greatest present. After all that time in the desert, sliding into lovely smooth sheets after a long hot bath was unimaginably luxurious.

'We'll pick you up at about 7.00pm. There's a party on in Swakopmund and we're taking you out to dinner afterwards,' John told me. 'Then we'll get your wheel bearings fixed.'

He could hear they'd been grinding. My car ended up spending three days in the garage and I was in the cottage for longer.

Benedict Allen was at the party. He was wearing a hairy springbok skin waistcoat, like the one I made Solly, and told me he was walking up the Namibian coast with the three camels.

'Oh, why?'

'I'm an explorer.' he informed me.

I thought Namibia was a rather modern country to explore, but interesting all the same. Extraordinary person. The Namibians couldn't understand him at all. He doesn't drive a car or use a penknife, he doesn't wear sunglasses in the desert, let alone sunscreen, but I think looking a bit battered and peely was good for the series he was making of the trip for the BBC. Being tall he has long limbs, so by holding a small video camera at arm's length he can film himself.

'Here I am, alone at last, (puff, pant) making my way deep into the interior…' (great intake of breath).

'Benedict, you pillock, you've still got the sea in the background.' Maria said, watching the rushes on her VHS. 'He's not really alone either; you'll see John's little blue van in a sec.'

This van was lined throughout in shaggy fake fur and known as 'The Love Bug'. It didn't look like a reliable back-up vehicle at all.

'No,' Maria said laconically.

We went to see Benedict's camels at the riding stables. A sign had been put up on the side of their kraal saying:

BEWARE – THESE CAMELS BITE/KICK, but I thought they were fascinating creatures. They have a hard callous beneath their chests for squashing predators. Not that there are any in Walvis Bay.

BRISKET FOR CRUSHING PREDITORS

Even after resting for a week, the camels didn't want to move anywhere. Benedict just hauled on the lead reins while they voiced their objection.

You have to admire Benedict's determination. And the sheer guts. He'd managed to persuade the SWAPO Namibian Government[xviii] to let him walk the camels miles through the Restricted Diamond Area where no one is usually allowed to go under any circumstances.

Up in Khorixas I had met a man who owned a chain of supermarkets and was driving through the desert, sponsoring Benedict by leaving food packages for him to find along his route. He seems to eat nothing but tins of curried meatballs.

John's mother, Denise, was a SWAPO Town Councillor.

'My husband said, "Someone has to do the job," so I stood for election,' she said. 'It's easier to do without Benedict in the office. My printer has not been quite the same since I found him standing about, with a helpless expression on his face, while reams of paper poured onto the floor.'

I didn't have the nerve to ask if I could use her photocopier after that. I was working on a decorative map of the Kunene for Blythe when I received a fax, via Vaalwater, from the BBC. I had to hire an office, there in Walvis Bay, and start finding new locations for *Global Sunrise*. They've now decided that they want to film leopard at dawn – for live television. Deary me; I've been living – working as a safari guide in the Waterberg, which probably has a higher density of leopard than anywhere in Africa and how many have I seen? In my whole life? Two. Now I have an aggressive (and therefore probably inexperienced) researcher demanding leopard in tree, with warthog kill, surrounded by hyena, at dawn on 1st January. I felt like replying: HAVE YOU EVER WORKED WITH WILD ANIMALS, DUCKY? But no, I pulled out the stops (my contacts book) and put her in touch with John Varty, whose mother's house I once painted. I also sent her information on some expensive (although somewhat *Afrique en plastique*) private reserves, which have about 100 game scouts per square inch (and are so notoriously well organized that they won't need me for the filming).

I had a lovely time in Walvis Bay though. A lady with a gold Mercedes lent me her big black thoroughbred to ride and I'd go out every evening. Maria took me off in a Morris pick-up, with her two Great Danes standing in the back, to walk with the flamingos at the salt farm at the far end of the lagoon as the sun sank into the sea. We watched dolphin from the balcony of the yacht club and then went on to an aquarium where we walked through an underwater arch, looking up at stingrays and sharks. They had brightly lit tanks full of jellyfish, sea slugs and crustaceans, and I stood there sketching for ages.

I badly wanted to go up the coast into Angolan waters on John's father's fishing boat. I could have gone out for a week. It's the only privately owned vessel of its kind; massive, with eight diesel engines - enough so that the ship can go sideways. I went round it in awe. It's a trawler with incredibly complicated radar and navigation equipment. John said going out into that sea is fantastic, and you see a lot of marine mammals.

In fact they have a terrible problem with seals, which leap into the nets, going into a feeding frenzy and making it complicated for the crew to haul their catch aboard. One was sucked up the pipe used to bring up the fish and found itself on the deck, barking and snapping.

John made one thing clear: you cannot go out if you have any tendency for seasickness at all.

'The seas are always rough and the smell of fish and diesel fumes takes a great deal of getting used to. There are no ports further north; nothing there,' he explained. 'If you start to get sick you are in real danger of dying of dehydration as there's no way of getting you off the boat until they return to Walvis Bay, the following Saturday night.'

I decided that physically it would be something I couldn't handle and sadly declined.

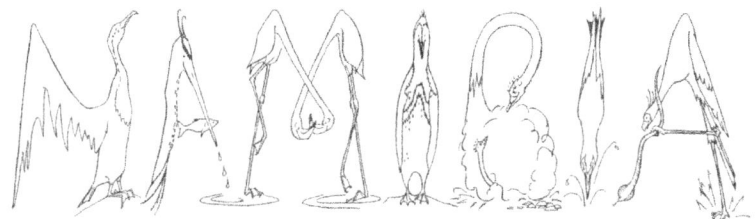

Instead I bought myself a permit for the Namib-Naukluft National Park and drove into nowhere. I found a tree under which I thought I would camp and had just organized myself for the night when a man appeared and started chatting to me in Afrikaans. It was obvious that he was trying to get something out of me but I knew not what. After a while I told him I was going off for a walk, only I soon found he was following me. It was a bit creepy, but I thought, 'I can't let him spoil the evening.' I turned around and said I was going to walk up the high sand dunes, the other side of the dry river, (only I didn't know the Afrikaans for dune so I had to call the colossal dune a hill. A sand-hill). It was about three hundred feet high and it was deceptively hard work wading through the sand. He watched me struggling for a while and then explained the easiest way to the top was to walk up a scree of rock.

Then he came up with me.

So I ended up sitting on top of this dune, looking out over the barren landscape with a strange Namibian man. What is a girl to talk about in such a situation? We talked about repentance. He thought it was an excellent idea. But by the time we reached my camp he was looking awkward again, his eyes shifting from side to side, and his breath coming in jerks.

I was just thinking that I ought to be sensible and lock myself into the front seat of my car when he closed his eyes, gulped and said, 'My mother sent me to ask you if you could spare us some sugar.'

He'd been so embarrassed about asking that he'd climbed the 300ft sand dune before he'd been able to gather enough courage.

I had to do a brave thing the next day. I had driven past an ecological research station called Gobabeb and thought, 'I would *love* to stay there.'

I knew they don't even allow visitors; that it's virtually impossible to see round, but I'd met the Director when I was with Blythe and thought she would like a copy of the map that I had just completed. I drove past the officious *Verboden* signs and found all the scientists sitting around drinking coffee.

They loved the map and asked to see all my other artwork. I brought out the graphics I had been working on only all I had were designs for children's T-shirts. To my delight they asked if I would be able to stay and design some for them. So I did. I took the word Gobabeb and drew the animals they study there, tok-toki beetles, scorpions, geckoes, golden moles, and drew them into the letters while I spent my evenings painting watercolours of the extraordinary landscape.

The scientists themselves were immersed in their strange work. I ended up accompanying an Israeli biologist, who declared she was studying the mating behaviour of melons. Nara melons. Off we went into the dunes in the middle of the day, walking on sand so hot it burnt me through the soles of my hiking boots. She started trying to catch the tiny beetles that pollenate the prickly plants.

'I need you to paint numbers on the backs of each beetle,' the scientist then declared.

'?' It was like asking me to paint a ladybird's wings. I thought this was idiotic but she was persistent. I managed to do it with Tipp-ex in the end, although it rather ruined my fine paintbrush. It was fascinating to be able to look at all the insects we found under a microscope.

I've reached Soussosveli, where I've been walking through more great dunes, accompanied this time by a South African sculptor. My plan is to drive on south to a harbour on the coast called Luderitz, which I'm told is a place one cannot not go to. I hope it will be fun there; it's a long way to drive.

Here are some shells and flamingo feathers that I found for the children,

Lots of love,

Sophie

Dear Perry,

I arrived in Luderitz and thought, 'Why on earth did anyone tell me to come here?'

It seemed stark and ugly with a constant gale blowing in from the sea. The light was blinding. I had driven 450 kilometres along gravel roads to get there, and had nowhere to stay.

I went to a dismal and expensive hotel to try the number of someone Maria told me to ring. She was out. I asked if I would be able to stay at the hotel, but it was full.

I then began to have the most extraordinary time. A girl with long, brown, shaggy hair and brightly coloured clothes drew up in a dormobile painted with daisies and shouted my name across the street.

'Hey, Babe. Groovy. We've been sooo worried about you. Follow me back to the pad.' I was shown into what she called *our music room*. 'Do you mind dossing down under the synth?'

It was full of black, electrical, sound equipment, microphone stands and a drum kit.

'Nathan has a really cool band.'

Then Nathan came in.

'Hey Dude. Far out. We were just speaking about you,' his girlfriend said, flinging her arms round him. 'He's been at sea an age-and-a-half.'

Nathan had thick, waist length, blond hair and was wearing a red wetsuit. He'd just come from having a piano lesson with Father O'Leary, the Catholic priest, on his way up from the harbour.

'I had to jump off the boat and run up there.' he said. 'Oh, Babe, it's fab to be home. Won't you comb my hair?'

Nathan, it transpired, was a diamond diver. Although the mineral rights on land belong to the Government, companies can lease concession areas of the seafloor.

'You must come and see our boat.'

Off we all went back down to the harbour. I boarded a small fishing vessel, about thirty-foot long. It had a three-sided wheelhouse with a two-ring stove, where Nathan told me he cooked stews, above steps that led down to an engine room. The crew slept in shifts on three mattresses around the open V8 engine.

'I tell you we don't get out of these wetsuits. We kip in them, jig in them; the lot,'

'How long for?'

'Something like ten days at a time, but I've just come in from three weeks at sea.'

The odd-looking jig was in the bows. One diver would go underwater with a thing like a giant Hoover, which would suck up gravel onto the deck. This was then passed through the tiered jig, where the other divers would feverishly sort the stones, looking for diamonds.

'Now the sea is cold. You keep your mask and your booties on and don't have an inch of skin showing.'

What a life.

We went out to a bar that night – a vast, dark panelled room built in the 1900s, where all the diamond divers were hanging out. I was plied with grapefruit schnapps. The atmosphere was smoky but electric; it must have been similar in the classic gold rush times; all the talk about diamonds, concessions and what changes might come in.

'What about sea life on the ocean floor?' I asked.

'We try to take care,' Nathan said. 'You see amazing creatures and it's not bad if you're working by hand with a small machine, but if the big boys come in, they'll chow the whole ecosystem down there.'

When we returned to the house Nathan plonked himself down on the sofa next to me and said, 'You know why I'm doing all this?'

'You want to start a recording studio.'

'Yes, that. But I need to train to be a surgeon. My folks are both dead so I must find my own fees.'

He dropped a formal-looking photo album in my lap. I opened it and took a deep breath. They watched me as I slowly turned the thick, black pages. They were beautiful photographs.

Heartbreaking. An Irish nurse was examining an emaciated woman, with huge terrified eyes. Another showed rows and rows of refugees patiently waiting for food, lined up against the setting sun. There was Nathan, looking younger with two tiny, dark, pot-bellied children sitting on his lap. He explained that when he was conscripted into the Army he became a war medic, operating in Angola and Somalia.

'You end up taking bullets out of arms that thin,' he said, holding his thumb and forefinger together. They often had limited drugs. 'I would end up having to perform amputations by blowing dope up children's noses or using amphetamines.' Horse drugs. 'You get a hella-va-lota experience.' He slammed the album shut and put it back on the shelf. 'But hey Chick. What makes you click?'

I ended up riding a racehorse along the rocky coast. It reared every time we came across flamingos but I rode up into the hills, finding a brown hyena den, and was able to explore the hinterland. I also wanted to get out to the islands.

'You can do WHATEVER you want to do, if you want it badly enough,' Nathan said. 'We'll put you into a wetsuit and you can paddle out on my surfboard.'

Puuunuff. The nearest island was about a mile offshore. I didn't use the surfboard. I arranged to go out with a girl called Imca who worked for Nature Conservation. She was off to release de-oiled penguins. I found her loading them into her Land Rover in plastic crates. Goodness they can peck.

We hooked-up a trailer with a substantial rubber boat on it and made our way along a rocky road, through the desert before cutting towards the shore.

'They'll smell the sea in a minute,' Imca said, 'And start to get excited.'

They did. A great eehawing came from behind the back seat as the penguins started to bray with excitement. They sound just like donkeys.

The sea was so icy cold that my feet hurt as we launched the boat. There's no way that I could ever have paddled in that sea on a surfboard. The current would have ripped me down the coast. We loaded the crates of penguins and roared out towards an island called Halifax where Imca wanted to let them go amongst an established colony. I arrived soaking wet from the spray. The sun was hot, but I was so cold that I ripped off my wet trousers and laid them under a rock so they could dry without blowing away. There were penguins everywhere, looking up at me as I stood there in my knickers. Imca tipped up the crates and the captive birds waddled delightedly into the waves.

There are a number of old buildings on the island, once used by coastguards. They were full of penguins. As I looked around they peered at me quizzically from around doorframes and jumped up steps in their shyness. Imca took me up a small mountain, telling me of all the other amazing islands along the coast; Roastbeef Island, Plumpudding Island, Possession Island…

There's an abandoned diamond mining settlement outside Luderitz called Kolmanskop. I was shown around by one of the divers' girlfriends who is a guide there. There used to be so many diamonds in parts of Namibia that at night you could see them lying on the sand, shining in the moonlight. Cash from sales enabled the importation of European possessions from teacups to entire skittle alleys. Extensive stone houses, originally built for the managers of the mine, are now filling with sand as the desert re-claims its own. Luderitz clings to this faded glory too. I walked into a once elegant, German drawing room, which is now a bakery. Looking past the counters and through a door into another parlour I saw a derelict old lady, sitting on a bed beneath a dirty chandelier in a high-ceilinged room. Her hands were smoothing a brightly crocheted counterpane. It was like a glimpse of a scene from *Cabaret*.

Someone asked me if I would like to sail down the coast on a yacht bound for Cape Town. One of the diamond divers would have driven my car to Johannesburg, but I declined, regretfully. I felt committed to the BBC project and that I should return home before too long.

I stopped at the Fish River Canyon on the way back but it was still a long, long way home. Nathan said I must call him if I broke down.

'I'll come and rescue you, wherever you are in Namibia, but Sister, once you're over the border, you're on your own.'

The journey ended up being 8,000 kilometres in all, by myself in a sixteen-year-old pick-up. But it was good. The things I've seen. The things I've done. And the people I've met. If I had travelled with a companion, or had money, it wouldn't have been the same.

Nina asked if I had ever felt in danger but typically it was when I was back here, unpacking, that I nearly trod on a scorpion – in my own bedroom. I killed it with a paintbrush and flushed it down the loo.

Let me know how you all are,

Lots of love,

Sophie

Hardacre Farm
- By hand -

Dearest Sib,

Here is a bit of your inheritance, you do realise. The zip-up number will do just the job to keep those winter chills at bay.

I now have no girl baby things left, but no doubt shall be given more. If she needs woolies I do have stacks, but you may want them for your own little Caroline and Herberts. Tracy said she was happy to bring all this out; I gather she is going to work at Horizon for a while. Do look after her.

Poor little Guy has had rather bad croup attacks and I've had to call the doctor out in the middle of the night (first time ever). It sounds horrendous – rather like a baby seal. Croup apart, he is a bouncy baby. Hughie has loads of friends – all of which are blond and all of which are boys, so it's rather hard to tell them apart.

Tractors remaining his favourite topic of conversation. We've had quite a few in and out, haymaking like mad. There's such a shortage of hay that it's selling for £7 to £10 a bale.. Last year it was £1.50 to £2.50. I sold some dreadful two-year-old stuff for £3.00 a bale; poor polo ponies.

We went to Johnty's Old Boys Dance. Nigel Bruce was there and sent you his love. He'd been in Scotland, being the Queen's Archer. (I don't think this involves bows and arrows exactly).

I felt an old frump with my farmer's tan, sitting in the freezing cold marquee as semi-clad nymphettes pranced around giggling. Do you know, what with lugging babies about and trying to stop my horse I've developed larger arm muscles than Nigel, and he's been in the Army.

One of the star attractions at the dance was a bucking bronco machine. I thought, 'Bod can be much harder to stay on than that thing' and being encouraged by Nigel, climbed aboard.

Well, it bucked but I threw back my shoulders, kept my weight in my feet and quite got into the rhythm of it. A great roar went up. I was rather chuffed. Instead of being thrown they had to turn the machine off.

Johnty was standing there looking wide-eyed. Nigel and everyone else including all the nymphettes were roaring with laughter. I hadn't realised that my dress had whizzed up under my armpits revealing everything. But everything.

Sophie, I had to have my mole removed. The day before yesterday. I have a sore armpit, a butterfly stitch and three other stitches to prove it… Quite interesting. When it has been cut off it goes away in a jar to be examined, so I felt at least it was not wasted. I'm a bit sad though as we've been together thirty years.

Our garden gate to the fields is now in place – such a difference to my life, and the Hindlesons have taken out half the downstairs cupboard… much better; my kitchen feels twice the size.

Eric and Mr. Hindleson arrived with sledgehammers, which was a bit scary. It's worse than having the PG Tips chimps in the house. Eric came in with a six-foot length of plasterboard.

Mr Hindleson yelled, 'Eric, the clock.' as he swung past the grandfather clock, missing the glass by about an inch.

'What did you say, Father?' Eric said, swinging round again and smashing the light fitting into a thousand bits. I cried.

Lots of love.

Tx

24 Rivers
Vaalwater
South Africa
21ˢᵗ January 1996

Dear Tamzin,

Thanks for all the baby clothes you sent out with Tracy. Marcus does look a bit hot but my friend Miriam was thrilled. He is a boy but it doesn't matter, the girl things disappeared quickly. Did Mum get back OK? She enjoyed Cape Town where we rode through the wine estates and were spoilt by all Dad's cousins.

She spent her first week on the farm, where Charles was holding his annual stock sale. Mercy-me: Mum nearly put in a bid for Lot 33 - one of the stud bulls. I'm not sure what she would have done with him. Poor Mum, she couldn't get over the fact that there are no pillar-boxes here, or that people drive over the lawns.

She was rather shocked to see a man I was taking into town putting the seat belt right over his head. 'He must be over forty-five. Doesn't he know how they work?'

'Well, he might not have sat in the front seat of a car before.'

'Used to torturing donkeys instead I expect.' Then, 'Why are these people so poor?'

'They each have nine or ten kids, Mum.'

'That's appalling. Doesn't the Government provide free contraception?'

'Yes, but they're going to give people grants for having children.' When I took her to the tennis club, she politely asked one of the ladies she was playing with what she did for a living.

'I cut up dead animals.'

'Oh, really; that's nice.' Gerda, Mum told me later, works at the butchery. Sarah-Jane wanted to speak to her mother once when she went shopping in Potgietersrus. 'I rang Mr Hassim, at the hardware store, asking him if Mummy had come in to pick up the U bends, as I needed to get a message to her. He said she hadn't yet but to hang on and he'd see if he could find her, looked out into the street and told me she was just walking up the pavement. He hadn't seen her in his life before but could spot an English woman a mile off.'

I think Tracy found our nativity play a bit of a culture shock. Charles sent some children off to get the donkey we'd been rehearsing with but the owner, who was drunk, said we couldn't use it anymore.

'That's no good. Go and steal the donkey!' Charles ordered.

The children herded it into the garden, only then the dogs chased it straight out again.

Mum was excited as I had asked her to do the make-up but we made the terrible mistake of scheduling the performance for 23rd December, which was Pay Day. I was meant to be the Stage Manager.

Well, none of my cast turned up. Juliet went to look for them but could only find two little angels playing in the sand. Mum insisted on putting them in the bath. They had never had one before. 'It's OK.' I said quietly, 'She's my mother.'

'Ooo,' they nodded, looking up at me with big, brown eyes.

I needed to know where their mother was since she was both the director and playing the part of the Angel Gabriel.

'*Qua,*' they answered. (Far away) She'd gone to Potgietersrus and was still there.

Mary was '*Qua. Qua.*' (far, far away) – in fact 150 miles away in a place called Hammanskraal,. The Wise Man, the main one, had simply gone off, '*Qua*' 100 miles in the other direction.

Charles Baber eventually found the rest of the cast outside the church, sitting on a trailer with two flat tyres. They were on their way back from Vaalwater, waiting to be rescued.

'Quick, Mum,' I said when they eventually piled into the garden, 'Get everyone into their costumes, I have to find another Wise Man.'

The only person who remembered to come on time was Miriam, who arrived with her baby clad in your zip-up outfit.

She stood in front of the gathering assembly and declared, 'I have brought the Lord Jesus.'

By now lorry loads of audience were arriving from all the neighbours' farms.

I thought, 'They're going to have to wait ages.' but Juliet quickly put together a gospel choir and got the audience singing.

My sin was deeper than the ocean,

My sin was deeper than the ocean, they told us,

My sin was deeper than the ocean, - were there diamonds down there?

When the Lord satisfied me.

'How could such lovely people possibly sin?' Mum asked.

Charles was driving around in his categorically unroadworthy Chevrolet, collecting anyone from the district who wasn't sloshed. Mum couldn't believe he was commandeering an audience but she quite approved.

'Right, you know the story,' I was saying to the chief cattleman. 'You've got to be number one Wise Man. Here's your camel, (my horse) and there is the star.'

A missionary visiting from Zambia called Bright had strung a large silver star on a wire running between the Jacaranda trees either side of our stage, which was the bit of lawn between the flowerbeds in front of the low, thatched farmhouse.

By now it was dark, but we had security lamps on dimmer switches to light the play and I gave Mum some trays to bash when Gabriel arrived.

'Darling, I need a script to know what my cues are.'

'Listen Mum, the dialogue is in SeSotho. You'll have to guess.' At this stage I became caught up in a rosebush and couldn't move at all but the show went on.

Crash! went Mum with the tin trays, and Gabriel miraculously appeared (having spent all day queuing at the bank). My horse's eyes rolled and he started prancing, but more stoic than an actor, the cattleman held him by the bit and staunchly led all the Wise

Men before Herod. The action rather ground to a halt when the star stuck fast to the tree but it eventually jerked across the sky with a Jacaranda twig dangling beneath it.

The girl who had never played Mary before put a cushion up her dress, jumped on the back of the donkey and rode into Bethlehem with great poise. It was the first time I'd ever seen a pregnant Mary.

Charles was worried the Inn Keeper might just spoil the whole thing by saying, 'Yes, come in, there is room at the inn,' and usher them all into the dining-room, but Joseph was rejected and the angels did their thing.

'It's such a good story,' Nina kept saying.

'I just want to show the children,' Juliet said, 'That Christmas isn't just a time for bingeing and drinking and fighting.'

Mum and I flew to Knysna on Boxing Day, arguing all the way. She couldn't work out how the seat belt worked.

But the cousins whisked us off to stay above a beautiful beach where the rainforest comes down to the shore. We saw a Cape clawless otter swimming in the surf and followed its tracks along the warm, black river under towering yellow woods.

I stayed on in Cape Town for a while after Mum left and went to see my friend Danielle, who is running a restaurant. They shouldn't have let me into the kitchen; I caused complete havoc. One thing that I am not going to be in this life is a pastry chef.
Love,
Sophie

Corsham,
Chippenham,
Wiltshire.

Late at night, 26th January 1996

Darling Sib,

When we drove out of the Channel Tunnel and told the children they'd arrived in England, Atalanta threw up her arms and declared, 'It's Grannyland.'

We are over for six weeks, all staying in such a funny set up - an Army camp full of 'transit accommodation' - mobile homes. I think it was originally a refuge for battered wives: I'm not allowed male visitors. But dead lux they are; three bedrooms, Army furnished and snug as can be. This is all so as to be together whilst Robert learns to be a squadron leader in Warminster. (A bit late. He's been one for ages).

A policeman arrived at the door late one night when Robert was away on exercise, out on Salisbury Plain. I thought, 'Oh no, this is it.' Terrible accidents happen on the ranges. But the young constable smiled and said,

'I've come from the main gate with a message from your sister about a tadpole.'

I dressed the pyjamaed children and trekked down the hill to the phone box. Tadpole was seriously ill. Tamzin didn't know whether she would survive the night. She hadn't held down any food for five days... I rushed to Hampshire in the morning, down a foggy motorway. It was a pitiful sight. My poor little girl looked more like a whippet. So thin. And her back legs were collapsing. Quite ghastly. After two visits to the vet for blood tests she rallied and has made the most remarkable recovery. There was a kidney scare, one is a bit iffy, but it was probably a virus. She is now eating well and roo, roo, rooing about. Robert meanwhile was sleeping in a trench - self dug - and nearly froze to death.

We've had such fun catching up with friends. It's Lu's wedding next weekend. No fairies in tutus for her; the outfits are very smart – navy velvet jacket and off-white trousers. For Hastings. Tamzin warned me NOT to tell Lu the clothes were plain – as if Mrs Tactful would. Lu's cousin had though and Lu was LIVID, nay, fuming.

Two more weeks left and then back to Germany. Big landmark for us in June when we find out where we are destined for next...

I've just been to the framers to get your picture of elephants mounted; it's going to look GLORIOUS.
Tons of love from us all,
Perry xxxxxx

5th February 1996

Thank you, dearest Sophie,

For the lovely time on the farm and for putting up with your embarrassing old Ma. I had such a fantastic, varied time.

Meanwhile, at home, POOR DAD; not only did he have to cope with thick ice, so bad he had to cross the lane on doormats to give Leonard his hay; not only did Josey-Joe nearly die from the change in air pressure and had to be force fed with Millupa baby food (parrots revert to babyhood when stressed) but, horror of horrors, the woman renting the cottage from us over New Year fell in love with Dad and put a disgusting and suggestive poem through the letterbox. He freaked out, locked up and fled up to Helen and Tony's.

Helen took a photocopy of the poem and tried to get Basil, her Rottweiler, to chew up the original. She thought if Dad could scatter the pieces around the woman might think our dogs had eaten it, but Basil didn't want to touch it. Poor Dad just had to pretend nothing had happened and avoid the woman. Any other action would have ruined the nice-seeming husband's holiday and problems could have escalated.

Johnty told him to chew lots of garlic in case she took him unawares and pounced. They left the day before I arrived back, which was a shame as I was dying to see what she looked like; obviously a sexual deviant. I went in and disinfectant-ed the place. Dad is in good company; Princess Anne has a stalker, *Points West* is full of it all.

We all went to Lu Llewellyn's wedding on Saturday; she looked quite BEAUTIFUL in a classic dress. The evening service was held in a huge, opulent church in Bayswater, lit by candles. Couldn't hear a thing but Atalanta was very moved and cried out, 'Jesus.'

Claridges was full of twigs covered in little gold lights and they had a three tiered, BLACK wedding cake. I've no idea why it was black, but it was.

I've been writing a lot of airmail letters to S. Korea as they torture dogs and cats before eating them – supposed to be good for sex drive. I ask you. They breed them especially for eating, as well as stealing pets. I want to organize a demo outside the Korean Embassy in London. Could you write to the President and ask him to bring in new laws to protect dogs and cats from being tortured?

Send to: Mr President, Blue House, Sejong-Ro, Jongno-gu, Seoul, South Korea 110-050.

I must get on (it's 6.30am) because Mary-Dieu and Co. are coming for lunch. I am Oscar-sitting again.

Thinking about you all the time,

God bless darling,

Mummy

The Claridge's waiter asked Hastings, 'One blob or two?' ~ of tomato ketchup. Hastings was most impressed.

We have a pair of swans on the lake – one is a Bewick all the way from Greenland.

I went by paddle steamer right along the South Wales coast to Milford Haven. Very few gulls or any life to be seen, but the Severn is getting cleaner and we saw salmon jumping on their way back to the sea.

We are off up to Yorkshire next, when one of the otters is to be in *All Creatures Great and Small,* the James Herriot series.

Your Mum has just found her parrot in the dishwasher, luckily just before I switched it on. We could hear her talking but couldn't think where the sound was coming from.

Has Billy become a tourist attraction yet?

Love to you,

Dad

Dear Sophie,

Here is a picture of a man to keep you company. A caveman.

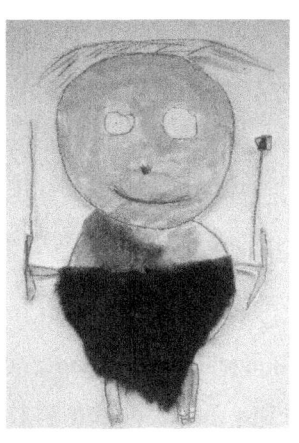

I've just phoned Mum. She was furious that I called, as I had got her out of the bath – typical. She said she has a job, training puppies for *One Hundred and One Dalmatians* and did I have her Ready Reckoner. I didn't even know what this is. It's a pocket calculator.

Actually I had a little adventure over a pair of shoes too; a modelling assignment. A friend of mine has started importing the most lovely loafers from Spain and asked me, yes, me and my thick ankles, to do some photographic modelling. When everyone went off to get changed, the photographer cornered me and asked if I could put on some really tarty, high, strappy sandals for a few shots – which, without thinking, I did. Big mistake. They turned out to be his ex-wife's. The photos were for himself. He had a SHOE fetish!

Otherwise life as a Hampshire Housewife trots along nicely. We went to see *Jude* at the cinema last night; such a stunning film. In the story the children keep being told what a financial burden they were by their parents. I had never read the book, alas, so when they walked into the bedroom to find their eldest child had hung himself and killed the other children I screamed loudly. Raddy shook so much I thought I would have to remove her.

The rest of the Basingstoke audience was totally unmoved.

Lots of love,

Tamzin xxx

Jacobus Bekkerlaan
Vaalwater
February 1996

Dear Perry,

I've just sent a crew from the Natural History Unit off, with all their excess baggage, to the Eastern Transvaal.

I need to decide if I want to start making my own films again, but the thought alone exhausts me. I would rather spend my days painting.

Dad's cousin gave me great advice. He said, 'Stay mobile and independent. Achievement? Paint a picture or write a play.'

Tell you something; I'm determined to enjoy myself, wherever I am; life is too short not to. And there are more important things to do in life than make television programmes. I'm going to plough ahead as a wildlife artist, difficult though it is, and help Michael Ramasodi if I can. Michael works with Juliet Baber running a mission for the poverty stricken people of the Waterberg, organizing youth camps and evening classes, that sort of thing.

After ten years of drought it doesn't want to stop raining. Water is literally coming out from the top of the mountains, cascading over the rocks. Charles told me that that is why the Waterberg is called the Waterberg; the whole plateau is like a giant aquifer. When the first Vooretrekkers came north the ground was so squelchy that their wagons kept getting stuck.

Shane and Laura are getting married next week. Laura's rather extensive family has just flown in from Westbury-on-Trym.

As a landslide washed away the tar road that normally brings people up the escarpment they had to take the old dirt road, through a pass called Tarentaal Straat. This means Guineafowl Street, you'll be glad to know.

Well, Guineafowl Street takes you for about forty kilometres through uninhabited, mountainous country and it had almost turned into a river.

Of mud.

The hire cars promptly got stuck. It was raining hard. Laura said all her relations, who were in their smart travelling clothes, had to get out and push. They were instantly covered in red, clayey mud. It was way past her knees and her brothers had to virtually carry the first vehicle through before tractors started towing them out. Instead of taking three hours to get up here, it took nine. None of them were happy about this or at all amused.

After being in the bush about three days Laura's sister-in-law declared that she HAD to shop, and without asking local advice, insisted her husband drove the family off to Potgietersrus. She returned looking shattered. It's always fiendishly hot in Potties.

'There were stalls running all the way up and down the main street,' she said, flopping down in a chair. 'But all they sold were enormous bras and ENORMOUS knickers.'

We could have told her. I think she was expecting a traditional African market but street trading was banned in most towns during apartheid and the contemporary stalls mostly stock goods imported from China.

Shane takes us to the Wimpy, as a treat, when we go to town, but this girl took her children to an African café.

'I peered at the food under the glass counter. It all looked like slops to me, but I pointed to a pan of yellow food, which was at least quite cheery.' Julie told us.

Laura looked at me as this was being related, her mouth slowly falling open.

'I said, "We'll have some of that."' Julie went on. 'But the shop girl said, "No." I said, "What do you mean, No? The children are hungry, I'll have some." She looked at me and said, "Not white food," but I wasn't going to be deterred. I said, "We want to try African food." I have to admit,' she said, finally slowing down. 'It wasn't white food. It was chicken's feet; the claws, cooked with chicken's heads; beaks and everything.'

Laura and I burst out laughing. The local delicacy is known as 'Walkie-Talkies'.

There's a big party on tonight for Ant's thirtieth birthday. I'm going as Minnie Mouse. Laura said, 'How are you going to pick up that eligible bachelor wearing big round ears and white gloves?' We'll see. I'll send you the answer on the back of a postcard.

Love,

Sophie

Dear Perry,

I was painting his house, not matt emulsion but a picture of it. An Italian haute couturier, long separated, recently divorced, living on his game ranch in the Waterberg. Although he looks like Stuart Granger, Giorgio is sadly a little old for me, but he enjoyed getting me dressed up as Minnie Mouse and did my make-up beautifully ~ using my watercolours. Giorgio of the Jungle. But he didn't come to the party at Windsong Cottage. Instead I danced with a rather gorgeous Julius Caesar all evening. Tracy, the other Minnie Mouse, was proposed to – becoming engaged to Shane's new guide. That evening.

So there you go. And very exciting; Tessa flew out from London dressed as Private Benjamin, which pleased Indiana Jones enormously. (She'd come out especially for his birthday). Love, Sophie

Church Cottage
Vaalwater
South Africa

Dear Tamzin,

I'm sitting happily in my art studio – a cottage I've been renting off the church in Vaalwater where I have a big room just for making a mess in. I actually paint in the sitting room or on the veranda, but I seem to have accumulated great stacks of frames and materials, with seven portfolios of work from my various trips.

I'm trying to sort out what is good enough to make into limited edition prints. I have six ink sketches of birds and a set of Namibian wildlife friezes, which I am going to make into lithographs. I want to get enough work together to be able to exhibit in England this July, so am drawing away and need to start on some canvases.

One great excitement is that I was asked to submit a painting of black rhino to be auctioned at Phillips in Bond Street. I sent them one of a cow and calf running over a hill, which in the catalogue, I see, has been titled, 'Bottoms'.

Shane and Laura had a cowboy wedding. Even the vicar wore a checked shirt and jeans. The idea was that Shane would canter into the garden at Triple B Ranch where the service was to be held, with his mates mounted on about thirty horses like a posse from a 1940's western. Laura and her father were going to arrive on a cart, pulled by Bismarck, with her girlfriends riding behind. It didn't quite happen that way.

Shane's Dad had never ridden in his life, so all the men arrived at rather a sedate walk. Meanwhile we couldn't get Bismarck to move at all. He had to start on an uphill slope around the back of the tobacco barns, which was difficult. It's easiest for him to pull at a trot. Tracy finally managed to get him going and I shot after them.

My *High Noon* dress must have started to tickle Sam because by the time we reached the drive he was bucking violently. '*Do not forsake me Oh my darling, on this our wedding day.*'

Bismarck was going full pelt, hurtling downhill towards the garden, where instead of sitting on their chairs like a proper congregation, the guests were waving and cheering around the gate. Laura grabbed the reins out of her father's hands and just managed to pull up before she flattened someone.

I did too, only as the bride was getting out of the cart, Sam decided to leap over a flowerbed. If you watch the video you just see me flying through the back of the shot while the doctor's wife is screaming in horror. I hit the saddle with an awful thump, and rather lost my bearings before realising that I had to tie up my wretched horse and run through the garden, grabbing my flute in time to play *The Wedding March* for Laura as she came up the garden path on her father's arm.

The Sotho Gospel Choir took over after the service. They had composed a special song:

'*Oh Shaney,*' it went, '*When you get drunk you must not beat up Laura,*♪♪ *And Laura, when you're angry at Shane because he did beat you, You mustn't pack your bags and return to your mother.*' ♫ ♫ ♪

A bit different from Mendelssohn. They had gumboot dancers too; boys from the farm doing their own version of a mine dance, while great joints of beef were being cooked on the spit.

I danced with Jez who was there in rather tight riding boots. Everyone danced, they danced until dawn, only my back was rather sore from the flowerbed leaping.

Off to Botswana next week; can't wait.

Lots of love,

Sophie

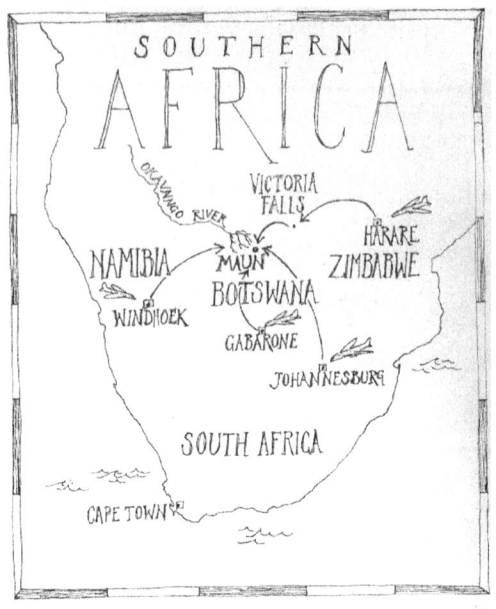

MACATEER'S CAMP
KER & DOWNEY
MAUN
BOTSWANA

Dear Perry,

One of the horses has been attacked by a lion. I drove up to Maun to paint but found myself being flown straight up to the camp to help deal with the situation, while Sarah-Jane tried to organize a vet. Herero, one of the best horses, had badly lacerated flanks. The lion had scored his rump, scratching him again, and then again. Not unlike Johnty's adventures with the Tom cat. It's amazing that he escaped but I think that being a stallion, Herero probably kicked the lion hard in the face. No one saw what happened. Herero had been grazing outside the electric fence which was surrounding the other horses. No one noticed that he'd disappeared until the end of the day when the grooms found him shaking in the bushes.

With the flesh cut to ribbons Rowena couldn't work out how to sew the wound together. The big threat, however, was from infection. In the end Sarah-Jane managed to find a lady vet in Gaborone who was willing to fly up, but it took two days to get her into camp. She overdosed the horse with antibiotics and made him dopey enough to pack the wound with a bright orange healing agent. It looks like stuff you would fibreglass a boat with. We have to carry on dressing the wound without anaesthetic, which is not easy since it's on his bottom. It's all so painful he kicks on reflex, up to five feet high.

Traditionally, camps in the Okavango close in January and February as it's meant to be the rainy season. I was told that you didn't want to be there then as it was seething with mosquitoes. Not a bit. Although towering rain clouds fill the skies we've had the most beautiful, sunny weather. All the wild flowers are out and there are butterflies everywhere. We rode over one plain, which was covered in fine, cloudy, Bushman hair grass. It was quite mesmerising, like plunging through a sea of mist or spun gold.

I've been riding a lot, getting the horses fit for the coming season and helping the grooms to qualify as guides. We'd been living off warthog pie and fried rice but some rather glamorous friends of Sarah-Jane's drove up from Johannesburg in a Landcruiser stuffed with delicious food and incredibly good wine. They've been laying on languid lunches under a huge fig tree with smoked meats, delicious fruit and Chardonnay that is seriously impeding the progress of my artwork, but quite a reward after spending so much time nursing Herero. Since Nicki arrived with a French boyfriend, life has completely dissolved into the wine glasses. I think even the animals are blitzed. Last night when we were eating dinner outside by the fire a small heron plopped out of a tree, high above us, falling onto the sandy ground. It must have fallen off its perch. It stood up looking embarrassed and stalked off.

One serious encounter was with the skull of an elephant. It was a bull that had been shot in the leg by poachers. They presumably never managed to track the body because the huge broken tusks were lying nearby. As Nicki's boyfriend is an osteopath, we collected the scattered remains and rebuilt the huge skeleton. But when we returned to the site later we found the bones had been flung about and a tree felled on the remains. The other elephants were furious that we had interfered with their dead.

'I couldn't work at this camp,' Nicki said, 'No ways. There aren't any taps.' Sarah-Jane does have one at the stables for the horses but the human beings have bucket showers and long-drops.

'Be careful that your penknife doesn't fall off your belt when you go to the loo,' was all she could say. 'I tell the guests it's a matter of being eco-friendly and that there are potties in the tents if they get nervous about going outside at night.'

Rowena says the arrangement is a great improvement on the Makgadikgadi pans where the staff were given an upturned oil drum as a lavatory. 'There was no shade and unless you went first thing in the morning the metal got so hot you couldn't sit down. I know some film-makers living up on the Chobe use an elephant skull as a loo seat but at least it's under a tree.'

We saw a saddlebilled stork catching a snake today. The snake promptly wound its body round the stork's bill. Try explaining that in French.

Lots of love,
Sophie

Hughie is nuts about zebras and wants to ask if you have ever ridden one. Could you?

Lots of love from us all.

Tamzin xxx

Dear Hughie,

Thank you for the lovely picture of the zebra. People often ask me why they have stripes. I think it would be quite fun to ride one, but I'm told they're bad tempered and try to bite your knees. They like braying early in the morning. I'll come over in the summer and we can go riding together.

Lots of love,

Aunt Sophie

My map of Sarah-Jane's concession area, in the western delta.

MACATEER'S CAMP
KER & DOWNEY
MAUN, BOTSWANA

March 1996

Dear Tamzin,

My letters do reach me in quite extraordinary ways. Hughie's zebra arrived by Cessna at Xudum, an airstrip deep in the bush. I've been up in Botswana with Sarah-Jane. The horse attacked by a lion is recovering well but she's worried about sleeping sickness, an African disease called Ngama. It's carried by the tsetse fly and poses a great risk to domestic stock, including horses. The tsetse fly is so prevalent in the Okavango that it has

actually kept cattle out of the area and has probably protected it from development, but she has to keep her horses alive. The Government have set large blue and black flytraps all over the place but I don't know how effective they are. The elephant hate the sight of them and we come across quite a few that they've trashed.

So, I've spent the last month talking about fly spray... and whether riding zebras would be an option as, like other wild animals, they've built up an immunity to sleeping sickness. The man who owns the supermarket in Vaalwater has an impressive photograph of his great-grandfather's stagecoach pulled by fifteen zebra. They can be stubborn, but this Mr Zeedeburg managed to break them in by hitching them, one by one next to a strong mule.

'You can imagine the fun and games they must have had hitching the whole team up.' Rowena said, 'The idea was that they could venture up into the tropics without having to worry about sleeping sickness but the zebra lacked stamina and always needed one lead mule.'

I was meant to be painting classic pictures of wildlife but ended up working on a series of cartoons, which I made into a map for Sarah-Jane. When it was finished I sat outside her tent painting the landscape but that somehow degenerated into an animation of Tigger. She spends her days dozing but at night turns into a banshee, voraciously chasing hyena out of camp. They come sniffing around the tents and steal anything made of leather. One took someone's boots, a wad of file paper and Sarah-Jane's black plastic office stapler.

Lion are a real threat. They don't seem to pounce on riders but nothing's more frightening when you're on a young horse than the sight of a little lion cub sitting under a tree; the females will be right behind it. We take a rifle with us but you need to be observant. Jez used to walk round with a safety flare in his pocket but these can cause bush fires if you let them off. The horses are kept in a barn at night, made of corrugated iron with great locked doors, but the lions prowl around.

'Once the horses smell them,' Rowena explained, 'they start kicking the sides of the barn. Sarah-Jane just pulls on her gumboots and runs out into the darkness, shouting.'

It wasn't an animal that attacked me but a falling sausage. A wooden one weighing about twenty pounds. They grow on trees. Sausage trees. *Kigelia Africana*. There's a big one in the camp. These missiles reach about eighteen inches in length and then drop off without warning, while girls like me are eating their lunch. I could have been killed. I asked what one could do with the almost solid fruit but Rowena hadn't found any use beyond using them to throw at the hyenas. Baboons and rodents like porcupines seem to gnaw at the ones on the ground and I think parrots nibble them but they smell bitter. It said in the tree book that Africans hang them in their huts to fend off hurricanes, but the Tswana girls in the kitchen looked at me rather dubiously when I asked them about this.

A Cornishman called John Sobey, who first came to Equus as a client, arrived here and asked if he could work as a guide. 'And what work experience do you have?'

'Stroking titties.'

'?'

'I was a dairy farmer.' As he's a confident rider, can shoot straight and makes Sarah-Jane laugh, she took him on. He thinks the sausages are the best thing out and found a number of things to do with them, all of which are rude.

I'm off to South Africa soon; a journey of 1,000 kilometres. Once, when I was driving back with Nick we hit a bump in the road so hard I knew something terrible was going to happen. An awful noise came from the back of my car and we saw one of the wheels overtake us. I couldn't understand how we could still be driving along. It was the spare wheel that had been jolted off its cradle. Nothing fell off last time but donkeys seemed to be mating incessantly, right in the middle of the road. What would Mum have said about this, I cannot imagine.

Love,

Sophie

Church Cottage
Jacobus Bekker Laan
Vaalwater

Dear Perry,

We've just had an horrific storm. One moment the sky was blue and the next hailstones the size of mothballs were pelting out of the sky. Fortunately most of the tobacco crop is in, otherwise the leaves would have been completely shredded. Shane says the horses should be fine, but if anyone had been out riding they would have had to take their saddle off, and crouch underneath to survive. Apparently the hailstones can grow so enormous they've been known to destroy orange orchards, tile roofs and whole fleets of brand new BMW cars. They had to sell the pock-marked ones off, cheap.

We've had so much rain this year that the crocodiles have come out of the river and have taken to walking through Vaalwater. One was found lying on the lawn in front of the hotel. I used some of my last BBC fee to put up a big old army tent as a church in the squatter township that has formed, quite suddenly on the outskirts of town. The rumour is that the ANC have moved 5,000 people there so they can win the local elections and it's clear that a great number of disadvantaged people have arrived on our doorstep.

'There's nothing for them here.' Michael Ramasodi said in despair, 'Just rain.'

He is going to use the tent as a base from where he can hold services and Sunday schools, run a soup kitchen and self-help groups. I'm trying to get school leavers and local people started in making crafts. The sewing club up at Triple B Ranch has taken off and attempts at making baskets out of fencing wire started at my cottage today. It was chaotic.

We had a bank robbery in town. They came in brandishing guns, leaving the poor teller who normally serves me a bit shaken, to say the least. 'Did the bank offer you compensation?

'No, just counselling.'

But they caught the robbers. Ant is in the Commandos. He said they formed road-blocks along the few routes leading off the Waterberg and stopped the getaway car as it headed north.

I had four punctures this month and have spent so long in the tyre shop that the owner is thinking of getting me to paint his portrait. I'm still a slave to my art commissions, but do have a few wildlife paintings to bring back. Mum has arranged for me to be the Artist in Residence at a gallery called *Nature in Art*, so I'll be back in England for about three months this year but I don't suppose I'll see you there.

Do you have any news of your next posting yet? I really pray that you won't be too isolated this time round. I don't know how you can stand moving house the whole time.

Lots of love,

Sophie

Church Hooker,
Near Winchester,
30th September 1996

Darling Sib,

We've arrived in an exhausted heap. Of all the places in the world, we've been stationed in a Hampshire village. I don't want to ever move again. After two days Robert had to go back on exercise in Germany and is there until 10th but that doesn't matter. I'm going to astonish him with my power drill – I'm astonishing myself.

It was a pretty bad move in that our first chosen dates fell through, so after packing up six weeks ahead we had to live another three weeks with a house stripped to the core. Our belongings finally arrived all in a higgle-de-piggle, resulting in a lot of damage and staining. Your African wire basket survived, but the packers put the lawnmower on top of my dining-room table, if you please. I suppose it could have been worse; once all our suitcases went off to the Falklands.

The house was filthy and I now have to clean out sticky drawers before I can even put my clothes away. To add to everything, I broke the glass on my dressing table - what a fool. Mum and Dad appeared out of the blue, as they do, with a chainsaw and we now have a view from the loo.

My children spend most of the time next door with Robert's second in command, as he has, wait for it, 'the sweetest little ferrets'. I'm afraid I can't bear them. They stink. I've been trying to plant things in the garden before it's too late; it has been terribly dry. Our hose seems to have been lost and it is a bit strenuous watering the whole place with a jug.

We spent a heavenly day with Tamzin yesterday - she is thirty minutes away. It's so exciting to have them all so close. H&H are as thick as thieves.

Sib, I'll write properly soon.
Keep safe and well and much love,
Perry xxx

Hardacre Farm

October 1996

Dearest Sophie –

Happy Birthday - Poor old thing.

Before I forget here is Perry's new address. I was so looking forward to having her over for lunch with Mum but it was all rather sad as she wept over Tadpole's grave, mourning the fact that her little dog died so young. I said all the wrong things and Mum bullied Atalanta endlessly about being a wimp over having a bottom tooth pulled out. Atalanta inevitably started crying which set off Guy. Then Mum grabbed Hughie and collapsed in tears for no apparent reason at all. At this stage a man arrived with a tanker to empty the cesspit. Why can't we ever have a normal family gathering without it turning into a theatrical drama?

Mum said her dogs have been accused of killing sheep. That must have been why she was nagging Atalanta. She doesn't believe they were capable of bringing one down but they certainly chase them. Lurchers do. I really don't want to end up looking after Shaddy. I thought Perry might like him but she says they're giving the children guinea pigs for Christmas. Well, you know what happened when Mum bought a little black guinea pig as a friend for her first otter. Shaddy is a carnivore too.

We were very interested to hear about riding zebra. Dad said that in the First World War the Germans had such problems with tsetse fly killing their cavalry horses in what was then Tanganyika that their officers rode eland, wearing their coal-scuttle helmets and all. They cut off their horns and made special saddles and bridles for them.

I rode in a cross-country event on Saturday wearing my new Pro Plus helmet. It's so massive I felt like a prat but had a lovely day relaxing in the sun, watching the autumn colours.

Bod, who has reached the age of seventeen, is getting stiff and quite lame on a regular basis. Fat Git Trevor, my Blacksmith, says it's probably arthritis.

'Chop his hooves off and stick roller skates on.'

I'm sad, as it seems like the beginning of the end.

I can't remember what you're doing, but have fun doing it anyway.

Love,

Tamzin.

7 November 1996

Dearest One,

Johnty took the boys to the tank museum, where Hughie chose to behave unexpectedly well and I was able to relax.

Perry and the children are all very chirpy. Not crying anymore. In fact the cousins get up to all sorts of mischief together.

Mum is having a 'Nappy Party' of all things, collecting baby stuff to take to a Children's Home in Moldova.

I don't actually know where Moldova is; somewhere once behind the iron curtain. My curtains look fantastic. Drawing room now finished; new chair covers too; looks smart, very pleased. A really lovely room now.

Lots of love,

TJH+G

Dear T.

Am in Zimbabwe fishing on Lake Kariba, with my friends Ged and Jane. Very hot. Ged said it can suddenly get stormy. He became so seasick on the lake once that he begged his father to leave him in one of the dead trees that stick out of the water. They collected him at the end of the day. I would have been a bit worried about them getting lost. Or of elephants, which we saw fighting on the water's edge. We had fun in Harare. Street stalls line the roads and you can buy good carvings. I bought a warthog scratching its ear. AIDS seems to have a grip on this country but all the farmers are optimistic and have been trying to persuade me to buy land there. It's so beautiful and vibrant with such a great craft movement I'm quite tempted.

Love, Sophie

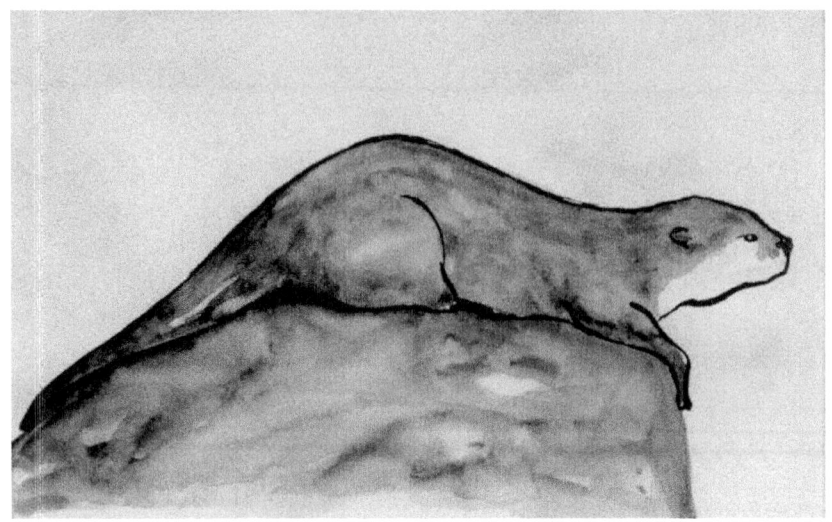

Darling Sib,

We were innocently watching the ITV 6 O'clock News last night when Mum came on with Glen Hoddle. She was in Moldova saying, 'If the RSPCA saw this they would be on the warpath. But these aren't animals, they're children.' She looked very emotional.

Meanwhile, since her own animals have been convicted of murder, we've adopted Shaddy. He's surprisingly well behaved. Tamzin said she would help me make a run for the guinea pigs. I'm envious of her woodwork skills; she thought nothing of making herself a dining-room table. Daisy and Oscar were with Mum and Dad when we went to collect the dog. They're such sweet, easy children – far calmer than mine. Far calmer than me. It's cold here. 'With a bitter wind,' as Granny would say. I wish I was WARM.

Love, Perry x

Dear P,

I'm suffering. Like no tomorrow. Unable to eat or drink a thing. The doctor put me on a drip but doesn't really know what's wrong, just kept flicking through the pages of his medical book umming, so I went to see the vet who looked up, saw me colliding with door post and said, 'Amoebic dysentery. Probably contracted in Cape Town.' Apparently it's rife there. I went with James Money-Kyrle who came out for Christmas. We made him be the angel Gabriel. This time our nativity play was at the church with a multi-cultural cast and two rather virile donkeys. Tracy and I took him on a horse safari. He rode the largest horse we could find and became rather intimate with what the locals call a *wag'n bietjie* – a hook thorn so tenacious you are obliged to 'wait-a-bit' and unhook yourself before you can go anywhere. Mum gave me a one-size-fits-all silky pink top, which I wore to a party with an orange bead necklace and a dark pink skirt. I though I cut quite a dash until James said I looked like a bougainvillea bush. I did.

Love,

Sophie

Dearest Sib,

Freezing cold here and fog quite dreadful. Deb has been given a huge black horse that now lives with us… it eats Bod's tail. We also have 300 sheep staying. Boys growing well. Hughie was given A* at school for not grabbing, so he must grab the whole time. Guy is going to be two soon; he still looks like a Christmas pudding. Delicious.

We might go to Wales in August; will you be around? Mum has returned from her mercy mission full of horror stories and has been staying here to recover. I said, 'But Mum what did you do once you arrived with the nappies?'

'Oh, I sang *Old McDonald had a Farm* with the retarded children. They adored me.'

T xxxx

PO Box 415
Vaalwater 0530
March 1997

Dear Perry,

    I thought Atalanta would like to know I'm about to be a bridesmaid (of all things). Rather an old one since I'm now thirty-six. I'm normally the video girl at weddings these days. 'The Tripod Bird,' someone called me. I've just shot Ant's. He married Tessa amid piles of white roses with horses galloping everywhere and glitzy people flying in from all over the world. The marquee is staying up in the garden for Juliet to go through the same process two weeks later. To the amazement of the population of the bushveld she is marrying a physicist called Phil from Philadelphia. No, he's from Worcestershire. It's just that since no one here has ever met him I could have a field day making things up if I cared to. None of his friends can come, so we are going to have two more weddings for them in England. All this bridal stuff is enough to make a girl feel quite left out, although rather be me than poor Tracy who is now suddenly unengaged and very unhappy.

    I've just returned from another trip to Zimbabwe. Sarah-Jane sent me to advise the owners of a newly formed reserve on whether they could operate horse safaris. Sophie the Consultant. I thought it time the executive ought to get herself (an impressive) four-wheel drive vehicle and bought one off Nicki. It was a big blue thing with roller bars, called a *Raider*. Only you have to roll the R's. *Rrrrrrraider*. What a mistake. It broke down seven times. I now know a great deal more about vehicle mechanics. And miracles. I bought it thinking I could fill it with aid stuff and drive up to Mozambique but it would never get there. On top of everything I've been told it must have been in a terrible accident as the chassis is bent; I'll have to return it.

The reserve was stunning. Near a town called Triangle and bordering Gonarezhou, it's being carefully developed by a wealthy American who is pouring money into the place. Billy's old boss is the Warden there. He drove me around, beneath majestic trees and tall waving grasses. They had interesting Bushmen paintings, but I did think the vegetation was a mite dense for riding safely amongst lion. Some areas were like a jungle with one narrow elephant path running through high rocks. Lovely, but what if you were on your pony and met elephant plodding towards you?

A student working on the reserve asked if I would give her a lift on my way home. After driving miles through sugarcane plantations in torrential rain we reached her sister's house. I climbed out of the blue truck and heard that particular sound that is made when hungry ponies grab at hay. I then felt searing pain from the top of my head and was nearly lifted off my feet. A giraffe had leant over and grabbed a mouthful of my hair, which it tore off and ate. It was a hand-reared foal that obviously had no fear of humans. I ran onto the veranda as it came bounding towards me, kicking in all directions. Terrifying. All the way home I was picking giraffe spit out of what bits of hair were left, thinking 'I'm going to be a bald bridesmaid.' A bald, old bridesmaid. Juliet says it's just a bit embrossé and that no one will notice as I'm tall. Ha.

I've been painting hard, although the wedding guests keep buying the best pictures, so I'll just have to paint harder. The sales have nothing whatsoever to do with talent. There's simply a huge demand for pictures of hippo and warthog. People get quite fond of these, loving them as they would pets.

I'll be home soon, for the summer. All I want to do is go to the sea but must try to have an exhibition in London this year.

Lots of love,

Sophie

Hardacre Farm

Dearest Sib,

Yesterday morning was spent at 'Fun Jungle' with Atalanta, Hastings and Perry. No elephants. A most un-jungle like place, which smelt of stale sweat, dribble and pee. Mostly of pee. The children adored it, jumped in ball pools and climbed things, using their tongues as sensors. I'm now waiting for various viruses to hatch out. What do you think; about three or four days?

Spring is springing madly ~ so many primroses and wood anemones. Bod had his last cross-country event two weeks ago, which was fun. It was such a hot day a butterfly flew past. We've been lent a miniature palomino pony called Patrick and I'm earnestly teaching the boys to ride. Raddy rode down to collect her daughter from school on her horse. She was given a talking to by another mother for not wearing a hard hat and setting a bad example for the girls. She calmly let the woman rage on, before declaring, 'No hat, no knickers,' and clattered off up the hill. I would never dare say anything like that.

Thank you for the boys' birthday cards; they loved them. Hughie shared his party with Alexander and they had Mr Cronky, who was inadvertently amusing. He had rather an obvious toupee that kept threatening to fall off. Despite being March it was so sunny I had to put up a garden umbrella. Guy took off all his clothes and danced around squeaking. Fourteen darling children and ten mothers came; can you imagine the fun and games?

Lots of love,

Tamzin

Triple B Ranch
24 Rivers
Vaalwater

Dear Tamzin,

You're going to have to come and ride my pony. We can take tents and set off into the bush like old *Vooretrekkers* living off oranges and *biltong*. Shane disagrees, maintaining that, 'You must always have delicious food like smoked oysters and bacon butties.' We ended up taking pork sausages last time, although he's not beyond encouraging the guests to fry up mopane worms – processional caterpillars about the size of your finger. John Sobey is worse. He eats flying ants, alive, at the dinner table, although he'll deign to remove the wings first. Very nutritious, but you have to crunch up the legs before they scratch your tongue.

Perhaps we are all getting bushed. The wilderness can have the effect of reducing one's inhibitions. I helped Shane to take a group of riders into the neighbouring reserve over the weekend. We had just lit the fire when one woman declared, completely out of the blue, that she'd recently had 3 kgs cut off her breasts. Even Shane was stunned into silence.

Barn owls have made a nest in the roof of the veranda at Triple B Ranch and are brilliant at keeping down the rodent population and thus snakes from around the house. I wish they would keep away the murderers. We have three on the loose, who could well be running around the property. Uninhibited indeed. They shot one farmer and then attacked a neighbour as she got out of her car to open her gate. Her face was slashed but she slammed the high gate as they were climbing over it and drove to her house where she had a short-wave radio. The Police and farmers rallied, homing in on the area with tracker dogs. Charles wouldn't let Juliet or me out of the house. We sat locked in the office all evening while the radio buzzed in Afrikaans with reports of the manhunt. There was a great crescendo of activity before it fell ominously silent.

'You can come out now,' Shane said. 'They've got 'em.'

Effie told me that she thought life was easier during apartheid, that she doesn't feel safe any more. I asked her if she minded the fact that there are still two different entrances at the surgery, not black/white anymore but 'Medical Aid' and 'Non-Medical Aid'.

'No!' she said, 'It costs R50 to go in one side and R30 the other.'

'Well, I know what side I'll be going in,' Laura said.

'No, my darling,' Effie replied. 'It's where they have to see the drunken people on Pay Day when they come in bleeding.' The medics need an examination room that can be hosed down.

'*N'kosi sekeleli Africa*,' Charles Baber murmured leaving the room.

'God Bless Africa.' It's the opening line of the national anthem.

A friend of mine who was once a producer on *Newsnight,* now working for the BBC in Johannesburg, says that crime and violence is no new thing, it's just come out of the townships and is more conspicuous.[xix] We are beginning to face awful problems in our local township. Most of the people who were moved there are destitute and there's little work to be found in the Waterberg; no factories or big plantations, just extensive farms which are looking for ways of reducing their labour force as the government makes employing people increasingly complicated. Any spare cash is often spent on alcohol. One man has just killed his wife, shot himself and left four children of school age orphaned. Michael Ramasodi says that the two aunts are arguing about who will get to bring up the kids, as both fancy receiving the welfare grant.

Since there was a hold-up at the other bank in town we now have security guards, dressed in black and carrying truncheons, posted at the doors. You're not allowed inside wearing a crash helmet. Although Laura got quite a dressing down for using a mobile phone, firearms don't seem to be an issue. 'Two old Afrikaans ladies had revolvers blatantly displayed in holsters on their hips, but it didn't seem to bother the guard at all.'

I'm coming home again for the summer. Fred and Josie, who met at Equus, are getting married in Suffolk, which is rather exciting. Everyone seems to be getting married.

Mum said, in her despair, 'I suppose you could always marry Nick.'

I told him. He said that Diana's father had actually asked him if he would marry her.

'If only she would have me,' he answered suavely.

You're chosen to be a diplomat. In fact he is off to work for the Prince of Wales, organizing his overseas trips and foreign visitors. No one is remotely worried about Nick not being married, but he's a man.

See you soon,

Love Sophie

Dear Atalanta and Hastings,

I'm at the seaside with Aunt Tamzin and the boys, while Johnty is working on the harvest. We caught 32 crabs today and went out in the leaky boat Granny bought off her dentist.

A man sold me a lobster he'd caught but Guy thought it was rather frightening and ran around screaming so loudly the other holiday makers must have thought I was torturing him.

Hughie spends all his time digging holes. He fell over the edge of a cliff but I caught him by one ankle. Then it was Aunt Tamzin who was screaming.

We are all sunburnt and sandy.

Lots of love,

Aunt Sophie. PS. Tell Mummy we will leave the mackerel lines ready for you, with all the salt rinsed off, as requested.

Love from Aunt Tamzin, Hughie and Guy.

CHAPTER FOURTEEN

The Plaza Hotel
Swakopmund
Namibia

Dear Tamzin,

I sit, stuffing my face with German pastries, watching dolphins swimming in the glittering sea, my skin covered in reindeer fat.

'Good for the face, good for the bottom,' said the rather large lady called Mini, who gave it to me.

Well, I slapped it on. Even my iron backside is sore. I'm afraid your tartan pregnancy leggings wouldn't stay up. I ended up riding across the desert in a pair of someone else's blue nylon jodhpurs, and when I say ride, we rode. The crossing was 400km, completed in nine days and my lack of fitness was quite apparent.

We would sometimes canter for twenty minutes at a stretch and were asked to trot along the stony roads standing in the stirrups. But I loved it. Can't wait to go again.

I'm not sure if Bod would have made it. The Namibian horses think nothing of walking along dry riverbeds full of boulders, hopping from one to another. At one stage we walked up a steep, steep path made not just of rocks, but rocks that moved and slid down on top of me from the horse in front. A large stone hit my horse's leg and he reared up in shock. I had to hang on to the reins to stop him falling backwards over the edge.

Our guide was a stock farmer called Lumpi, whose grandfather had first ridden across the desert with the German Army in 1902. I'd offered to draw a map of the safaris he and his wife Waldi now offer and sat sketching as we rode along. Well, not when we were trotting.

They had a Mercedes truck that was sent on ahead to meet us at the end of each day with food for the horses. And for me. I ate as I've never eaten before, huge quantities of meat from their farm where we'd started our journey. I'd start with two chicken drumsticks and then tuck into rump steak with baked potatoes and still have room for steamed pudding.

'If you get constipated, tell us,' Waldi declared to all and sundry.

I took two clients with me; a girl who chose a Lipizaner to ride and an English chap called Steve who was given a stallion called Baron von Wolff, named after the Commandant who left a breeding herd of horses to go wild in the desert near Luderitz before the war.

Baron von Wolff was indeed one of these wild horses. He was quiet to ride but had a strong and inexplicable desire to head north. We'd be cantering along and suddenly see Steve heading for Angola. The horse would literally do a right angle turn and go off on its own mission.

After three days of this Steve got so fed up I said I would ride the Baron. There I was, going westwards into the sunset with everyone else when, completely without reason or warning, the horse beneath me would turn to the right. Even if it meant going into a wire fence. I was left sitting there kicking and slapping him with the reins like a frustrated child.

I don't know why all these stallions keep coming into my life. Shane has one on loan from the AWB [xx] at the moment. It's been trained to walk up the steps to the Voortrekker Monument with a huge, grumpy-looking man on its back.

After riding through the mountains, past vast cattle stations and woebegone goldmines, we dropped down the Kuiseb Pass.

I've never been hotter, but we trotted along the road as if we were in the cavalry.

'During the Second World War German settlers in South West Africa, as Namibia was then known, were interned by the British,' Waldi explained 'but two geologists fled into the desert where they managed to hide in caves and live off the land for quite a time.'

They got a bit desperate at one stage. I'm reading a fascinating book about them called *The Sheltering Desert*. We camped at Aruveli, the thorny oasis where they originally hid their vehicle, and Lumpi pointed out the deep, rocky valley where they spent most of their time.

You often see trees in Namibia that look as if they have haystacks in them. The dry grass is collected by birds, community weavers, who adopt the strategy of living together, I suppose for mutual benefit, only they built such a massive nest in one thorn tree that the branch supporting the nest broke and the whole colony found itself on the ground. We saw quite a few telegraph poles that had acquired what amounted to high-rise apartments full of chattering birds.

When we hit the flat plains of the Namib Naukluft I found birds that had opted for a completely alternative strategy. My horse would seem to avoid something on the ground, only when I looked behind me I could see nothing there. It turned out that he didn't want to tread on a small bird's nest, made in a hollow in the stony desert, with two perfectly camouflaged eggs. The adults didn't seem to be around but the sun would have been hot enough to keep the eggs warm during the day.

A chap called Welwitsch, one of the first Europeans who made it to the Namib, was convinced he'd found a monster in the desert. What he'd actually come across was a huge, prehistoric plant. I'd seen the *Welwitschia Mirabilis* in Damaraland, where the rhino had been eating them, but here they have grown unchecked. Lumpi said that some are over 1,000 years old. The plant has a woody centre and two thick, leathery leaves, which grow continuously, shredded by the winds until they resemble green tapestry wool overflowing from a basket left on the floor. Mist blowing in from the sea condenses on these leaves, enabling the plant to survive without ground water.

After passing great underground lava flows, now exposed as craggy hills, we found ourselves looking down into a mass of ridges known as The Mountains of the Moon. I couldn't understand how we were going to get through the violently hostile looking landscape, but we dropped down into the Swakop river gorge.

It was like being in a cowboy film, only with more extreme scenery. Sheer, red cliff faces rose six hundred feet on either side of us, dwarfing the horses. You could see how the rock had been viciously carved at times when the river was in spate.

But now it was a mere stream and we could gallop down the firm, sandy floor of the gorge until vegetation choked the way.

We slept beneath palm trees and, after nights spent out in the silence of the open desert, I was woken by the sounds of their leaves, blowing in the wind. They sound like rain.

I had imagined myself cantering up the high sand dunes nearer the coast, but the horses didn't like them. They sank deep into the hot sand and were rather unnerved by the experience, confused as to why on earth we should want to climb up.

Until we saw camels. A herd was grazing freely near the river mouth. I've never known horses to be so terrified. They were completely uncontrollable. Lumpi commanded us to get off and let the horses run while he chased away the camels with a little stick.

We eventually managed to re-mount and rode in triumph down to the sea.

It was the first time I had ever ridden along a beach. We made our way up the icy Skeleton Coast and into Swakopmund to drink huge glasses of German beer and eat platefuls of gherkins and salami while the horses sighed with relief and were taken home in their, now empty, Mercedes truck.

I'm having tea with John's mother Denise tomorrow, which seems strangely demure after all we've just done; days spent singing that song, *I rode through the desert on a horse with no name*.

She says she'll come next time; only wearing Lycra cycling pants so as not to get chafed.

Raddy would love it, but I have to say I think Johnty would rather drive the truck.

Thank you for the excellent pneumatic sports tops; they were very useful.

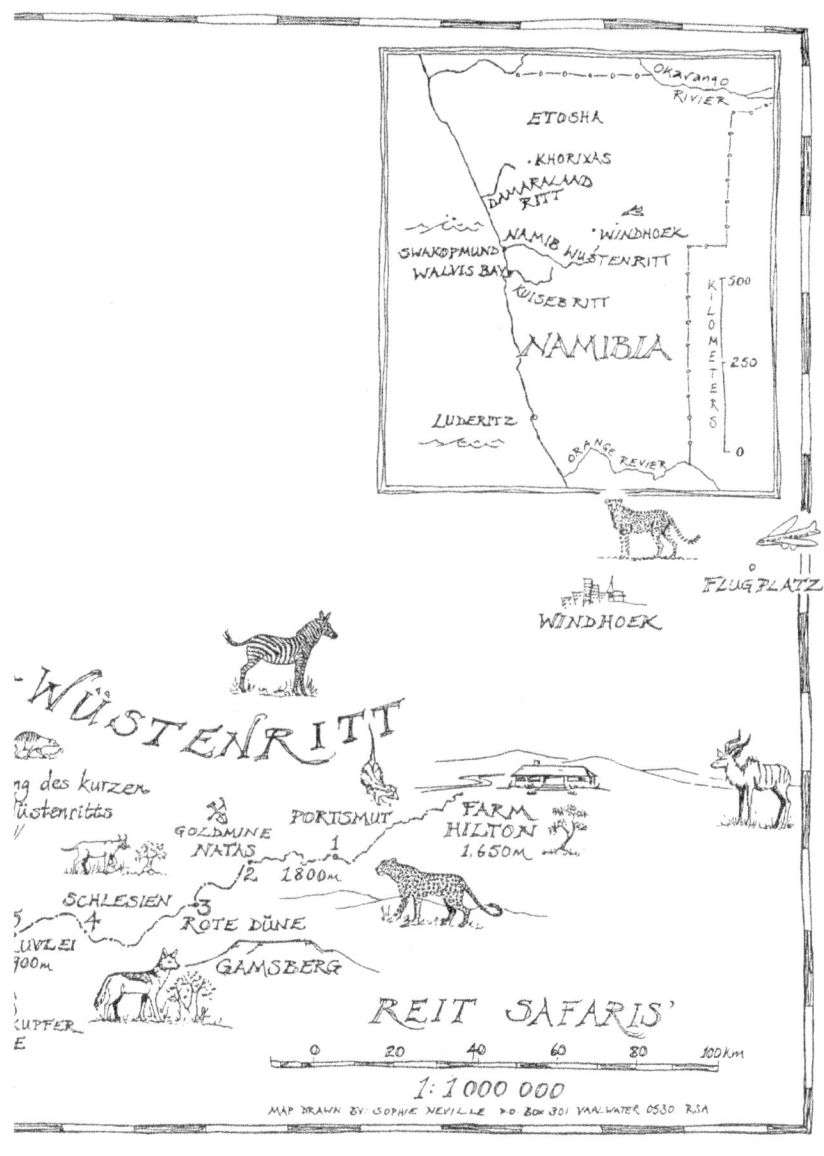

Love,

Sophie

September 1997

Darling Sib,

It's suddenly autumn, with leaves falling and all the garden stuff stashed in the garage. My bairns are upstairs playing with our old dolls house. They spent a happy day with their cousins getting lost in the tall maize growing on Tamzin's farm. Hastings now wants a ferret, but I've said NO.

I've been up in Nottingham of all places, filming a sweet children's programme called *Bernard's Watch*. The director has invited me to be in the next series. It was strange staying in a hotel in a town where we once lived.

Then I did an unexpectedly good day's work on a Paramount picture. I had to be in Southampton for five a.m, so worried all night about waking up on time, but it was worth it as we went out to sea on a steamship. It was bliss; the sunniest day of the year with *Clinique* Factor 25 supplied by the make-up girls. A nice way to earn money.

England, of course, has been shot to pieces by the Princess of Wales' death. Did you hear that Mum took a stool and sat outside Westminster Abbey to watch the procession? She saw it all. And met a one-toothed funeral director who told her that Diana was in the coffin that had been made for Prince Philip. They didn't have one ready for her and she was too tall to fit in any of the ones waiting for the older royal ladies.

The most remarkable sight on television was the crowd lining the whole of the M1 for about forty miles - astonishing. The hearse had to keep its windscreen wipers on to see through the flowers that were being thrown onto it. Apparently it broke down as soon as it got through the Althrop gates. One of Robert's soldiers was a coffin bearer.

Do you know the life expectancy of hamsters? Monty is getting rather old. I feel under his bed for heat every day, just in case. I think it might be rather shocking if his death went undetected for too long.

Lots of love,

Perry xxx

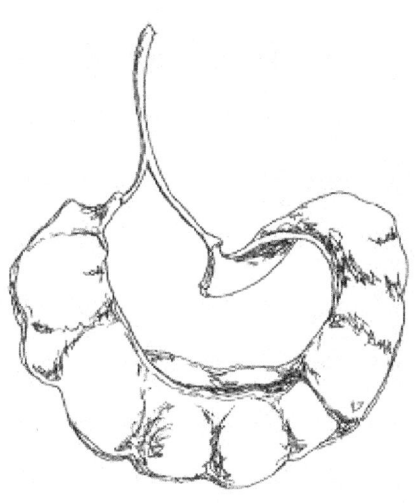

>Horizon Horseback Adventures
>Triple 'B' Ranch
>PO Box 791
>Vaalwater 0530
>South Africa

Dear Perry,

I was with Andrew, driving south from Etosha when I heard of the car crash in Paris. The news had a mirage-like quality out there, until I found CNN blasting into Windhoek and sparing us no detail.

A safari company wanted me to draw various maps of Ongava, a private reserve bordering the National Park, and flew me up from Swakopmund in a small plane. After a spectacular flight over the country, we dropped altitude and looked for rhino along a range of stony hills running through the reserve called Ondundozonananandana. Andrew, who can pronounce this perfectly, was there to greet me when we landed on the chalky white airstrip. He is managing the lodge and seemed very grown up, only I'm not sure if it wasn't just the relative length of his shorts. He has a pet vulture, which jumps around on the rocks above his office and came hopping towards me in rather an alarming manner when I brought it a bone.

I spent my days sketching from the game drive vehicles, making up a map with the help of the rangers, and dodging enormous African masks that hung from every wall of the lodge.

I met another pilot who took me for a flight over the great salt pans in the pink, dusky, evening light.

It was an amazing sensation.

We found ostrich and gemsbok moving far, far out into the pans, so that they could spend their nights in the open with a better chance of avoiding lion.

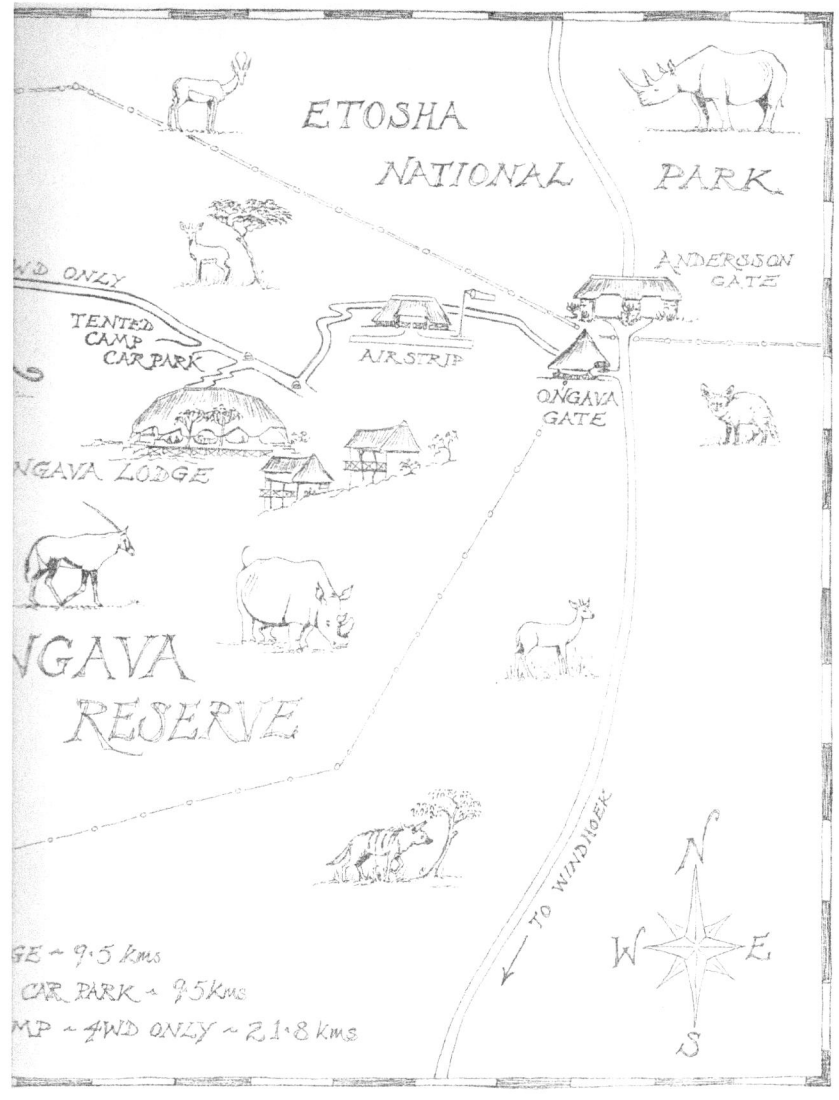

As it was, the predators were coming our way. I don't know if it was Granny's prayers or pure chance but I did two things I wouldn't normally do. I kept meaning to give Andrew my passport and money to lock up in the lodge safe, but didn't think my things would be pilfered from the guide's room where I was staying. After all the gadding about I was tired, sitting up unusually late. Every sinew in my body was demanding sleep, but Andrew had clients who were keen drinkers and I was sharing the grinding task of having to watch over them. We couldn't go to bed until they chose to, when Andrew would accompany them past the possible dangers posed by nocturnal beasts, to their chalets.

Andrew and I eventually staggered sleepily up the steps to the lodge reception.

The whole place had been smashed up. Lights were broken and there was glass everywhere. The safe had been ripped open. I'm so grateful I hadn't decided to go to bed earlier. I might well have walked into the thieves alone. My face would have been left on the wall with the African masks.

I flew back to the Waterberg to find I have a new vehicle, a long wheel-base, four-by-four Toyota, born in about 1988 but sprayed green and re-built specially for me by a friend who lives on the mountain. I asked him to cut a panel out of the roof so that when you come to stay you can stand in the back.

You must come, sooner or later.

A girl with a truck, but no abode. The church needs my cottage to house old people. I feel a bit ousted but it's probably no bad thing to have to relinquish material things from time to time. Whilst I used to look out onto the bush, I now see signs of suburbia threatening to grow up around me, which is something I couldn't stand. It would be stifling.

Laura was great, she said, 'Come and live with us.'

So I'm back on the farm, staying in their house near Horizon where my horse is stabled.

I'd forgotten how dire the antiquated wind-up telephones are. There's only a single party-line for five different families, two businesses and the mechanic's workshop. It rings non-stop, in seven different ways, driving us all bonkers. You never know when it's free and have to lift the receiver and ask if it's busy, although this is normally obvious as you can hear the chat. This means that when you do have an important phone call, Mrs van der Merwe, an old Afrikaans neighbour, is bound to come on the line unexpectedly and ask, loudly and deliberately, *'Isit busy op die lyn, ass-e-blief?'* I'm sure she knows perfectly well how busy we are, as her evening's entertainment is to listen in on conversations.

Everyone on the exchange calls me Mrs Neville. It makes me want to go and call for Mum. I keep being presented with air tickets that pronounce me as Mrs too. Do I sound married? I don't think I look it. To everyone's amazement it is Sarah-Jane who is getting married. I'm off to Botswana on Saturday to officiate. As I might as well stay there for as long as I can, I've packed most of my possessions, tents and camping stuff into my new vehicle. Nina ran up to me as I was leaving saying how she hates it that I have to travel alone, but I've no choice.

I can, henceforth, be contacted C/o African Horseback Safaris, PO Box 20538, Maun, Botswana.

Do write. I will.

Lots of love, Sophie

I don't know anything about hamsters and they're not listed in my game book. Ask Mum.

Hardacre Farm
20th October 1997

Dearest Sib,

At last a letter. Firstly, thank you for the stunning glass you gave me for my birthday ~ it's heavenly. I love it. I hope you had a wonderful one; we all thought about you lots.

Tonight Hughie read some words and (most exciting of all) wrote his name. He is really keen, loves school and his teacher; so very thrilling.

We had just finished supper on Friday night when there was a knocking on the door.

I opened it and found Mum, sobbing on the doorstep, very, very upset.

'Mum, what's the matter? Have you left Dad?'

'Of course not,' she said, 'I'm lost.'

'You're not lost, you're here.'

But she was meant to be in Kent with the otters. She'd been endlessly orbiting the M25 looking for the exit near where she was meant to be giving a lecture. It's about two hours drive from here.

On Saturday we went to a ploughing match. They really exist. Hundreds of tractors. Hughie could hardly contain himself. He ran one way, his arms and legs ran the other and then he fell down a rabbit hole, face smack in the mud. On Sunday they came to harvest the maize in the largest combine you have ever seen… the excitement. There's a fierce looking contractor called Gary, a skinhead in a sleeveless, orange boiler-suit who scares all the mothers rigid. All the little boys adore him. He drives the harvester round in ever decreasing circles. After a while, all sorts of small wild animals shot out of the maize where they had been living. It was astonishing; I had no idea there were so many there and was rather shocked to see a snake. Guy was interested but quite careful and took no risks. Very sweet.

We found a well in Cecily's meadow – I knew there had been a house there. Looney Len the metal detector man (do you remember he keeps saying, 'Possibly Roman' and always has his fly undone) stumbled across it and nearly fell in.

'Very dangerous, possibly a cavern,' he declared.

Perry is in flying form, although Atalanta is not long away from going to boarding school; she has to go when she is eight, which seems very little. Poor Perry. No doubt she'll tell you all. Take care of yourself, Mum is worried you will catch malaria in the swamps.
Love,
Tamzin

Dear Sophie – P.T.O. – Hastings was thrilled to find his name on twenty-three signposts! Lots of love, PRHA + Shaddy

MACATEER'S CAMP
AFRICAN HORSEBACK SAFARIS
OKAVANGO DELTA
BOTSWANA

Dear Perry,

Sarah-Jane was married under a wild fig tree with water lilies in her hair. She wore a gold dress with what Andrew would call 'gladiator boots' underneath ~ strappy sandals with gold buckles. Tigger was a bridesmaid. Atalanta would have loved it. I made the video, filming everyone in their hot suits helping to get the table laid. I caught Sarah-Jane's father looking intently at something and panned down to see what it was. He was reading the newspaper that the plates had been wrapped in.

Everything for the wedding, including an enormous amount of glasses, tables, chairs and the photographer, arrived on the back of a lorry, which had broken down about two hours into lion country. They had to spend the night in the bush with a large group of school children who were also on the back. 'What are they doing here?' The teenagers were all smartly dressed in blue uniforms.

'They've come to play their marimbas.' I didn't know what a marimba was but a number of African xylophones were coming off the back of the truck. They made the most beautiful sound, playing during and after the service while the African guests sang choruses.

The minister and most of Peter's family were flown in by helicopter at unexpected times. Sarah-Jane rode up the aisle on a white Arab and went away four times: once on a raft constructed by the grooms, once in the helicopter, on the horses, and finally in Peter's muddy hunting vehicle. They went to spend the night in a tent Rowena had put up on a fallen baobab tree but didn't know that John Sobey had hoisted a handheld radio into the branches, so they had to contend with his comments on their wedding night.

'You won't believe it but the day I arrived back from honeymoon,' she told me two weeks later, 'we got involved in a shootout, in Maun.'

It would happen to Sarah-Jane. A drunk Motswanan hunter armed with an elephant rifle was on the rampage.

'Why? What happened?'

'He was upset that his girlfriend had rejected him,' Sarah-Jane went on. 'I wasn't surprised. He started firing at our house, which was really quite frightening, you know.'

'What did you do?' I knew they had no telephone.

'Peter told me to get upstairs and hide in the cupboard. So I sat there, making my body as small as possible, while the lunatic kept firing rounds into the building. As the man had an elephant gun the bullets were coming right through the walls. I thought, "I've only been married ten days. I don't want to die yet." Peter was hanging out of a window, trying to persuade the man to calm down. He really was in danger, except that the looney clearly has a hatred for women, and Peter has a moustache. None of the locals alerted the Police for a long time. Eventually he fired two shots into the engine of a Land Rover standing outside and stormed off. All I wanted to do,' Sarah-Jane said, 'was have a bath and get to bed, but then the Police did arrive and we had to spend the night sitting in Maun Police station making statements.'

'Did they catch him?'

'Oh, yes. But he's Motswanan. They let him off with a warning.'

'What about the house?'

'Yes, well that is full of holes and has a lot of broken windows.'

Meanwhile I was sitting under the sausage tree chatting to her clients, without a care in the world. The tree is safe at the moment as it is flowering. Every morning the ground beneath it is strewn with dark, velvety red flowers the size of teacups. I scoop them up to decorate the table. Sausage trees are pollenated by small fruit bats, which are attracted to the flowers, as they smell of fermenting fruit. The flowers of baobab trees, which are pollenated by flies, smell of rotting meat.

When not flower arranging I seem to spend my time drawing cartoons of John Sobey:

> 1. John, the safari guide showing the guests a python, which started to constrict him.

2. John shooting someone's Cartier engagement ring out of a tree.

JOHN AND THE HEART SHAPED BULLET

3. John chasing off a lion on foot. It had come running up to us as we were sitting near a pool having a picnic.

4. John with a naked lady sitting on Jigsaw.

I wasn't sure about the lady but John said he wasn't either. She was one of the few people who has taken him entirely by surprise.

'One minute her husband was politely asking if he could take some photos of her on the horse without a saddle and the next, well, I looked up to find she was not only starkers but wanted me to give her a leg-up.'

Laura once had exactly the same experience. Does this sort of thing ever occur in Hampshire?

Lots of love to you all, Sophie

MACATEER'S CAMP
OKAVANGO DELTA

The day of my indignation

Dear Tamzin,

Topgun, one of Sarah-Jane's grooms, has declared that I don't seem to be able to ride very well. It was Jigsaw's fault. Sarah-Jane insisted on putting his saddle on too far forward and he got upset about it, bucking me off into the water, right outside the stables.

'Are you intending to join the Botswana Underwater Cavalry?' one of the clients asked.

I did a little bit of submerged galloping yesterday. It doesn't do your camera any good. We were racing down a floodplain, water splashing up around us, having a glorious time when my pony must have come across a hippo path and we both plunged into a pool. John said we quite disappeared from view. I opened my eyes underwater, seeing fish whizz by as I travelled quite a way before hitting the sludgy bottom.

Mum says that Granny is adamant I'll die of malaria. Please persuade her not to worry. There are not many mosquitoes here in the wild; dragonflies eat their larvæ. They only breed in stagnant water, like town drains. Anyway, the mosquito is only the vector for malaria; you catch it from other people. Like any disease. I bravely gave the grooms a lecture on the dangers of contracting STDs. Topgun said haughtily that he's not concerned since he condomises, but that isn't failsafe. I saw a hand-written poster in town saying:

AIDS IS REAL. GIVE YOUR PARTNER A CONDOM FOR VALENTINE'S DAY TO SHOW YOU CARE.

One. I hope that they don't think it will do the trick for the rest of the year. I felt sorry for our dear little kitchen maid called Independence. When she cut her finger the infection went flying up her arm. I found myself soaking her hand in Epsom Salts but her body is so wasted that it's evident she is HIV+. If her name is Independence it means she was only born in 1966. She refuses to go to hospital and scurries off to the witchdoctor instead. These wretched sangomas tell men that if they sleep with a virgin they'll gain immunity or be healed of AIDS. This has led to little girls and even babies being raped, often by five or six men at a time.

A hyena stole my Rice Krispies. Stupid of me to leave the packet in the dining-tent. The kitchen has been raided so regularly that John's had to put an electric fence around it. They even managed to open the chest freezer.

'We got up before dawn once,' Sarah-Jane told us, 'to take the man shooting our promotional video off to film the sunrise. I saw an odd looking creature out on the dry floodplain making a strange noise. It was quite far away,' she explained, 'and I couldn't think what it was. It seemed to have one straight horn.'

The cameraman found it with his long lens and started laughing. A hyena had a cooking pot with a long handle stuck over its head.

'I didn't know what to do about it,' she went on. 'We needed to get going before we lost the early morning light, so we hurried off.'

When Sarah-Jane returned she found the kitchen ladies had armed themselves with brooms and had chased the hyena into the back of a vehicle. By now it was going berserk.

'There was a teaspoon in the bottom of the pan, clonking around.' Her husband managed to catch the animal and they filmed the saucepan being wrenched off. 'The hyena looked rather dazed, roared into the camera lens, leapt off the Landcruiser and disappeared into the bush. Peter smelt horrific for days.'

There are an extraordinary number of giraffe in the area. We quite often come across groups of sixteen and Rowena once saw eighty, all standing together. They rather shape the landscape or certainly the vegetation. The trees tend to protect themselves with thorns but the giraffe couldn't care less. Apparently the trick when you want to eat an acacia is to produce copious amounts of saliva but I haven't tried this myself. The trees continue to retaliate by producing tannin in their leaves after the giraffe start to browse. This substance is bitter and ultimately poisonous. As it's released the tree automatically sends out chemical signals on the wind to urge nearby trees to do the same. The giraffe counter this by nonchalantly browsing into the wind.

Sadly the lion round here have developed a taste for giraffe meat. Since they are about fourteen foot high I didn't think the adults would be at risk but the prides can number up to ten lion. A giraffe was chased into a clump of trees recently and pulled down about 500 metres from the camp. We were surrounded by howling hyena for nights on end. Actually hyena don't howl, they whoop. I've decided jackal don't howl either; they wail. Tree frogs ping. It's all very noisy.

The days whizz by. The whole scene created for the guests must be a bit like an English house party in the 1920s. They're met off their little charter planes by a driver and brought back to the camp where the staff line up to greet them, (not in an English way though; they sing and clap and dance harmonious songs of welcome while Tigger leaps about wagging her tail).

After being shown to their tents the guests are veritably pampered. Rowena is like a chatelaine, offering drinks or tea, hosting dinner at night. She's a one handed hostess at the moment. As Jigsaw broke her wrist I've stayed on for a while and take the guests off riding with John.

When they've been out for about three hours and are beginning to get a bit peckish, we surprise them by coming across a beautifully laid table in the middle of nowhere, with bacon and eggs cooking on the fire. Rowena always delights in coming out from hiding in the bushes and opening champagne for everybody. They love it.

I'm getting spoilt too; having my knickers ironed and tea brought to my tent on a tray every morning. It's rather difficult to leave.

Lots of love,

Sophie

Hardacre Farm

October 21ˢᵗ

Dear Sophie ~

We've just returned from Thurlston in Devon where we stayed for a week with some friends, whose aunt has part of a large Victorian house looking out over the sea.

The boys loved it; everyone loved it, especially the dogs. We sat in the autumn sunshine and the children dug holes. They dug so deep we thought we might see you. Harry swam and Maudie-spoilt-brat barked. They found washed up dogfish day after day. The weather was simply magical, not a drop of rain or puff of wind. Saw lots of birds – herons, sea egrets, buzzards etc.

All was well, thank Goodness, on our return. Bod looks like a teddy bear with a huge coat inspired by deep Hampshire frosts. We missed them while we were on the coast.

Mum and Dad came to lunch yesterday bringing a six-stone pumpkin they had grown, which we hid in the wood for Hughie to find. The boys were in their element.

Mum, as ever, was not disappointing; she is having yet another battle with a neighbour, had been to 'a ghastly wedding' and had lots of local gossip, slagging everybody off.

She is 'involved in a dispute with Stroud District Council over an incident connected with a missing traffic bollard outside the White Hart public house.' The engine was nearly dragged out of her car when she drove over some sticking up bolts where the bollard was meant to be. Dad had to pay for the repairs of course.

Yesterday I took part in a cross-country event. Bod had a lovely day with lots of jumps, and is a bit stiff this morning.

Today, poor Deb (my neighbour) broke her nose in two places. Her mad horse threw its head up. It's a bit crooked but she is thrilled as she can breathe through it now. Very odd; she was always bunged up before.

Have a wonderfully Happy Christmas; I hear Mum is coming out to see you. We will too soon I hope. Alarming news to hear you're under canvas again. Is this OK?

With all our love,

Tamzin xxx

MACATEER'S CAMP
OKAVANGO DELTA
BOTSWANA

Dear Tamzin,

Just when I was thinking, 'I must tell Tamzin how lovely it is to sleep in a tent,' a hyena tore through the side of my store tent and stole my laptop. The grooms found it down by the horses, and luckily it was not chewed up.

Another hyena ate the indicator lights off the water bowser and 35 metres of electric fencing. The wild animals seem to be asserting themselves; Sarah-Jane walked into a leopard making its way along the path to her tent, and a baboon pooed on John Sobey. From a great height.

Rowena seems to be plagued by a belligerent elephant called Royd. She hates him because he keeps knocking down all the most beautiful trees. He has pushed over so many John had to buy a chainsaw so that he could clear the track into camp.

Rowena lost her temper with Royd in the end and tried to shoo him off. He turned and without warning charged her, ears flat against his skull. She ran behind a tree but John could see that the elephant was coming round to get her. He whipped inside his tent, grabbed a safety flare and fired it off. It hit Royd high on the forehead a moment before he lunged at Rowena. She only just missed being speared by his tusks. The elephant wasn't hurt but the flash rather stunned him and he ran off.

I was responsible for sending a nineteen-year-old girl to the camp to help during the weeks before the wedding. 'Was she useful?' I asked Rowena.

'She was good at entertaining the clients,' John said smiling.

'He refers to the time I caught her snogging a guest behind an anthill.' Rowena replied.

'Really?'

'Yes, and Royd was the other side, munching away on Mokolwane nuts. Bloody dangerous.'

'She did manage to convince an old German tourist,' John said, 'that warthogs lived up trees and there was a family of piglets living in an old hammerkop nest near the camp.'

I thought that was quite an achievement.

Royd ended up nearly killing me last night. I woke to the sound of terrific creaking. I must have instinctively known that a tree was about to fall and rolled out of my bed. A palm tree, about eighty foot high, crashed down, landing alongside the tent. It could quite easily have fallen through the canvas.

I crawled back under my covers and peered out through the mosquito netted window beside me. There was Royd carefully walking over the guy ropes. With three boyfriends. They tore strips off the fibrous trunk of the palm tree, munching away on the woody mouthfuls, making terrible smells all night long. There was no way I could escape.

We've had the most unbearable man staying; a sixty-five year old Texan dry-cleaning tycoon who thought he'd lose weight by coming on a riding holiday. Only he doesn't know how to ride.

'I can't git this horse to steer,' he barked furiously, cantering along out of control and was most offended when I suggested pulling on the reins.

We've been trying to work out how to spare the other guests his company. To enable us to explore a wide area every party is taken out on what we call a Fly Camp for a couple of nights. The term implies that you just take a flysheet but we've been using a beautiful camp called Eden where there are tree houses built on stilts. The horses are picketed along a rope and need to be guarded at night. I was the one who had to keep the midnight watch with the Texan, who predictably was drunk. He'd shriek at even the slightest sound, 'Git the gun. Git the gun.' More dangerous than Royd. I found out in the end that he had terminal cancer and had probably come to Africa in an attempt to die in action. I would so much rather he hadn't tried.

FLY CAMP

It's getting late. I can hear the sound of hutus calling; ground hornbills – turkey-sized birds with large bills and red face pouches, which patrol the grasslands looking for snakes to eat. They've become my favourite birds. I must go and make everyone drinks. We are having gemsbok steaks tonight and mushrooms fried in garlic butter with Crêpes Suzette for pudding.

I think if they want to ban fox hunting they must certainly make it illegal to keep domestic cats; they kill millions of completely innocent songbirds; you're certainly not allowed to keep them on a game reserve. Slag in Afrikaans, by the way, doesn't mean quite the same thing as in English. It is, indeed, the word for slaughter. A butcher's shop is called a *Slaghuis*, selling *beeste, vark* or *skaap*, although last year, at the Melkrivier Slaghuis, they held a beauty contest.

Lots of love to Johnty and the boys, Sophie

MACATEER'S CAMP

Dear Perry,

The Maddens are out for a fortnight and send their love. After spending a week riding we went by dugout up the Borro River and drove into Moremi in my new Toyota. Right into the water.

We started off one morning, taking a track that seemed to cross a shallow river only to find water coming up over the bonnet and pouring into the cab. It was my fault, I'd told David to keep the revs up and keep driving. Fortunately a safari guide drove up behind us and offered to tow us out. Two bewildered English tourists were sitting on the back of his open vehicle.

'Are you on holiday?' They asked us.

Unbelievably my engine started first time. It could have been ruined. The portfolio with all my watercolours was in the back, but as that end of the vehicle was sticking up in the air only the very corner of the large paintings got wet. Every time we came across a stretch of water after that, two of us went ahead of the vehicle, me carefully investigating hazards with a stick. We must have looked like the troupe of baboons who cross the submerged stretch of track beyond the camp with great caution, hating the idea of getting their feet wet.

Even David loved the horse safari so much we returned to Macateer's for their last two days and we've been lying in the sandy shallows all afternoon, watching Tigger trying to catch fish with her mouth.

The floodwaters of the Okavango are receding, leaving great open areas where the elephant graze. Cries of the fish eagle fill the air. We came across a cheetah yesterday and have been getting close to tsessebe; high-shouldered antelope of the hartebeest family that I'm told are the fastest buck in Africa. I saw a serval cat here for the first time, honey badger and marabou stork, which have been landing by the pool in front of camp like gawky pterodactyls. Two warthogs have made themselves a bathroom right outside my tent. I think Tigger would rather like to play with them but despite a great deal of flirting they trot off indignantly with their tails in the air as she makes her way towards them.

We continue to live quite happily with the baboons, who never touch our fruit or anything else belonging to us. Once Sarah-Jane picked a bunch of wild dates though and the monkeys screamed down, snatching it from the tea table; it was food that belonged to them. Peter said that it's a good idea to camp beneath a baboon roost when you're in the bush as they bark, warning you if lion or leopard come along.

We found Topgun, one of the grooms, sleeping in the tack shed this morning. He said that there was a terrifying animal in his tent. Rowena went over armed with a broom to find there was indeed something rather large under his bed. It wasn't exactly a predator. It was an angry porcupine.

Mum's visit went well in parts. She was badly affected by the heat and went round in a voluminous kaftan. Although oblivious of any embarrassment this might cause, she was terribly concerned about other people's appearance.

'Imagine being married to a man with a moustache,' was all she could say about Peter. 'Like kissing a Dandy brush.' And, 'What distresses me about John,' she said, 'is that he rides in bare feet.'

He actually wears *strops* - rubber soled sandals - because he gets so wet riding through the water.

'Well, I'm going to suggest he wears gumboots.'

We put Mum on Herero, the small chestnut stallion who was once attacked by a lion, and off she zoomed, looking determinedly over his ears. She ended up alongside Rowena, galloping with the zebra. To my surprise she rather enjoyed going fishing, so I took her into the western Okavango and we explored the whole region in boats gliding through tall papyrus reeds to forgotten islands, finding huge herds of lechwe under whole glades of baobab trees.

I had a shocking time after she flew home. John and Rowena, whose hand is better at last, had taken the clients on a fly camp. Most of the staff had gone over to look after them, and Sarah-Jane was in town, leaving me at the main camp with the rest of the horses, two grooms, the laundry maids and Tracy - Raddy's erstwhile nanny from New Zealand. It was her first day working here as the horse manager. I'd got her the job.

'Mrs Sophie, Mrs Sophie!' I was in a deep sleep. 'Fire! Fire at the horses.' Two large Tswana ladies were pulling me out of bed. 'Come. Come quick. Fire.'

It was three o'clock in the morning. I pulled on my boots, grabbed a huge torch Mum had left me and ran towards the barn. I could see flames leaping thirty foot high into the trees.

'The horses. They'll be trapped,' I was thinking. I thought the hay in the barn must have caught. But the horses were fine. The flames were coming from beyond the feed room where the staff have a village of tents and wooden huts.

Bang! An explosion went off. I came swinging around the high reed fence to find one of the huts was ablaze, sparks flying and explosions coming from inside it. One groom had a feeble hose on the fire but Topgun was rolling around in a puddle of water just beyond the flames, as if in agony. I shone the torch on him. He was panicking and his skin looked terrible, burnt from the neck down like a crispy joint of lamb.

'We must put him in water,' I shouted.

The ladies couldn't understand why, thinking I wanted to put him in the Okavango, but Sarah-Jane had just bought a new horse trough. We carried him over and lowered him into it. I sort of stirred the cold water around, keeping Topgun under the surface. He wasn't happy about this but by now the ladies had begun to realise that his body needed to be kept underwater, so he didn't have much of an option. I left him with them, leapt in the old Landcruiser, which was still smelling of hyena, and drove off to find the First Aid kit kept in the kitchen. The prospect of saving Topgun's life was daunting.

'He seems to have third degree burns all over his body,' I hurriedly explained to Tracy as I was getting her out of bed. 'They won't fly planes after dark. We are going to have to wrap him in cling film or something and drive him to hospital.'

I had only driven across the Okavango to Maun once before, with a guide, in daylight. It took five hours, scrunching through thick sand that would be too impossibly jarring for a burns patient to endure.

'It would be best to stabilize him and radio for a plane first thing in the morning.' Tracy said.

'If he survives that long.'

By now we were back at the barn. Topgun was out of the horse trough and on a mattress, with the ladies standing over him looking annoyed. Far from being in agony he was sleeping peacefully, like a baby. I gently drew back the blankets to show Tracy the burns. He was completely unscathed, looking clean and wearing nothing but white satin underpants with scarlet roses printed on them. The burns had disappeared. There was one, small blister between his fingers. I couldn't understand it.

We still had to put out the fire. It had made its way up into a tree and sparks were flying everywhere. Tracy found a knap-sack pressure spray in the tack shed and used a rake to reach a burning branch that we pulled down onto the blackened remains of the hut now burnt to the ground. Everything inside it had been completely incinerated and Topgun's tent, which had been next to it, had simply melted. Aerosol cans lying charred in the smouldering mess must have caused the explosions.

It was only in the morning that the whole story came out. One of the guests who returned with John and Rowena happened to be a pædiatrician and said she'd seen similar cases in England. She examined Topgun and told him he was lucky to be alive.

'He fell asleep smoking dope,' was her diagnosis. 'That's why his finger was burnt.'

He must have woken up to find the bed on fire and come hurtling out, only to fall to the ground. He would have been hot enough to want to roll around in the wet mud until, by torchlight, the leaf mould and earth made his skin appear badly burnt. It transpired that it wasn't his hut. It belonged to one of the ladies.

I'm flying back for my old flat-mate's wedding in Derbyshire this January and will be around for a couple of weeks, so I'll see you all soon. Can't wait.

Lots of love,

Sophie

CHAPTER FIFTEEN

Hardacre Farm

3rd March 1998

but such amazing weather the magnolias are out.

Dearest Sib,

It was wonderful having you here; the boys loved it too.

Mum has just rung. 'I'm most upset you didn't ask me to The Tower of London.'

'I didn't go to the Tower of London.'

Actually it was Raddy who went, as her father is in charge of it this year. She took Alexander, who is still rather young to endure the waiting around involved when the Queen comes to see things like that. He stood on one leg, then on the other and eventually couldn't wait a minute longer. The press missed it, but he ended up peeing on the Queen's shoes.

We had the cousins to stay over Half Term. Aunt Perry was glitzing in St. Moritz. Hastings was fantastic and taught the Spy how to ride his bike without stabilizers. In fact the weather was wall-to-wall sunshine. The children spent all day cycling in the farmyard and Hughie had his party on straw bales. He'd wanted and wanted a hamster for his birthday. In an instant I thought of Monty-One-Gulp who I invited to join the cousins. The scheme worked beautifully.

Now, if you ask Hughie if he wants a hamster he gets quite upset and says, 'No. They bite.'

Indeed they do… three children in as many days:

First: Alexander, straight through his fingernail.

Second: Guy who SCREAMED.

And the Grand Finale: Rosie Hampton-Smith, on the very tip of her nose. I cannot tell you…. The blood. In the end we gave Hughie a real tool-kit in a dear little wooden box, which he loves with all his heart and even took into Prayers at school on Monday. Much, much better than a hamster.

We've been having a local altercation. The people who bought the twenty acres of land next door to us are getting around Green Belt planning restrictions by claiming that they want to set up a rabbit farm of all things. In order to supervise the breeding the farm manager needs, of course, a five bed-roomed house, which they want to build on virgin soil. I'm getting upset about this ploy. They've already erected a number of sheds and installed a big, white caravan. The whole thing means going to endless Parish Council meetings and is quite depressing as we lose at every stage.

I've been team-chasing quite a bit. Bod jumped the most enormous ditch you have ever seen on Thursday. I heard a little cry as we sailed over and found we had leapt clean over a spectator sitting eating a sandwich.

Raddy-Radish has bought an old horsebox for £250. It was originally designed to load horses backwards. That's why it was so cheap; you can't actually get horses to walk into it. I even have to give Bod a smack on his bottom to get him loaded. Thanks to her

Range Rover it pulls well but you have to get out and flip a lever to reverse. Maudie was nearly killed by Deb's horse during this process, but she survived.

Lots of love,

Tamzin xxx

Horizon Horseback Adventures, Vaalwater, South Africa

Dear Tamzin,

A friend of mine was at a dinner party, held before a Charity Ball, when the hostess was serving soup, ladling it out at the table. There was a splosh and after fishing around a bit she removed a small, wet, furry animal.

'Oh, it must be the hamster,' she said. 'I was wondering where it had got to.'

She put it on her side plate and went on ladling soup for everyone. My friend was telling this story at another dinner when one of the guys looked up and said,

'Oh, yes. I'm afraid that must have been my mother.'

I arrived back in the Waterberg to find Shane has built a great pitch outside our house and has everyone in the district madly playing polocrosse. The Springbok players have been up for the weekend coaching us. It's a game like lacrosse on a horse; thrilling and completely addictive. Raddy would love it. I'm not good at playing but my pony is. I just have to learn how to get hold of the ball but this is not easy as on the whole it has to be done as you're cantering along.

I've been trotting eight kilometres a day in order to get fit. This nearly killed me. I was going quite fast, down through the cattle lands thinking,

'I ought to be carrying a mobile phone or something when I ride alone,' because no one would find me if I fell off, when my horse went straight down an aardvark hole.

Sam had been going at such speed that I somersaulted straight off without time to roll out of the way. I thought he would never be able to avoid falling on top of me, but my loyal little horse twisted back on his haunches, wrenching himself out of the hole. My hands should have been badly grazed but it was the one morning that I went out wearing gloves.

The inhabitants of Vaalwater still think of me as a creature from another planet.

The Afrikaans lady at the bottle store said, 'Why aren't you married?' in an abrupt, demanding way.

I looked at her and said, 'Do you know, I think it's because I don't brush my hair.'

She took this as an entirely reasonable answer. Shane once heard someone asking, 'Do English girls know about shampoo?' which delighted Laura who is astounded that Afrikaans women have so much time to spend on their appearance.

'I've never seen a Tunnie without earrings, nail varnish, full make-up and bouffant hair.'

'But Laura, they all have housemaids.'

The Sotho ladies actually put us all to shame; they always look both immaculate and fashionable. Most of them have huge families, wash all their clothes by hand in cold water and only have old-fashioned, fire-heated irons.

Laura couldn't believe it when I told her the Afrikaans word for a cucumber; it's a *komkommer*.

'I'm never going to conquer Afrikaans,' she said, laughing in despair. 'Every time I ask the exchange to put me through to someone in Potgietersrus they say, "Oh, Laura, please say that again." I think it's me Pontefract accent.'

I still can't speak the language properly either, but our friends the Whitbreads are worse than either of us. They had a carol service for the neighbours on Christmas Eve. Everyone was given a song sheet with the words for *Silent Night* in Afrikaans but there was a typing error. Instead of writing *vrede* for peace they typed *vors*. How, I don't know. *Vors* means sausage. I suppose we all ended up singing about heavenly sausage.

A bit like the sausage tree sausages. Or Gregory the sausage dog. Sarah-Jane had a client with a sausage stuck down his throat once. He could easily have choked to death. He was a big fat Bavarian and the blood vessels were bursting in his eyes. His daughter did the Heimlich manœuvre on him but it had no effect. What worked was that Sarah-Jane put her fingers down his throat, grabbed one end of the salami and pulled.

I'm painting away madly in an attempt to get enough artwork together for another exhibition in London this year. I sold 200 pictures last year but somehow still don't make enough profit to warrant paying income tax. So that's my new aim; to become a taxpayer. The *David Shepherd Conservation Foundation* have asked if they can sell my Namibian prints in their mail order catalogue, which will hopefully raise funds for large mammal conservation projects as well as for me.

Save the Rhino Trust auctioned my bird prints in Windhoek and managed to raise N$23,000 or something, which was pretty good.

Enthusiasm for the craft projects has rather waned but Stevens Mokwena, my one keen student, has won a scholarship to train as a boilermaker at the local coalmine. I suggested he took his wire-work along to the interview, telling him to look the personnel officer in the eye and shake him by the hand. Well brought up Sotho people look away in deference when greeting a superior but white people often receive this as rudeness.

'I did what you told me,' Stevens said. 'The man smiled but said, "Who taught you that trick?"'

Stevens told me there have been riots in our township.

'Oh, no. Why?'

'The mothers were very cross.' He looked quite daunted. 'You know everyone has been given electricity?'

'Yes,' I'd heard the houses had been connected.

'Now they are not being given it.'

The women were furious, because after one month and six weeks this supply was cut off. They got together and marched, bearing down on the house of the ANC Town Councillor.

'You have to know that your power will be cut off if you fail to pay your bills,' he explained.

'But what about you?' they retorted. 'You don't pay for your electricity.'

Stevens said they were all pointing to a loopy cable coming down from a streetlamp to supply the Councillor's own house.

Off to practise catching a ball from on top of my horse.

Lots of love,

Sophie

Church Hooker

4th March 1998

Darling Sib,

We've returned from the most magical holiday in St Moritz. It was all blue and white and dazzling - like staying in Narnia. It's quite the easiest place in the world to let time slip by - glorious blue skies every day.

I had pleurisy again, which spoilt things a bit. Cough, cough, cough. Instead of skiing we walked around the beautiful lake and saw *Titanic* in a funny little red velvet cinema. They had an interval. I must look trustworthy; Robert came back with an ice-cream to find me looking after a pile of mink coats belonging to the good ladies of the town.

Granny said that she wanted to give me a fur coat to wear in Switzerland. I know Mum can't bear them on principle, but I did think it would be rather glamorous. A huge brown paper packet arrived in the post all tied up with knotted string and sealing wax. It contained a stiff jacket, cut in a curious 1930's way. The hair was very short. I didn't take it with me. Sophie, it was made out of a horse. A bay.

We had lovely sleigh rides at night and stayed in an old-fashioned hotel, eating five course dinners. Heavenly. You could lie in the bath and look out over the lake. They have a polar bear in the reception, padlocked to a pillar since one of our friends took it on a drinking session. The manager caught him trying to take it up in the lift.

Robert went skiing every morning and won a race on his traditional toboggan. He took 54 seconds to complete the course, which is a mile long. Sheer ice. He came in late at night after celebrating his triumph to find a man at the reception desk wearing nothing but a pair of boxer shorts, asking the polar bear for a wake-up call.

The children went to stay with Aunt Tamzin for five days, returning all rosy cheeked and exhausted. She insisted they bring their hamster, Monty, for some reason. She didn't have to have him.

Now back to reality: builders are in for three weeks and it is quite hideous. It's especially difficult to endure when you don't own the house or have any control over the builders. They're making a pig's ear out of everything and there's thick dust everywhere. Today constitutes day seven of my nervous breakdown; the kitchen ceiling was pulled down. Robert says it's similar to living in the Spotty Dog.

I have another photographic shoot, modelling for *Take a Break* magazine. Hysterical. You have to act (overact) a character for their short story. I was Lorraine the Lynched Lover in a green suit. This time I'm going to be Shrewd Sharon the Salon receptionist. I reckoned that none of my friends would read it, but Mary-Dieu does and rang to declare me famous. Did you know that *Take a Break* has the largest circulation of any magazine in Britain? Mum now wants to appear in it.

Hastings is very earnest about his appearance these days and insists that he has to wear everything to be exactly like Robert. He tried to take a horsewhip into school today as Robs carries one as part of his uniform. I told him the headmistress didn't allow them and he said he'd ask her...

It's the school Bonfire Night on Saturday. Two people have been killed by fireworks blowing up in their faces this year, including a headmaster.
But love from us all, in our life of Hampshire happiness,
Perry xxx

Hardacre Farm

Dear Sophie,

The warthog tusks you sent were a great success and are currently part of our nature display. Hughie has drawn this lovely picture of a muck-spreader to thank you for sending them.

As you know, we had a battle preventing our neighbour's field from being turned into a rabbit farm. We won the appeal, but guess what? They've moved in another mobile home and twenty-eight ostriches. It's just like being in Africa. The strangest thing was that all the wild birds stopped singing when they arrived and stayed silent for days. Having moved the ostriches in without a *Dangerous Wild Animal License* the field shelter, which they need for this certificate, blew inside-out and they have no cover. They make the most bizarre noise and run around like crazy things. Deb's children stroke them, which is quite brave. I just get cross. The horses could not believe their eyes and went totally scatty except for Patrick, the miniature Shetland, who couldn't think what all the fuss was about. He can't see over the hedge.

Bod and I took part in another cross-country event, which was great fun. Johnty dropped us off and we made our own way back. I've started feeding him (Bod, not Johnty) cod-liver oil and cider vinegar for his arthritis, and it's now like riding a four-year-old. A handy hint for you to pass on to your pony friends. (Perhaps I ought to give it to Johnty too).

Love,

Tamzin

Horizon Horse Trails
Triple 'B' Ranch
PO Box 791
Vaalwater 0530
14 April 1998

Dear Tamzin,

You will never guess. We've just won a steam iron. We spent the weekend at a polocrosse tournament when everyone had the pleasure of seeing me in white jodhpurs. I must have looked odd because to avoid getting bruised I wound thick felt horse bandages round my lower legs, which with Laura's half-chaps and kneepads meant my legs looked fattest lower down. I think the iron prize was a joke. As it is my legs are fine but my right arm was caught in a horse's mouth at full gallop and I'm left with a graphic imprint of the teeth.

It was a tremendous tournament with 156 players. I couldn't believe I was competing. It's exciting because, unlike polo teams, we are split into two sections, so you play one chukka and then sit out the next, watching your other half scoring goals for you. The horses spin. One of our players spun off over the back of another horse, landed on her feet and spun back on again. She is 22 years younger than me. We had a big back-up contingent including Shane and Laura's four-week-old baby and camped by the trucks with the Zulu grooms who sang late into the night. We sat round a big fire on the first evening, chewing dry *wors* while our supper was heating up.

'Some horses seem to have got loose,' a disconnected voice said through the darkness. 'We haven't identified whose they are yet, but…'

'They'll be ours,' Shane said standing up.

They were. Of all the 200 or so horses there, our eight had run into someone's bean field and were hurtling around in the dark. It was a fifty-hectare field. A flat, square one. As we started to walk through the beans, grasshoppers jumped up, zinging in all directions. They sent the Thoroughbreds into a frenzy. My horse led them, galloping around in the darkness with his tail in the air.

The farmer was furious. He kept going on about his boing-kies and providing a 9mm solution. It took us two hours before we caught them. Our supper had solidified.

Sarah-Jane had a terrible shock transporting her horses. Ours travel in a big, open cattle truck but she bought an impressive steel horsebox. Only the bottom fell out. John had bought two chestnut Hanoverians in Namibia and was driving them back through the Kalahari. He said he felt something was wrong and stopped to check the tailgate. As he got out the floor literally dropped out the trailer. One of the horses cut its lower leg superficially but they're fine. Can you imagine what might have happened if he hadn't stopped? He had to leave the horses in a field by the side of the road and drive off to get the trailer welded together again.

We are now all sitting on the back stoep - a veranda comprised of a sheet of corrugated iron and a lot of plants - trying to recover physically from the weekend. It rained until everything I am and everything I possess became covered in thick, red mud. My white jodhpurs shrank so violently I had to get into the bath before peeling them off; an endeavour, which as Shane said, turned into a community project in its own right.

After six years of living out of bags and rucksacks I'm afraid I finally cracked.

'All I want,' I said to Laura, 'is a chest of drawers.'

And I burst into tears. What a silly girl.

Lots of love, Sophie

Triple B Ranch
April 1998

Dear Perry,

I've just come in from riding through the tobacco fields in the rain. The workers' bright yellow overalls stand out dramatically against the green leaves and they call and wave as I ride by.

'*Dumela.*' (Good morning).

'*Dumela, Lekae?*' (Morning, how are you).

Rupert Baber, who has returned from Oxford with a PhD to take over from Charles, says this must be the last tobacco crop. I'm glad, not least because the fumes from the drying ovens were making me quite ill. The plants must be full of poisons. Rupert wants to stop growing it for moral reasons but it means putting over 100 people out of work. He is planning to grow geraniums organically instead and extract the essential oils for the perfume industry.

Everyone seems to be getting their PhDs: Rupert's beautiful fiancée Tanya has one, and Juliet's husband another. Our nearest neighbour in the Okavango was doing a PhD on termites. His stories were so fascinating that we used to get him over for dinner to entertain the clients. One night he brought a queen in a jam jar. She was the size of a fat chipolata and lived until she was about twenty years old.

'Died of alcohol poisoning,' he said.

He'd pickled her. Termites in Africa are so numerous that there's a greater biomass beneath the ground than above it, ie: more termites around than everything else put together. I've learnt that they never sleep and will eat anything containing cellulose ~ grass, animal dung, wood, bales of straw, fence posts, books, your knickers. Harvester termites collect so many grass seeds it's possible to dig into their storehouse and find six kilograms of grain. I suppose cellulose rots in Europe but it's too arid here; we hardly get any mould.

I've just been given a chest of drawers; I'm so pleased I've categorized all my terrible clothes. A very constructive thing. Tanya has been given the most destructive thing; a tiny wild cat that someone found abandoned under a tree. It looks like rather an energetic tabby kitten, but it's certainly aggressive. It ran straight up Rupert's chest and hit him on the nose.

Walter said, 'If it's a wild cat it will be able to catch a fly.' Right on cue the kitten swatted a fly in mid air and ate it up. 'It'll be capable of killing steenbok when it's older.'

One little kitty-poosie.

A number of hippo have taken up residence in the lake in front of Horizon, where they've been terrorising the grooms but delighting the guests, as one has produced a baby. Juliet is due to have her first baby soon too. Shane and Laura were told, point blank, that it was medically impossible for them to have a child but everyone prayed for them and they now have a beautiful little girl called Jesse. Jesse means 'God Exists'. They found a way to buy their own farm nearby and are thriving. Shane is giving courses in natural horsemanship whilst breaking in the colts reared on Triple B Ranch and seems to spend a lot of time rescuing horses. Sarah-Jane does too. She has a cob called Livingstone who has been branded so many times he looks like a Scrabble board. He is being retired to the Waterberg, living with Ant and Tess on their lovely game ranch. It's called Ant's Nest.

'*Mais pourquoi les fourmis?*' some French people asked me looking perplexed. I had to try and explain.

I'm coming home for the summer and staying a good, long time, migrating like the swallows. Can't wait to get to the sea. Tamzin wants me to go with her again and Mum has asked me to find the boys a pony.

Here is an organic geranium leaf for your bath.

Lots of love to everyone,

Sophie

CHAPTER SIXTEEN

Gloucestershire
August 1998

Dear Perry,

Poor Shaddy had to travel all the way to Norfolk sitting by my feet in the front of Tamzin's car. He was so patient and good. I wish I could be as trusting as he was, but like the children I moaned, even though we knew we were going somewhere lovely. After five hours we finally reached the coast, and Shaddy was able to run out over the mud-flats in delight. It was all worth the squash.

Everyone I grew up with seemed to be on the beach with their little children. The only thing about going on a family holiday, is that some people don't like it if you don't have a family too.

'Let me take a photograph of you,' one girl said. 'It must be ghastly being single and not having a man around to take photos of where you've been.'

This is something that had never even occurred to me. And it isn't true, since you can simply hold your arm out and take shots of yourself like Benedict Allen. If you want photos of yourself that is. But, anyway, I was made to feel lacking. Lacking children, lacking in the experience of pregnancy and childbirth (the excruciating details of which they seemed to think I long to hear of) and lacking a man.

I had to go off to the other end of the beach with my camera to escape. As I did, a man called to me, walked over, took me in his arms and kissed me. This wasn't something that I expected but it happened. Perfect timing. I looked up to see the Mothers' Mafia watching, intrigued.

'This is Steve,' I said, introducing the man a little later. Steve, it has to be said, is extremely good-looking.

'Oh, hello,' said one Mother, instantly pulling her tummy in. 'Are you here on holiday too?'

'Not really,' Steve said. 'I've just bought a house in the village.' He pointed to the most desirable location in the whole place. 'I've decided to retire.'

'But you don't look old.' He is my age.

'No, but early retirement is one of the advantages of having worked in computers.' In other words, he has made a fortune.

'Where did you and Sophie meet?'

'Riding across the Namib desert.'

The next time they saw him was outside the cottage at 8.30am. He'd come over early to sort out Hughie's fishing tackle, but I had to laugh, as all the Mothers thought this glamorous being must have spent the night with me, and that the grass looked greener on my side of the fence.

It was greener until I arrived home and had to contend with being the unmarried daughter. Mum had left a second-hand pram, saved from the neighbour's rubbish, in my bedroom (what a terrible hint) and Len the donkey was dead in the field with his legs sticking up in the air. Apparently this was all my fault. I can't think why; he was twenty-five and had a seriously swayed back. I didn't know what to do with the body of a dead donkey without any lion about but rang the Hunt who mercifully took him away.

Raddy bought an oil of a lioness I had painted from my Okavango sketches, which was encouraging and I'm revving up for my art exhibition in London. Thank you so much for offering to help. I was rather counting on you and Tamzin to be my gallery girls. You don't have a black trouser suit do you? Tamzin said she would wear hers with big pearl earrings and look vacant. Mum offered to bring the otters along, but I didn't think it appropriate. I must go and look at this pony for Tamzin tomorrow but otherwise am slaving away framing as I reckon I need 180 pictures to fill the space available.

It's good to come back to England for a longer time. It takes a while to decompress and acclimatise. The culture shock isn't in going away, it's in coming back.

As Nicki said, 'It's weird in England: there are traffic circles everywhere (roundabouts) and all the houses go up (consist of more than one storey)'.

I'm certainly struck by the volume of traffic and the astronomical rise in house prices.

Love,

Sophie

Hardacre Farm

18:10:98

Darling Sophie,

The day you left, heavenly Eric arrived and Building Extension: Phase One began in earnest. Foundations were dug, drains laid and (after a wet start) amazing sun shone on our ever-heightening brickwork. As we drove off for our annual Devon adventure the roof was almost on. When we woke up on our first morning home the internal walls were being knocked down. Despite polythene, there was so much dust that my hair never got greasy – what heaven.

But now we are, Johnty being the only exception, ill. Just when the Irish pony you had found for us arrived too. We have had the weekend from hell. I've lost count how many times I've been puked on, from the bedroom to the kitchen. The boys' temperatures range from 103°~105°F. Sleepless nights of hot, kicking, sobbing, screaming children. When one stops the other starts. To top it all, I had the worst tonsils – great scarlet punch-bags joining in the middle and sandwiching two thick cushions of bright, white …pus. I felt so ill I couldn't open my eyes, but I couldn't sleep either. It was impossible to swallow. Even our doctor was quite impressed. I'll have to have them out. I still look grey and feel mouldy.

Quite funny. Mum found herself being investigated by the CID. The real business: they came to the door wearing suits when she was out, asking about her car and if 'anyone fitting her description' was at home. She sat in all the next day waiting for them to return, imagining herself on manslaughter charges for knocking someone off a bicycle.

'Madam, we wish to enquire as to whether you're a member of *The Animal Liberation Front?*'

'I am not!' she retorted. 'Do you realise what those people are responsible for?'

The detective had to listen to the whole saga of Animal Rights people releasing farm-bred mink from their cages and how, with mink now populating every watercourse in Britain, this has contributed to the decline of the otter.

'Madam,' he said patiently, 'were you in the vicinity of Hellingbrough Down on the first Tuesday of this month?'

'Well, I've no idea, I'll have to look at my diary.'

She then refuted this adamantly as she does not actually know where Hellingbrough is and had not written down that she'd come to visit me that day. But the Police knew she had. She'd been reported as *a person acting with suspicious intent.* This outraged her, but it was quite true. What she'd done was go round to the rabbit farm next door for a good old snoop. We are still having problems with their ridiculous planning applications. She wanted to see whether they did have rabbits there or if the whole set-up was just a con. I thought this was quite a good idea. I've never seen any evidence of rabbits at all, well not captive ones, but wasn't brave enough to go onto the property and confront the people. When the owners caught her peering through the shed windows, she brightly declared that she'd come to buy a bunny for her granddaughter. They knew she was lying. She had to convince the Police that this was reasonable, showing him Atalanta's school photograph, and in fact through her entire collection of children's baby albums.

'My brag books. I mean, Officer, one does expect to be able to buy a bunny at a rabbit farm.' The owners told her they only sold rabbits for slaughter, which of course had brought tears to her eyes. 'But really, do I look like a member of *The Animal Liberation Front?*'

The policeman then startled her by staring at her bosom, which made her even more indignant. Dad by this time was doubled up with laughter. She was wearing a T-shirt emblazoned with the slogan, *'Don't Badger the Badgers'*.

Before all my ailments, I did a bit of team-chasing with the Hampshire girls. Bod at last has had a total clip as things were getting a little hot under the collar. Quite amazing. People who didn't even notice him when he was trace-clipped come over and say, 'What a wonderful horse', 'Such a handsome fellow' etc.

One girl even said to Raddy (and this will make you roar with laughter), 'Gosh, Tamzin must be the most brilliant rider to have a horse like that.' Not true... he is just like riding a Chesterfield sofa.

Guess what Guy's Godmother has given him? Yes... a red, velvet *Teletubby* outfit. (Can you imagine a full size, darling Teletubby Guy?) Divine.

Mum is portrayed in the enclosed article entitled, *'Do your parents ever embarrass you?'*
She is very proud of it.
Lots of love,
T x

Church Hooker

16th November 1998

Darling Sophie,

Panic stations here in Hampshire. Tamzin went into hospital to have her tonsils out, then had an anaphylactic fit and stopped breathing. As she had no breath she couldn't speak to let anyone know she was suffocating. It took them an hour and a half to get her to come round. As she is still in tremendous pain, Mum is looking after the boys. This does not suit them as she is very strict.

'She screams at me,' Guy complained, 'and hurts my tiny little ears.'

I think she is rather terrified about cooking on the Aga, but loves the constant source of heat for making her chicken stocks and 'nourishing' stews. The boys refuse to eat them.

I'm taking A + H for an audition tomorrow – a national advert for 'toilet tissue'. What a screen debut that would make.

We went to see *Aladdin* at the Richmond Theatre on New Year's Day. They asked for two children to go up on stage with Bonnie Langford and Christopher Biggins, who presents Children's TV. Well, Hastings RACED. He told the audience that he'd been given flies for Christmas (????) and chatted perfectly confidently.

What Mum hasn't told Tamzin is that she has appeared in *Take a Break* as Moody Marge married to Bill the Budgie fancier –

played by Dad. Their photo illustrates an article called, '*Who's a Pretty Boy, Then?*' It's not quite the same as appearing in *The Field*.

Granny is the same as ever, driving us all bats with her constant phone calls. One really doesn't know what to say, I mean she rings before lunch and then straight after lunch.

'Have you had lunch?' she demands.

I can't wait until this winter is over. By the way, don't worry about what mothers on family holidays might say. Has it occurred to you that they might just be a teensy bit jealous of your freedom, independence and apparent lack of responsibility? Not to mention a maddening husband.

Lots of love,

Perry

Dear Tamzin.

This is to wish you a speedy recovery for your tonsil job. I was given my first job as a professional cameraman, filming the polocrosse. Sam thrives on the sport and I won a cup for winning the Waterberg Tournament. Or rather for being on the winning team.

I have to admit that we won because a girl who plays for Zimbabwe at International level was scoring our goals, but still; a moment of glory to make up for all the hard work.

Sam no longer bucks or leaps in the air unless there's good reason. Neither does he stand with his feet together.

After all this time I'm convinced that his behaviour was all due to a sore back. I now have an Australian stock saddle, which must suit him. Perhaps it was my hot seat. When I went to stay with Perry I went and broke the children's swing. Hastings put up a sign on it saying, 'No Fat Bottomed Aunts.'

Lots of love,

Sophie

Triple B Ranch
January 1999

Dear Perry,

I never knew having your tonsils out could be so dangerous. Tamzin said it's an incredibly painful experience when you're an adult. Is she OK now?

Thanks for the Superwoman t-shirt. I had to open it under the Christmas tree and put it on in front of everyone. Do they come any tighter? I wore it (once) to dinner at Horizon.

'Are they made of kryptonite?' Shane asked.

It did inspire me to go to a fancy dress party with a Hollywood theme dressed as Wonderwoman. Do you know, I stopped at the filling station in Vaalwater wearing a red satin cape and wristbands, Laura's hairpiece with a tiara, and the petrol pump man didn't bat an eyelid?

I was hoping Lawrence of Arabia might be at the party to notice, but he didn't pitch. Still, having turned into a bouffant-ed brunette, with earrings and eyelashes, I attracted the attention of all the Afrikaans men and was presented with an Oscar for the best make-up, which was nice. You will be glad to hear I was also given a hairbrush for Christmas. I'll have to tell the lady at the bottle store.

I'm plodding on with my art, working on larger oils of animals, including one of Lucas, The Prize Brahman Bull (much more difficult than painting an elephant. Walter the vet had to go through every muscle with me: 'More brisket.' He was very kind and spent hours helping me get it right).

I keep having to draw cows these days. A friend of mine asked me to draw a picture of a Friesian, 'a Cowmercial,' she said, for her trading company. This involved trying to avoid a lot of cowpats and getting licked while I was sketching. I would rather concentrate on chameleons that I could paint quietly in my studio, but would they sell? Perhaps I ought to stick to functional stuff. Virginia McKenna's charity, *Born Free*, published the Christmas Cards I designed in the Okavango and they sold out almost before everyone had received their mail order catalogues.

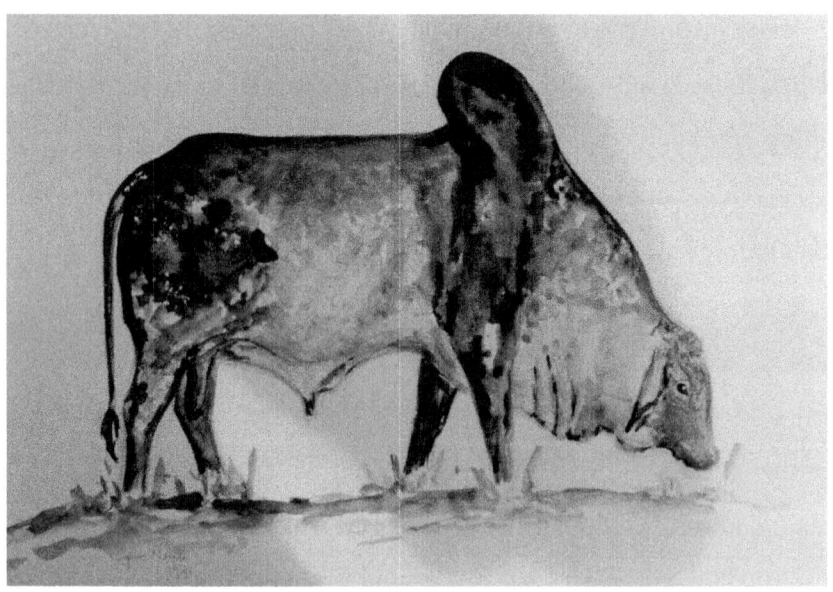

'You're rather a famous artist in our part of the world,' a girl told me.

'Am I?' (Really pleased).

'Oh, yes. Your name hangs in everybody's loos.'

They had all bought the septic tank notices I had drawn and printed all that time ago.

PLEASE THROW NOTHING MORE THAN LOO PAPER DOWN THE LOO AS THE SEPTIC TANK HAS A LIMITED DIGESTIVE SYSTEM.

It seems that the mother hippopotamus with the baby who lives at Horizon may well be Motla, the abandoned orphan that our neighbour Conita brought up. She has a distinctive stumpy tail and seems to have no fear of humans, which can be quite alarming.

My old boyfriend had rather a shock recently. Bwana, the tame black rhino, which is quite big now, got him in the bum. The horn went in just under his belt and came out at the top of his leg narrowly missing his femoral artery. He was tossed against a branch and was in great pain, but has recovered amazingly well and is back working as a game ranger in charge of anti-poaching.

We sent thirty local kids off to the Wilderness School on Lapalala where they learn about the environment. Michael Ramasodi said that climbing the mountain nearly killed him but that many children saw giraffe for the first time in their lives.

I'm worried about how many of them might be left orphaned by AIDS. The local doctor says that the entire population of Vaalwater is in denial; they don't want to know they have it and don't care who catches it from them.

'You can warn them about it until you're blue in the face, but no one will listen until they see people actually begin to die.'

I spoke to the girls on this farm who said, 'Yes, it's the boys. They want to sleep and sleep and sleep.'

But it's the girls who contract the infection most easily. HIV/AIDS has a ten-year cycle. The shocking thing is that girls are dying between the ages of nineteen and twenty-four, so you can work out how old they are when they contract the virus. Many of them leave children with no father.

I've decided to go and see what is happening at an orphanage I heard about in Mozambique and have appealed at church for things that they need up there. My friend Rebecca and a cricket correspondent from the *Daily Telegraph* called Geoffrey want to come too.

It's so annoying; the electricity keeps surging or cutting out altogether. I'm glad I'm not trying to run a business. Nina said so many people are illegally tapping the mains supply that it's being strained and overloaded.

Probably not unlike Tamzin. Please take her some jelly and ice-cream from me.

Love to you all,

Sophie

Dear Arnt soifie,

   I think you know why I am writing to you. But incase you don't I will tell you. It is because i'v not written to you for a long time. Also uther things two witch I hope you will notice reading along. eney how? How are you doing with your art and what are you drawing? I also hope that you have been erning lots of money. At the moment in art we are doing things a lot about Moneh, who was an epresenist. Writ back soon.
With lots of love from Atalanta
Hope you like the pitcher on the back. You can couler it in yourself.
(This was of a girl in a riding hat sitting on a horse wearing a purple bridle).

Dear Sofe

   thank you very much for the monkey shirt I wore it to a place called Chessington. The cukoo clock is cukooing.
Love Hastings

Dear Tamzin & Johnty,

I've just come out of Mozambique with Rebecca and a tortoise that we had to buy before it was eaten. The woman said they were delicious served with chips.

Zimbabwe seems changed since I was last here. Once the streets leading out of Harare were lined with colourful fruit stalls; they're now selling coffins and wreaths. Factories are closing due to labour shortages since AIDS has bitten in. Menial jobs seem to be accomplished by gap-year students from Britain. I met an eighteen-year old boy working on a game reserve here who said he came from Parrog in Wales. He was building an aviary for Alastair Fothergill who wants to film quelea, small birds which form huge flocks and raid the harvests. I saw great clouds of them against the sunset as we drove south.

I hope the Irish pony I found for the boys is working out.
Love,
Sophie

Dear Perry and Robert,

I wrote this report on my trip to Mozambique for friends who supported us and thought it might amuse you to have a copy.

Lots of love,

Sophie

Report on Recce to *Maforga Christian Mission* in Mozambique

I first heard about the orphanage at Maforga three years ago from people I met at Rome Airport when I was in transit, waiting for a flight on to Johannesburg. I thought it would be useful to see how an orphanage could be run on a farm and that I could use my large vehicle to bring up supplies from South Africa. Rebecca was keen to come with me.

The orphanage told us they needed children's shoes, clothing, crockery and sheets. I rang various chain stores and asked everyone in Vaalwater for donations but nothing seemed to come in. Five days before leaving I realised I would have to drive to Johannesburg to get my visa, but instead Geoffrey, a journalist who was up here to write a travel article on the horseback safaris, took my passport and said he'd go to the visa office between cricket matches. This was a tremendous relief and freed me to go to church where I was hoping people would bring along donations. Nothing arrived, however an American missionary was giving a talk and mentioned aid work in Mozambique. I spoke to her husband after the service and he said he could supply me with medicines. I was hesitant because the orphanage hadn't mentioned drugs. Also, I didn't want to lengthen our journey north by going via Potgietersrus to collect them.

When I drove to Johannesburg to collect Rebecca off her flight I learnt we would have to stay the night there to collect Geoffrey the following morning. I asked my friends, the Galloping Grannies, if we could stay. They should have said No; Annie had roaring tick bite fever and Rose had four Zimbabweans staying that particular night. The miracle was that the Zimbabwean farmers lived near the Mutare border post and knew all about the orphanage. They insisted firstly, that we should take in as many medicines as possible and secondly that we should come and stay on their farm when we came out of Mozambique.

'But we'd arrive in the dark without being able to give you any warning, probably filthy dirty and with vehicle problems.'

'That,' they said, 'is almost inevitable.'

A minor miracle was that although British Airways had refused to let Rebecca bring in clothes for the orphans as extra luggage, she persevered. Since she only had a tiny case for herself, the air hostess at the check-in counter let her fly with two bags, containing 100 cotton outfits she'd carefully sorted out for the children. Unknown to me, Rebecca had received donations from two primary schools in England, selling the winter clothes so that we could afford to buy new sheets, plates and mugs when we reached Zimbabwe.

I drove back north to the ranch where I found my friends had delivered five bags of clothes and shoes. Charles Baber gave me twelve Bibles, 'In case you have trouble at the border' and Shane and Laura lent us their tent and camping mattresses. I found the missionaries in Potgietersrus had sorted out four large bags of medicines for us to collect, worth hundreds of dollars. My vehicle was full. On top of the pile was an awful old yellow camping chair of Shane's that Geoffrey insisted on taking.

Everyone in South Africa said it was too dangerous for girls to travel through Mozambique alone. The civil war is over but it's pretty dodgy there. Crime is rife and yet, get on the wrong side of a policeman for the smallest motoring discrepancy and you could find yourself in gaol for three months. If you break down you're in trouble as you can't buy spare parts. Geoffrey was no mechanic but was deemed large enough, in Charles's opinion, to qualify as a protector of English girls. In fact he never made it. He decided to stay with friends of his in Zimbabwe, as he was offered the chance to shoot a baboon. This was beyond Rebecca's comprehension. But it gave us more space.

As we drove towards Mozambique laden with crockery bought in Mutare, I prayed that it would rain. If our vehicle was searched and we were asked to pay import duty at 50% we simply couldn't have afforded to take in the medicines. Technically they were gifts and exempt from duty but I wasn't convinced we could prove this. Charles has always said that Africans do not enjoy working in the rain. It rained hard; really hard on the border post.

Right over it. 400 yards before we got there it was dry, 440 yards beyond it was sunny. All the customs officers could see through my streaming windows was the awful yellow camping chair.

It occurred to me that I ought to ask about taking out local third party car insurance. It was not made clear that this was obligatory but without it we would never have passed the first policeman. He was very strict, tested our indicator lights and inspected our tyres. What he didn't ask to see were my reverse lights. One had stopped working.

We drove for two hours along an empty road and reached the orphanage just before dark. To our huge surprise we were accommodated in a log cabin, which in the heat made us feel as if we were on a skiing holiday in an overheated chalet. An old Zimbabwean nurse called Joan Goodman made up our beds. She was exhausted and I felt that we were an added strain. They had been getting over sixty patients a day at her clinics and they were running desperately short of supplies.

'I just hope we've brought things you can use,' I said.

'Have you any medicines with you?'

Rebecca and I brought the bags down for her to sort out. Joan just kept saying, 'Praise the Lord,' as she looked in box after box and, 'I've been praying for this for days.' The Americans had packed exactly what she needed; vitamin B, antibiotics and cream for tropical ulcers. 'There's just one thing I'm short of now, which they haven't included. We've a terrible eye infection going round and I'm almost out of ointment.'

'How much did you need?'

'About two dozen tubes.'

'I've put them all in your fridge.' Rebecca said.

I discovered that I'd actually met the elderly German Baroness who had once owned the farm that is now Maforga Mission at Mum's house. She'd been a contemporary of Aunt Reinhild's when they all lived in Tanzania. They still run the property as a farm, employing about 100 locals and trying to become self-sufficient with citrus, vegetables, sheep, goats and chickens, a milling machine and forestry projects. They have a carpentry workshop, make bricks and have a curio shop on the main road where they sell carvings and batique prints made in their own workshops. There's a school for 450 children and a centre for the very young, elderly and disabled in the local town, which acts as a soup kitchen.

The mission once looked after 250 children displaced from their families during the twenty years' war. Many were claimed by relatives when the fighting stopped but there are still 100 children there, including twelve toddlers and ten babies.

'Don't, whatever you do, start an orphanage. It's far better,' the nurse went on, 'to help the extended family bring up the children naturally, within the community. Don't institutionalise. It's not a good way of raising children and costs a fortune.'

They had no option but to take in kids during the violence but they try to keep new arrivals away, insisting that grannies or aunts bring up motherless children.

Running the place during the war must have been extraordinary. Joan told me about how she and five others from the mission were captured by RENAMO guerrillas in 1986, forced to walk miles through the rainforest, held hostage for three months and eventually marched up to the Malawi border. She spent the whole time in her nightie as they were seized at 1.30am and weren't offered any other clothes except for woolly tights, taffeta ball dresses and high-heeled stilettos left over from raided aid consignments.

The next day was Sunday, so after church we played with the children before lunch with the thirty or so volunteer staff. The woman in charge of the kitchen was in a terrible flap.

'We don't have enough plates.'

'Oh we've brought plates,' I said. She gave me a rather long-suffering look and said,

'We need twenty.'

'Yes,' I said. 'We bought twenty for you in Mutare yesterday.'

We had also bought mugs but they needed a lot more. There were no glasses, no jugs; the water was poured from battered kettles into teacups. They're supported by a British organization and one housewife raising funds in Australia. She'd managed to send in an enormous amount of supplies after the war but import duty has now become so high that they couldn't afford to accept the last container that came in from Australia and the customs officers confiscated it. That is why they were suddenly short of drugs.

On the Monday morning we visited the clinic, which was unbelievable. There were about seventy mothers with little children, old men and the ill of every description. They had just been given a lecture on how to avoid contracting cholera, which is prevalent, and were now anxious to be treated, pushing in on the nurses from every door and window. The facilities were distinctly African. Joan was battling her way through a huge variety of cases. An old Mozambiquian nurse, wearing thick spectacles, was consulting a lady with five children and newborn twins, her face crumpled with stress. One assistant was inoculating screaming toddlers and another distributing ointment and tablets while her own baby hung from one breast. Everyone was squeezed together amongst ancient hospital furniture. We left to have a look at the carpentry workshop. They were making coffins. It was an interesting morning.

On the whole, the people of Mozambique were relaxed and kind but we were robbed three times. They didn't want the yellow chair. The people are so poor you can understand the temptation, however it made us wary, which was probably just as well. I'm sure a Portuguese man tried to hijack us on the road. He had the bonnet of his car up and stood asking us for water, but Rebecca saw there was lots of water in a pond the other side of the road and shouted, 'Drive' before he could grab us.

Then torrential rain set in. As soon as we reached Zimbabwe my gearbox bearings started to go and oil began to leak out of the differential. Water from the flooded tracks we'd driven through had been sucked into the castings but the farmer we had met staying with the Galloping Grannies sorted us out and, by driving back using only first and fourth gear, we made it home. All anybody wanted to know when we arrived in the Waterberg was whether one of us had ended up engaged to Geoffrey. We couldn't think for a moment who they were talking about.

CHAPTER SEVENTEEN

Hampshire Clinic
21st Dec 1998

Dearest Sib,

I'm in hospital again and have been since the 17th with bacterial pneumonia (which has gone), viral pneumonia and a few broken ribs (acquired coughing). This is a Victorian illness. You can do nothing but convalesce. I ought to be in Brighton or some other seaside town. To think, poor Perry had exactly the same in Germany without Rob. I now know how terrible she must have felt.

I feel such a fraud though; I eat smoked salmon and sleep all day whilst people around me have things removed (wombs, guts etc) and get thrown out within seconds. But I don't think I look all that wonderful.

Everyone, including Dr. Brown who has been a doctor for a *long* time, keeps saying, 'You look very, very ill,' and, 'You *are* very, very ill.'

Visitors come and start to cry but I think it's a combination of Christmas and me not wearing mascara. Mum is at home cooking gallons of broth.

'Eat up your delicious vegetables; they've been cooked in pure chicken fat.'

Johnty heaving in the corner, no doubt. He can't bear using a tea bag twice, whereas Mum enthusiastically re-cycles every leftover. Apparently we now have four ice-cream containers full of breadcrumbs in the freezer. I am grateful, but Mum is so strict with Hughie and Guy. Unlike Daisy and Oscar they're rude and naughty and fight.

'Now Hughie, say your prayers.'

'Eerrrrh'.

'I hate Granny Otter.' Guy shrieked.

Guy loves the electric organ you gave him. The only problem is that all the little boys love your organ too and come from miles to play *Teletubby* music. I don't think Mum can cope. I've told the children they're lucky to have her but they don't like going in her car. It does smell of fish. Oh dear, the boys were so excited about Christmas and due to me being ill will have a ghastly one. No snow. I'll be in bed. I am so, so sad for them – we haven't even got any holly in the house; this pneumonia is so bloody unfair.

All my love,

Tamzin

Church Hooker
28th December 1998

Darling Sib,

Tamzin, as you will have heard, is keeping us all on our toes. She was close to death. I think it all started when she was schooling the Irish pony you found for her. It was naughty, refused a jump and fell on top of her. Did she tell you she'd been in Casualty overnight having her brain X-rayed? The Pro Plus helmet saved her life, but Mum thinks that her chest was cracked when the pony rolled over her and that the pneumonia virus took advantage of the weakness. I suspect Tamzin just got rundown.

When she was first at the clinic Hughie and Guy were dropped at our house by Johnty on his way to work and collected on his way home, with grocery shopping and hospital visits filling the rest of their day. Tamzin is now at home, in her own bedroom but has been too ill to see visitors.

Mum said to tell you she saw Sarah-Jane's horse safaris featured on *The Holiday Programme.*

'John Sobey was actually wearing riding boots,' she said. 'I didn't know he possessed any.'

She can talk; when Tamzin's kind friends come round they're told to 'Go away!' by Mum screaming at them from the kitchen door, wearing **carpet slippers**.

I would think this rather embarrassing, but Tamzin is too ill to care.

Dad had the rest of us over for lunch, cooking a massive turkey, which Mary-Dieu, Daisy and Oscar helped gobble up. Mary-Dieu still had her holey bottomed leggings on but was wearing knickers this time. She is planning to go to Ibiza with her friends this summer and made me laugh with hair-raising stories of what can happen on a Girl's Night Out. I was really rather shocked. We will try to get Daisy over during the Easter holidays. Both my children are now yo-yo experts. Atalanta can get two going simultaneously and is longing to teach the cousins. Robert is starting a new Army job next week, which will take him all over the country so he'll be away a lot. Again.

Lots of love,
PRAHS xxxxx

Hardacre Farm

10:1:99

Dear, dear Sib –

Happy 1999 and Happy Christmas. Gosh, lucky you being in hot Africa. England is cold and wet, with mud everywhere. No lovely sounds of the African night here.

Guess what? I'm still ill, so feeble I only ever get up to go to the loo. The last time I wrote I was in hospital going through great troughs of deep exhaustion. My body simply gave up. I slept and sweated for five days, so done-in the nurses called me 'The Dormouse'.

Thank you for all your presents. The mugs are fab but I'll give the exercise video a miss for the moment. I'm still in bed and still grey.

Poor 'Granny Otter' has been looking after the boys for three weeks now. They've been fighting non-stop. Johnty's mother is coming to look after them soon. I dread to think what will happen, but the children will be back at school so it shouldn't be too bad. Bod hasn't been ridden and has taken to eating the hedge to get his own back.

Looking back on the whole illness thing I was so stupid, so very stupid to go on working the horses – but after the tonsillectomy I was told to carry on as usual. When you feel faint and unwell but are told you aren't ill at all you want to cry ALL the time and think you're going mad. Until you get up one morning and collapse, and Johnty has to call an ambulance. The antibiotic for the bacterial infection made the virus very cross… Because viral pneumonia is so rare I was not diagnosed correctly when I did go to see the doctor and despite, or perhaps because I broke my ribs coughing I was told I had pleurisy, which you don't get with a virus.

Oh, it has been Bloody Hell. I really thought I was going to die, but I haven't so that's good.

25: 3: 99 - I've retrieved this letter from the bin. When I wrote it I was not feeling happy, but now am much, much better, although not quite up to full speed. Reading it back is quite amusing. Johnty's mother came for a week, which was kind of her.

Then came the saddest day of my entire life. We had to have my darling angel dog put down: poor, poor Maudie. Sophie, it was so sad. The pain was just below my heart like a sore, sore wound, aching and aching. Maudie had been getting more and more senile and one night just wandered off into the dark. I found her outside, six hours later. She cried like a child. In the morning Johnty, Guy, Hughie and I went off to the vet with her in my arms. She was so weak.

I looked up at the vet and said, 'I fear the worst,' and he said, 'You fear right.' As he gently put her to sleep I saw her soul walk past me. She is now buried in the field, under an oak tree.

I phoned Mum the next day, to tell her the sad news. She paused and then said that she'd some even sadder news; her agent (who is 82) has decided to retire. At that point I gave up.
All my love,
Tamzin x

Oh, Tamzin,

Poor Maude; I'm so sorry you lost her. And all this sickness. I do feel bad. I was away for a month and have only **just** heard about your pneumonia. It was the one time that not even Laura could track me down. I gather you're feeling better and getting out and about. Nina says you must come and stay out here where the air is warm and dry. At least you're not stuck in Mozambique with malaria with nothing to eat but tortoises. (A thought to keep you going when things look bleak). I nearly was, you know. If Rebecca hadn't insisted on driving through the rain we would still be there as floods brought bridges down all along the coast the day we reached Zimbabwe.

Do you want some more horror stories to cheer you up? Well, I was attacked in Harare; walking down the street in broad daylight. I found myself being lifted off my feet like a child as a huge man cut the money-belt from my body. I still can't get to sleep without the physical memory of the jarring impact before he dumped me and twisted off, leaping into a waiting getaway car.

Rebecca shouted 'Stop! Thief!'

A passer-by threw a rock at the car windscreen, but the best thing seemed to be to get out of the whole country.

I returned to the Waterberg to find a tractor towing a trailer that looked like the back end of the white Chevy.

'Yes.' Charles declared unsentimentally. 'I've re-cycled it.'

I also learnt that Miriam's sister has died, I think basically of AIDS, leaving a girl of eight and a little boy who has the same symptoms. The children do have a father but Miriam said, crossly, that he'd only paid R400. Her sister had died before even 10% of the bride price had been paid. Poor Miriam. Poor little children.

The farm computers have all died too. They had such a bad lightning strike that even the one that wasn't plugged in was exterminated. The people in the house were fine and seemed to be quite energised by the whole experience. We are no longer in danger of getting zapped by lightning in the ear when on the phone. The manual exchange has finally been replaced by French radiophones. Huge, striped transmission masts dominate the township, where no doubt they're frying everyone's brains, and the telephone lines are coming down for good. Charles Baber was wondering where the swallows are going to perch. The old system was tiresome but did have its advantages. Five minutes before I left for Mozambique a message came through saying that I must ring the Visa Office immediately. They didn't have my phone number but got through to the Vaalwater Exchange who, knowing me well, connected the call. There was a fuss over some technicality to do with payment and I would have been stopped at the border if they hadn't been able to speak to me.

Mozambique was beautiful. Empty, but war torn, with dilapidated towns. There's not much there; you can't buy a postcard. We began to find out that the campsites had recently been battlegrounds. In some areas land mines had been planted round waterholes and we were told categorically not to drive off road. Of course we already had. But we walked along coral beaches, swam with turtles, ate delicious fish and had a lovely time. I've never been as happy as I was at the mission. I'm hoping to go back soon.

When the Vaalwater Exchange finally closed I actually got to meet the Tannie, who turned out to be much younger than me. A complete stranger came up to me when I was down at Horizon, and chatted away for ages. I couldn't think how this girl, who I had never seen before, knew so much about my life and future plans; quite secret things. Laura was looking at the perplexed expression on my face and killing herself laughing. 'This is Hester,' she said. 'From the Exchange.'

Shane says it's high time you came out to ride my pony. Come and stay for as long as you like; you can either ride all day or laze and do nothing at all. Alternatively I can easily fly back to look after the boys; just say.

With all my love,

Sophie

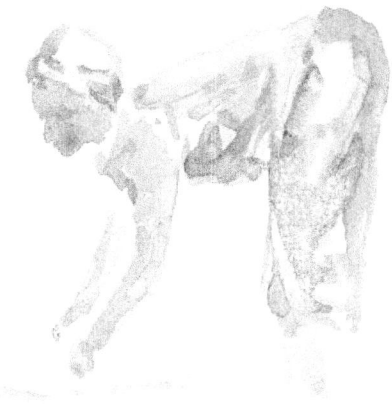

Church Hooker
12/03/99

Darling Sophie,

    Tamzin says you're not to worry at all. Johnty is taking her off to Florida to lie in the sun until she is fully recovered. Poor Robs has had to go off to climb Snowdon with the ladies who work in his office today. It's pouring so he's not happy about it. Hastings is not thrilled either. He is to be the small cockerel in the school play and has to wear brown tights with a pink rubber glove on his head.

    We went to see the cow parade in Berkeley Square – a whole herd of life-size fibreglass cows painted by different artists. 'The Cowmercial' you originally designed was standing there looking like a cow.

    After all our striving for stardom, it was Dad who was given a leading role. He went up to Edinburgh, expecting to be a 'Featured Walk-On' and was handed seventeen pages of dialogue – huge long, complicated speeches, the night before filming at the Royal College of Surgeons. I expect he'll be brilliant on the grounds that he'll come across as a real person, not an actor.

    Raddy is giving a hippy party. Tamzin did a raid on Mum's wardrobe (which goes to prove she is recovering well) and found loads of stuff – there was a huge selection, including some red patent leather boots that lace up the front and a purple Donny Osmond cap. I don't think Johnty will enjoy wearing the pink kaftan we chose for him. It was the one Mum wore the time she came out to see you.

Atalanta went back to boarding school on Monday. She said she cries with sadness to leave home, but cries with happiness to be back at school. I cried hysterically all the way home and am all on my lonesome again. I don't want her to go away at all, at all, at all, but it's a good, happy school and the alternative would be uprooting her at every posting.

Hastings is still around. He is funny. Last night he came into my room dressed in his smoking jacket (velvet pageboy's outfit) and a bowtie. He formally took me by the hand and led me into the dining-room. The table was bedecked with pretty flowers and napkins; a candlelit dinner for two. He'd made strawberry jam sandwiches. I cried. He wanted to thank me for taking him to *Monkey World*.

It's our turn to pack. I'm trying to book tickets so we can come out and stay with you. I want to bring Tamzin if I can. Can't wait to see you and have a good old natter.

Lots of love,

Perry xxxx

EPILOGUE

Sometimes, perhaps once in a lifetime, when you fall in love it's completely unavoidable and all consuming, dominating all you think and do. It doesn't seem to matter what age you are. Perhaps it can be more intense when you're older. All I can say is that it all happened here in the Waterberg when I was least expecting it.

Not to me but to Sam. He has fallen head over heels for a pretty grey mare at Horizon. So obsessed is he that he spends every waking moment jealously segregating her from other members of the herd and is covered in scars from fighting off her younger admirers. He's behaving far more atrociously than any stallion either Shane or Sarah-Jane ever took on and whinnies constantly as I ride along. And all this after Walter had tried to extract his teeth due to the onset of old age.

If this was a novel I might try to surprise everybody by saying I married Walter but I didn't. Real life isn't like that. Walter has been married for forty years or so. Topsy, his wife, has just pointed out that instead of the sign saying *Dit is die Volkstaat* on the way into Vaalwater, there's a cemetery now. She said it was instigated by the former PAC activists, who run the Town Council these days, and is growing rapidly. Under their constitution white people have to pay R300 for a space, black people R10.

Michael Ramasodi joined us saying, 'That's not important any more, not a problem. The problem is, everyone is dying, dying, dying.'

He should know; he has to take the funerals. Pandemic HIV/AIDS is biting into South Africa, which by the year 2000 had the highest rate and the highest rate of increase of HIV infection anywhere in the world[lxxi].

It seems worse in Botswana. Sarah-Jane has a formal policy in place to help her staff cope with the AIDS crisis, 'ensuring they get regular, professional advice.'

My friends in Zimbabwe were trying to help up there, but Robert Mugabe had other plans. We started an NGO and UK charity to care for those infected and affected by the pandemic, the Waterberg Welfare Society, to help people and ensure the orphaned children were provisioned for and could grow up happily within their community.

The ANC have not made major changes in our lives but it has to be said that the names of the towns are dramatically different. The Northern Province has become the Limpopo; we had to buy new number plates with baobab trees on. Potgietersrus has been re-named Mokopane.

'Quite ironic really,' Charles Baber pointed out. 'He was the chap who murdered the original Voortrekker, Potgieter.'

Whilst the crime rate has risen things are not all bad. Clear sunny day still follows clear sunny day. People are no longer expected to feel guilty about travelling to South Africa. Shane and Laura have done well; Horizon is fully booked with English people coming on riding holidays. The dam down there is full, with so many water lilies it smells like the Okavango and I canter Sam through the shallows on our way back from riding in the mornings.

Laura put her little girl up in front of her and took the clients swimming on the horses almost every day in the summer. The tourists don't sit around on canvas safari chairs anymore – No, no they lie around on loungers in the shade of a huge, exotic, siringa tree.

Before he fell in love, my horse, who'd been allowed to graze on the lawn one day, joined the guests in queuing up for one of the delicious buffet lunches; he was after the homemade bread. Jack, the horse I always thought looked like a camel, was transformed. He became a champion show jumper in Johannesburg, having won the Novice in the three-phase horse trials Walter and Topsy put on at Triple B Ranch. While Laura has named one poor pony Malaria, Shane's favourite mare is an endurance horse called Ghanzi. I haven't told Jez. Jez went from being a cowboy to a City slicker, with an apartment in Notting Hill.

Ant's Nest is incredibly popular. Ant and Tess spend their time entertaining rather grand visitors from all over the world, showing them their game reserve. They have a chef called Innocent and three Maria's on their staff: Fat Maria, Sexy Maria and Bush Maria.

'You can't give your employees names like that!'

'I didn't. They wanted to call themselves something original.'

I suppose it's not unlike The Spice Girls but I don't know what Raddy will say. She is taking her whole family out to ride and stay at both lodges.

Fred and Josie, who tell me they were merely innocent bystanders at the nativity play, now work at the smartest of Game Reserves. Josie's recipe book, *The African Kitchen* sold well, and was even translated into Latvian. Fred says he drives a computer now but he is into wildlife management and manages to capture and translocate up to 2,000 animals a year.

'Forget penguins,' he says, 'It's the black rhino who are micro-chipped these days.'

They insert one into each horn so they can always be traced to help ensure the animals are protected from poaching. Nina now tells me that *Bliksem* is a rude word and that I mustn't let Fred teach me anything else.

Andrew is still in Namibia, running his own horse safaris near the great dunes of Soussusveli.

He said he has horses for all types of riders, 'I've got smart horses for smart riders, I've got average horses for average riders, and for people who hate riding, I've got horses that hate being ridden too.'

Billy now works freelance as a Professional Hunter, spending his winter days happily looking for buffalo: The Black Death he calls them. Wayne is hunting in Tanzania. Grant has become the epitome of the handsome game ranger, never out of the pages of *Country Life* - the South African version - on the front cover, in articles on tracking game and featured in monthly advertisements with his beautiful blonde wife. The last I heard of Nicki was that she was as happy as anything, riding through the mountains of Wyoming but misses not being able to chat away in Afrikaans.

Wendy moved Equus across the river to Lapalala and finally onto her own property in the Waterberg, which she calls a 'mountain preserve'. Like jam. Sarah-Jane runs horse safaris in the Namib. After spending most of her life curled up on the sofa, Tigger sadly died of sleeping sickness but as she went a baby came along; a little girl called Zoe.

'I wanted to call her Sage, but Peter wouldn't let me.'

I tried to strap Zoe to Sarah-Jane's back like an African child but she didn't like it and was happier talking to the horses. She rode across the Masai Mara before she was born. Sarah-Jane, who didn't realise she was pregnant, took me on the trip for my birthday. We stayed in Nairobi with Rowena, her husband and baby ~ two boys gained it seemed in the twinkling of an eye.

I went to stay with Nick in Norway, where the Foreign Office in their wisdom had posted him, and found myself being confronted by a giraffe standing in the hall. It was Rowena's.

'Ugly thing,' Nick said, 'I'm still waiting for her to come and pick it up.'

Nick did find the girl of his dreams and now lives in bliss, commenting on my life from the Baltic. Lucy, having been so cynical about marriage, met a charming man who is, by coincidence, called Ant. She sends me Christmas cards of their adorable children.

Granny was right; A-line skirts came back into fashion but I was still single.

My friend James, who once appeared in my life as Julius Caesar said, 'So what? Anyway, being single is fun.'

He reckons I couldn't have had a better life. My only problem is having too much choice. Now and again my vehicles conk out. Last time I was having my *bakkie* fixed half way up the mountain an Old Afrikaans farmer asked me in for tea.

'Do you take sugar?' he asked.

'*Nie danke*, no, thank you,' I replied. 'I'm an English girl.'

'Not really,' he said, shaking his head. 'You're one of us now.'

After living in the Waterberg for ten years I drove down past Pretoria and collected Perry and her family from the airport. They had finally managed to come out to see me. And finally understood why I wanted to live out in the bush. Atalanta saw the rhino and started to draw, sitting on the red sand, happily sketching away. Hastings had only ever ridden four times in his life, but he clung on to a little horse I gave him and we rode off over the hills, past confused looking wildebeest and up to ethereal giraffes. Robert, having emerged from the Ministry of Defence where he'd been incarcerated following the latest terrorist strike, rode Bismarck. He loved cantering with the game and said he could easily get addicted to polocrosse. The night before they left I took them to a farm high in the hills where I wanted to build a house for myself. Water was flowing from numerous little springs in the bedrock and Perry had sunk into a bog, getting her shoes muddy.

'Sophie Neville!' her voice called out over the mountains. '**Where** are you taking us?'

PLEASE BE CAREFUL WHAT YOU THROW DOWN THE LOO AS THE SEPTIC TANK HAS A LIMITED DIGESTIVE SYSTEM

Character List

My life seems to have a massive cast list. For the clarification of those readers who might get lost, here is a list of those who do appear in the letters.

My Family:
- My sister Perry, her husband Robert, their children Atalanta and Hastings, and their dog Tadpole.
- My second sister Tamzin, her husband Johnty and their boys Hughie and Guy, their dog Maud, horse Bod, cat Thelma, Labrador Harry & pony Patrick. Johnty's mother.
- My third sister Mary-Dieu, her children Daisy and Oscar.
- My mother Daphne, Dad, donkey Leonard, lurcher Shaddy, parrot Josie Jo and Bee the otter. Gregory the Dachshund who always comes to church.
- Albert, Helen and Tony, and their Rottweiler Basil.
- Granny, Aunt Hermione, my cousin Jamie and his wife Julia. Aunt Vera, Uncle Tony and Aunt Reinhild.

- Tamzin's friends: Raddy and her children, her father and mother. Debs and her children. Johnty's friend Nigel

- Other children: Rosie Hampton-Smith, and Asa & Amber

- Locals: Dr. Eldred, Ian T………., Mr Dan the farmer, Maureen Winterman, Lady Quellington, Fat Git Trevor the blacksmith, the builders Mr Hindleson and Eric, Gary the maize contractor, Loony Len the metal detector, Dr Jones, Mr Cronky.
- Perry's friends: Liza, Godfather Jiminee, Lucinda, Lu Llewellyn and Leanda.
- Perry's au pairs, including the hungry Hungarian, Tanja the thin Finn and the Kamilla the cross Czech.

- *Equus Horse Safaris* ~ Sarah-Jane, her partner Wendy and Donald. Sarah-Jane's mother.
- Guides: Andrew, Andy, Nicki, Wayne, Fred, Brian, Vincent & Grant.
- Chefs: Rebecca, Danielle, Josie, Jez, Claudia, Kate and Sherman.
- Staff: France, Somewhere, Nelly, Madula, Wisdom, Lindizwe, Lazarus, Macaroni,
- Bullterriers; Tigger and PK
- *Horses* ~ Jigsaw, Smokey-Joe, Zambezi, Nicholas, Xian, Limpopo, Patches, Rocky, Marshmallow, Red, and my pony Sam the Great.
- Rhinos; Tracy, Rodney and Desmond.

- Locals: Johann, Meisie, Dupe du Plessis, Oom Hennie, Dr Grobler, Jane and Ged, Solly, Hano Gerkin, our vet Walter and grain merchant Janneman. Conita Walker with her orphaned rhino Bwana and hippo Motla. Hester from the Exchange.
- Clients including: Helen, John Varty and Gillian van Houten, Alan Dryden.

- Triple B Ranch ~ Charles and Nina Baber and their offspring Juliet, Ant and Rupert. Juliet's Godfather, Michael Cassidy. Ant's girlfriend Tessa and their employees Innocent and the three Maria's. Rupert's fiancée Tanya. Marty, Effie, Miriam and her baby Marcus, Bright the Zambian missionary.
- Shane and Laura running Horizon Horse Trails with horses like Thunderhead, Bismarck, Massey, Jack, Ghanzi, Crash and the Hellbitch. Laura's sister-in-law.
- Locals: Gerda, Mr Hassim, Giorgio, Michael Ramasodi, Mrs van der Merwe, the Whitbreads, Stevens Mokwena, Julius Cesar & Lawrence of Arabia.

On my travels:

- South Africa ~ Judith, Billy, Ronnie the mechanic. Joseph, Assistant Warden Victor
- Botswana ~ Rowena McIntosh, Randall Moore, Tim Liversage, Ken Oake, Ralph, Rose and Annie the

Galloping Grannies, Giorgio of the Jungle, Truman, John Sobey, Manuel, Topgun, Independence, Royd the elephant.

- Namibia ~ Blythe and Rudi Loutit, Jan, Hoffy, John his wife Maria and mother Denise. Benedict Allen and his camels. Nathan the diamond diver and his girlfriend. Imca and the penguins. Lumpi, Waldi, Mini, Steve and a horse called Baron von Wolff.
- Zimbabwe ~ Pixie and her children Burgundy and Summer Rain. Theresa the giraffe
- Friends serving with BMAT and farmers near Mutare.
- Mozambique ~ Joan Goodman.

- My friends and visitors: James Money-Kyrle, Nick Archer, Fiona, Diana and Lucy, David and Juliet Madden, Geoffrey the journalist.

- BBC Television ~ Alastair Fothergill, producer Robin Hellier, Bill the *Blue Peter* director.
- Contributors: Mark Marks Great White Shark Researcher, Colonel Ekestein of Correctional Services.

~ Some names have been changed ~

Others mentioned ~ The Queen, Princess Alexandra, Princess Michael of Kent, Prince Andrew, Princess Anne, Diana Princess of Wales, the King of Swaziland, Washington Okumu, Lord Carrington, Kissinger, FW de Klerk, PW Botha, Eugene Terre'Blanche, Tony Leon, Nelson Mandela and his grandchildren Zidwa and Wolbo. Norma Major, Cherie the Prime Minister's wife, Robert Mugabe, Michael Caine, Wilbur Smith, Jilly Cooper, James Herriot, Sly Stallone, Billy Connolly, Judi Dench, Roald Dahl, Gerald Durrell, Hannah Gordon, Kate Adie, Virginia McKenna, Donny Osmond, Bonny Langford, Christopher Biggins, Glen Hoddle, and The Spice Girls.

I knew many more people at this time, who must either be relieved or forgive me for not mentioning them, although they might want to brace themselves for the next instalment.

If you would like to come on a horse safari e-mail me at
safaris@sophieneville.co.uk
If you need a septic tank notice email *art@sophieneville.co.uk*

For further insights:
http://ride-the-wings-of-morning.blogspot.com

ACKNOWLEDGEMENTS

This book tells a real story. It's written from the letters sent between me and my sisters Tamzin and Perry, Granny, my parents and the children. They are letters I edited or amalgamated, letters I added the odd story to, but it's also their writing.

I didn't include, but was inspired by letters from Olivia Spencer, Nick Archer, Diana Vernon, Lucy Woodd, James Money-Kyrle, Alastair Fothergill, Rose Persson, Augustus Persson, Lucy Thellusson, Charles and Jane Johnston, Serena Jebb, Robin Parish, John James, Hetty Williams, Juliet Madden, Pippa Gillespie, Tracy Mitchell, Sarah-Jane Gullick, Andrew Gillies, Wayne Hendry, Fred Stow, Josie Fison, Nicki Nettman and many others.

I would like to thank Lucy Thellusson, Henrietta Mayhew, Henrietta Joy, Mark Chichester-Clark, Roger Vlitos, Charlotte Peters, Kathy Meyers, Rose Alcock, Lesley Wright, Camilla le May, Caroline Eldridge, Lleuella Wynne, Phoebe Wynne, Dawn Bernard, Megan Clarke, Christopher Davis, Billy Howard and those who appear in the book for reading drafts.

I am ever grateful to Lisa Scullard, for formatting such a complicated anthology.

BIBLIOGRAPHY

'*Long Walk to Freedom*' the autobiography of Nelson Mandela, *Macdonald Purnell 1994*

'*A Witness Forever*' by Michael Cassidy, *Hodder and Stoughton 1995*

'*Dawn to Dusk*' a safari through Africa's wild places by Jonathan Scott, *BBC Books 1996*

'*Back to Africa*' by Randall J Moore with Christopher Munnion, *RMP 1989*

'*Contraband*' South Africa and the International Trade in Ivory and Rhino Horn by De Wet Potgieter, *Quelliere 1995*

'*Kaokoveld*' The last wilderness by Anthony Hall-Martin, Clive Walker & J du P Bothma, *Southern 1988*

'*Southern Africa's Threatened Wildlife*' by John Ledger, *EWT*

'*Painless Afrikaans*' by George Holloway, *Juta & Co 1975*

'*Roald Dahl's Revolting Recipes*' edited by Josie Fison, *Jonathan Cape 1994*

'*African Kitchen*' by Josie Stow, *Conran Octopus 1999*

'*Is that really you, God?*' by Loren Cunningham, *YWAM Publishing 1984*

'*The Sheltering Desert*' by Henno Martin, *Kimber 1957*

Reference books:

'The Safari Companion' – *a guide to watching African Mammals* by Richard D.Estes, *1993 by Chealsea Green Publishing company, USA*

'Southern Africa's Threatened Wildlife' by John Ledger, *Endangered Wildlife Trust 1990*

'Newman's Birds of Southern Africa' by Kenneth Newman, *Southern 1983*

'Trees of the Kruger National Park' by P. van Wyk, *Purnell 1974*

'Damaraland Flora' by Patricia Craven and Christine Marais, *Gamsberg Macmillian 1992*

'The Shell Field Guide to the Common Trees of the Okavango Delta' by Veronica Roodt, *Shell*

'Common Wild Flowers of the Okavango Delta' by Veronica Roodt, *Shell 1998*

Programmes & Films mentioned ~ *Play for Today, Tumbledown, House of Eliot, My Family and Other Animals, Beautiful People, Love in a Cold Climate, Doctor Who - Vengeance on Varos, Dawn to Dusk - on Safari, Bird Brain of Britain, Really Wild Show, Animal Magic, Blue Peter, Global Sunrise, Fawlty Towers, Newsnight, Bernard's Watch, The Ten O'clock News, ITV Six 0'clock News, The SABC News, Points West, Teletubbies, Round the World in Eighty Days, The Power of One, Black Beauty, Mrs Brown, The Jungle Book,* Walt

Disney's film of *The Old Curiosity Shop*, *Monty Python's Flying Circus*, *Local Hero*, *Cabaret*, *Judge Dredd*, *All Creatures Great and Small*, *The Full Monty*, *Jude*, *One Hundred and One Dalmatians*, *Private Benjamin*, *Indiana Jones*, *High Noon*, *Titanic*, *Wonderwoman*, *The Holiday Programme*, *Some of My Best Friends Are Afrikaners* and Benedict Allen's series on *The Skeleton Coast*. *Gate Masters of the Universe* is not a film, but the name of a South African electric gate company.

Publications mentioned ~ *The Guardian* quoted, *Country Life*, *Country Life* - the South African version, *Cosmopolitan*, *Magnum*, *Cape Times*, *Private Eye*, *Farmer's Weekly*, *Boys Own*, *News of the World*, *Take a Break*, *The Field*, *Daily Telegraph*.

Alice through the Looking Glass by Lewis Carroll, *The Burning Shore* by Wilbur Smith.

Songs mentioned ~
'*The Ballad of Spotty Muldoon*' by Peter Cook/Dudley Moore
'*Deeply Dippy*' by Right Said Fred
'*Mercedes Benz*' by Janis Joplin
'*Girls Just Wanna Have Fun*' by Cyndi Lauper
'*I'm Gonna Wash That Man Right Outta My Hair*' (Hammerstein) from *South Pacific*
'*Rhinestone Cowboy*' by Larry Weiss

'*Do Not Forsake Me, Oh, My Darlin'* (Washington/Tiomkin) from *High Noon*

'*Horse With No Name*' by America

The scout chorus '*You'll Never Get To Heaven In A Chevrolet*'

The Gospel chorus '*My sin was deeper than the ocean*'

'*N'kosi Sekeleli Africa*' The South African National anthem

Mendelssohn's *Wedding March*

'*Old McDonald had a Farm*'

'*Silent Night*' by Father Joseph Mohr and Franz Xaver Gruber

Other Companies and organizations mentioned include ~
BBC Television, Central Television, Radio Jacaranda, Paramount, The R.A.C, Youth With a Mission, The Blue Cross, The Pony Club, The David Shepherd Conservation Foundation, Save the Rhino Trust, Animal Liberation Front, Maforga Mission, Mombo Camp. Deadline, Fairy Liquid, Mr Kipling's Cakes, Copydex, Phileas Fogg crisps, Holiday Inn, Claridges, Big Bend Motel, Penguin (Foods), Coca-Cola, Speed Queen, Vaseline, Brylcream, Wimpy, British Telcom, Peter Jones, Laura Ashley, Woolworth's, Fortnum and Masons, Chanel, Quality Street, Tipp-ex, Hoover, Millupa, Land Rover, Volkswagen, Nissan, Toyota, BMW, Mercedes, Chevrolet, Morris, Lufthansa, British Airways, Phillips of Bond Street, Clinique. Elstree and Shepperton Studios.

Postcard of Hastings Fish Market 1912: creativecommons.org/licenses/by/2.0/deed.en

HISTORICAL BACKGROUND

[i] The national South African referendum was held on 17th March 1992. 69% of white voters supported FW de Klerk who continued negotiations with the African National Congress, the ANC, showing they were in favour of dissolving apartheid. Nelson Mandela recognised 2nd February 1990 as the date that marked the end of apartheid when de Klerk announced, 'The time for negotiation has arrived' and lifted the bans on the ANC, PAC, South African Communist Party and thirty-one other, previously illegal organizations. Mandela was released from prison on 11th February 1990.

[ii] Eugene Terre'Blanche was leader of the Afrikaner Resistance Movement (AWB ~ *Afrikaner Weerstandsbeweging*), a khaki-clad and bearded individual of strong character and determined right-wing views.

[iii] On 16th June 1992 ANC 'mass action' consisting of demonstrations, boycotts and strikes commenced. On 17th June armed Inkatha forces killed 46 people, most of whom were women and children in the Vaal township of Boipatong and four days later the ANC suspended talks with the Government.

[iv] According to the *Sunday Telegraph Magazine*. This was inaccurate. Wise King Sobhuza II reigned for 61 years. When I went to Swaziland I asked everybody there how many wives had. No one could tell me, but they thought about 120. The present king, Mswati III chose his eleventh wife in August 2003.

[v] I think he was referring to time the Afrikaans defeated the Zulus at Blood River in 1838.

[vi] In 1992 there were 15,000 murders in South Africa and personal security was a concern. The slogan 'One settler, one bullet' or 'One boer, one bullet' was still being bandied about by

the Pan Africanist Congress and caused concern for the safety of those living on remote farms.

[vii] Sir Herbert Baker was a leading British architect famous for designing the Union Buildings in Pretoria.

[viii] Chris Hani, Secretary-general of the South African Communist Party and one of the most popular figures in the ANC was shot outside his house in Boksburg on 10th April 1993, two weeks after publicly deciding to become a Christian. Over 30 million Africans rose to condemn his murder. Five people died and 300 were injured in the 'Labour Stayaway' following his funeral and the political crisis in South Africa deepened further.

[ix] In 1993 50% of black South Africans were functionally illiterate, 25% had no formal education at all. Illiteracy was as high as 80% in some areas. Only 7% of the total population was receiving higher education.

[x] By the year 2003 many countries were forcing immigrants to take HIV tests including USA and Australia. *The Daily Mail* June 2003

[xi] 15th October 1993, the day Nelson Mandela and FW de Klerk won the Nobel Peace Prize.

[xii] Long Tom was a French 155mm Creusot cannon used by the Afrikaners during the Boer War. It is still up there.

[xiii] In 1993 some 240 policemen were killed in South Africa. In December 1993 there were 127 murders in one week.

[xiv] 10th May 1994.

[xv] 139 politicians attended the Kolobe weekends from December 1992 to November 1993. *Kolobe* means warthog in Sesotho.

[xvi] Read *'A Witness Forever'* by Michael Cassidy founder of African Enterprise.

[xvii] Quoted from John Ledger, Chairman of the Endangered Wildlife Trust in *'Southern Africa's Threatened Wildlife'* published by the EWT.

[xviii] SWAPO ~ *South West Africa People's Organization* who gained independence in 1990.

[xix] Tony Leon, leader of the Democratic Alliance, following a 2003 Parliamentary debate on the question *'Have conditions improved in South Africa since 2003?'* wrote, "Unemployment has increased dramatically since 1994, rising from 24% to 32%. And social problems have worsened. Serious crime has gown by 24%, while prosecutions dropped 23% and convictions by 19%." *SA Sunday Times 13:4:03*

[xx] AWB ~ *Afrikaner Weerstandsbeweging,* the Afrikaner Resistance Movement.

[xxi] Dr D Bourne, Medical Research Council, Cape Town speaking at an AIDS Conference in Johannesburg I attended in February 2002.

Printed in Great Britain
by Amazon